Practical Microsoft® Office 2007

Includes a multimedia BookOnCD with the entire contents of the printed book, interactive step-by-step animations, pop-up definitions, skills tests, and more!

June Jamrich Parsons

Dan Oja

Donna Mulder

COURSE TECHNOLOGY
CENGAGE Learning™

Australia • Brazil • Japan • Korea • Mexico • Singapore • Spain • United Kingdom • United States

COURSE TECHNOLOGY
CENGAGE Learning

Practical Microsoft Office 2007

Acquisitions Editor: Kristina Matthews

Senior Product Manager: Kathy Finnegan

Product Manager: Erik Herman

Associate Product Manager: Brandi Henson

Editorial Assistant: Leigh Robbins

Senior Marketing Manager: Joy Starks

Marketing Coordinator: Jennifer Hankin

Production Editor: Heather Furrow

Media Specialist: Donna Mulder

Layout: Tensi Parsons

Content QA: Deborah Elam

BookOnCD Technician: Keefe Crowley

BookOnCD Development: MediaTechnics Corp.

Prepress Production: GEX Publishing Services

For product information and technology assistance, contact us at
Cengage Learning Customer & Sales Support, 1-800-354-9706

For permission to use material from this text or product, submit all requests online at **cengage.com/permissions**
Further permissions questions can be emailed to
permissionrequest@cengage.com

ISBN-13: 978-1-4239-0604-9

ISBN-10: 1-4239-0604-7

Course Technology
25 Thomson Place
Boston, Massachusetts 02210
USA

Cengage Learning is a leading provider of customized learning solutions with office locations around the globe, including Singapore, the United Kingdom, Australia, Mexico, Brazil, and Japan. Locate your local office at:
international.cengage.com/region

Cengage Learning products are represented in Canada by Nelson Education, Ltd.

For your lifelong learning solutions, visit **course.cengage.com**

Purchase any of our products at your local college store or at our preferred online store **www.ichapters.com**

Printed in the United States of America
4 5 6 7 8 9 10 11 10 09

■Preface

About this book

Practical Office 2007 provides a state-of-the-art introduction to Microsoft Office 2007, written in an easy-to-read style. Every book includes an action-packed multimedia BookOnCD. Each page of the BookOnCD looks exactly like its corresponding page in the printed book and contains interactive elements such as pop-up definitions, interactive animations, and interactive end-of-chapter material. The BookOnCD requires no installation, so it is easy to use at home, at school, or at work.

Practical *Office 2007* provides a focused introduction to the most important features of Microsoft Office 2007. It is designed to teach you what you really need to know about this popular software suite so that you can use it for practical tasks at school, at work, or at home.

The first page of each chapter introduces chapter topics and lists the chapter contents. Each chapter includes:

- ■ **FAQs**, or "frequently asked questions," which explain and demonstrate how to use key features of Microsoft Office 2007, and give specific tips for becoming a more proficient Office user.
- ■ An **Assessment** page that contains self-test activities including two sets of QuickCheck questions and four interactive Skill Set tests. These assessment activities provide essential feedback that indicates how well you mastered the chapter material. Data from the Skill Sets can be stored in a Tracking File. An instructor can consolidate data from all students and generate a variety of reports.

About the BookOnCD

Every book includes the innovative BookOnCD, which is loaded with the following features to enhance and reinforce learning:

 Play It! buttons provide animated screentours that demonstrate how to accomplish various tasks.

 Do It! buttons launch interactive simulations that let you try your hand at activities presented on a page.

Get It? The Get It? section at the end of each chapter contains an auto-graded interactive review of skills.

QuickChecks Interactive end-of-chapter QuickCheck questions provide instant feedback on concepts you've learned.

Pop-up Definitions & Glossary Clickable boldface terms display pop-up definitions. A Glossary button provides easy access to all definitions from any page.

Projects A set of projects located at the end of the book provides structured practice for the Office 2007 skills presented in each chapter.

Use this book because...

- **You want to learn how to use Microsoft Office 2007**. Practical *Office 2007* will help you learn how to use the essential features of Microsoft Word, Excel, PowerPoint, and Access in the most efficient possible way. You won't find excess pages or coverage of features you'll never need. Instead you'll find a focused, efficient approach to learning how to use Office 2007 to complete real-world tasks.

- **You want to learn Office 2007, but don't have it on your computer**. Practical *Office 2007* uses interactive simulations to show you how to use Office 2007 modules. You don't need to have Office 2007 software on your computer to use Practical *Office 2007* CD. You only need to use Office 2007 software if you decide to complete the projects at the end of the book.

- **You're looking for a product that teaches you how to use Microsoft Office 2007, but that also serves as a handy reference**. Practical *Office 2007* is designed to work as both a learning environment and as a quick reference. We recommend using the CD to learn new features. After you've mastered Office 2007, keep the printed book nearby as a quick reference.

- **You've used previous versions of Microsoft Office and want to get up to speed with the 2007 version**. Practical *Office 2007* makes it quick and easy to get up to speed on the latest versions of Microsoft Word, Excel, PowerPoint, and Access.

- **You're a beginning or intermediate computer user**. Practical *Office 2007* is great for beginners, but it also serves as a quick reference or refresher for intermediate users. You can skim over the features you already know and quickly learn how to use features that are new to you.

Teaching Tools

Course Technology and MediaTechnics offer a wide range of instructional tools that can be accessed from the Instructor Resources CD or www.course.com.

An easily customizable, electronic **Instructor's Manual** is provided for each chapter in the book. Each Instructor's Manual includes a chapter overview, bullet point lecture notes, key terms, classroom activities, quiz scenarios, and teaching tips.

WebTrack provides automated delivery of tracking data from students directly to instructors with minimal setup or administrative overhead.

The **ExamView Test Bank and Test Engine** offer a user-friendly testing environment for producing paper-based, LAN-based, and Web-deliverable exams. The ultra-efficient Quick Test Wizard is designed to create an exam in less than five minutes. Exams can be based on Course Technology question banks or can be totally customized.

PowerPoint Presentations for each chapter are designed to help instructors deliver engaging and visually impressive lectures. Slides can be edited and posted on school networks for student review, or saved to the Web for Distance Learning students.

A **sample syllabus** covers policies, assignments, labs, exams, and procedural information, all of which can be easily customized for your course.

Online **distance learning** content is offered for BlackBoard and WebCT platforms and includes topic reviews, case projects, PowerPoint presentations, practice tests, and a custom syllabus.

There's More!

Course Technology and MediaTechnics are dedicated to bringing you the best tools for teaching and learning. Look for additional titles in the Practical series and the New Perspectives series. SAM provides even more interactive content related to the topics presented in this book.

Acknowledgments

The successful launch of this book was possible only because of our extraordinary "ground crews." We would like to extend our profound thanks:

To the students at Northern Michigan University, the University of the Virgin Islands, and countless other universities who have participated in classes and corresponded with us over the 25 (or so) years since we began teaching.

To our development team—Donna Mulder, Tensi Parsons, Keefe Crowley, Sue Oja, Deborah Elam, Kevin Lappi, and Marilou Potter—for media development and testing. To Chris Robbert for narrations, Christopher Schuch for audio processing, and Donna Mulder for content and media development.

To our team members' patient and supportive parents, spouses, children, and significant others.

To the New Perspectives team at Course Technology, who once again provided professional and enthusiastic support, guidance, and advice. Their insights and team spirit were invaluable.

To Kristina Matthews and Erik Herman for their editorial and logistical support; to the Software Quality Assurance team for their valuable QA test comments.

To the crew at GEX, and to Heather Furrow for her careful and cheerful production management.

To the professors and reviewers who expressed their ideas and shared their teaching strategies with us for the Practical series: Dennis Anderson, St. Francis College; Mary Dobranski, College of Saint Mary; Mike Feiler, Merritt College; Shmuel Fink, Touro College; Dennette Foy, Edison Community College; Nancy LaChance, DeVry Institute of Technology; Janet Sheppard, Collin County Community College; Pauline Pike, Community College of Morris; and Linda Reis, Garland County Community College.

Media Credits

All media elements for *Practical Office 2007* are copyrighted by MediaTechnics Corporation.

▪Brief Contents

■Contents

■Contents

■Before You Begin

You're going to enjoy using the *Practical Office 2007* and the accompanying BookOnCD. It's a snap to start the BookOnCD and use it on your computer. So don't delay—the answers to FAQs (frequently asked questions) in this section will help you begin.

■FAQ Will the BookOnCD work on my computer?

The easiest way to find out if the BookOnCD works on your computer is to try it! Just follow the steps below to start the CD. If it works, you're all set. Otherwise, check with your local technical support person. If you are technically inclined, the system requirements are listed inside the front cover of this book.

■FAQ How do I start the BookOnCD?

The *Practical Office 2007* BookOnCD is easy to use and requires no installation. Follow these simple steps to get started:

1. Make sure your computer is turned on.

2. Press the button on your computer's CD drive to open the drawer-like "tray," as shown in the photo below.

3. Place the BookOnCD into the tray with the label facing up.

4. Press the button on the CD drive to close the tray, then proceed with Step 5 on the next page.

To use the BookOnCD, your computer must have a CD or DVD drive. If you have any questions about its operation, check the manual supplied with your computer or check with your local technical support person.

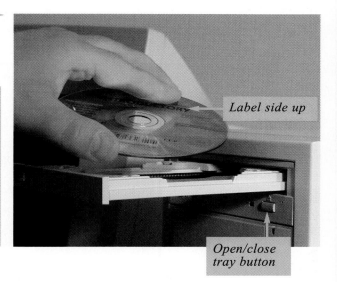

Label side up

Open/close tray button

Before You Begin

5. After inserting the CD, wait about 15 seconds. During this time, the light on your CD drive should flicker. If your computer displays an AutoPlay window similar to the one shown below, click the appropriate option.

On some computers, an AutoPlay window appears when you insert CDs.

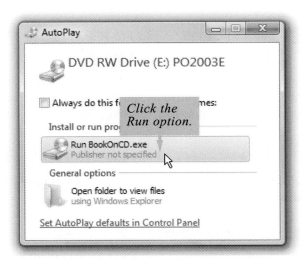

6. If the AutoPlay window does not appear and the Practical Office title screen does not appear, you can manually start the BookOnCD by following the steps in the figure below.

Some computers are not configured to automatically play CDs and DVDs, but you can play them manually.

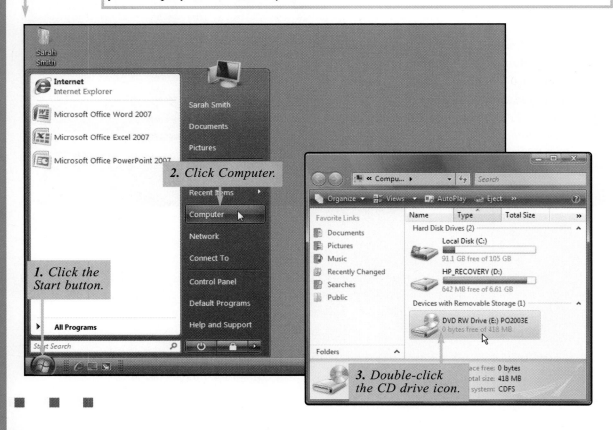

■FAQ How should I set my tracking options?

When the BookOnCD starts, it displays the Practical Office 2007 title screen and a Tracking options window. To proceed, you'll need to select your tracking settings.

A Tracking File records your progress by saving your scores on QuickChecks and Skill Sets at the end of each chapter. If you don't want to record your scores, simply make sure the *Save Tracking data* box is empty and then click the OK button to proceed straight to the first chapter.

> *Use the Tracking Options window to activate or deactivate tracking. You can also create a Tracking File or select a file as described below.*

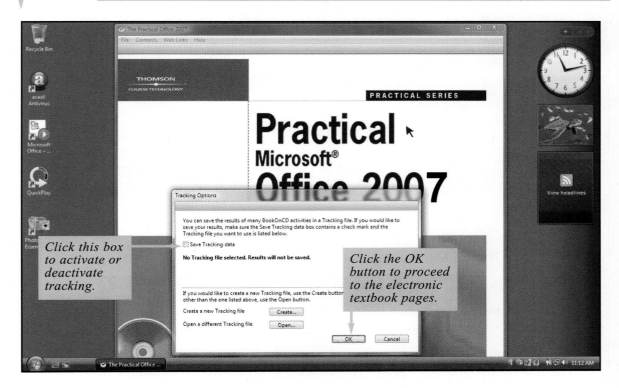

If you prefer to track your scores, then you must create a Tracking File. It's easy! Click the Create button and then follow the onscreen prompts to enter your name, student ID, and class section.

When the Save As window appears, you can select the location for your Tracking File. If you are using your own computer, the default location in the Documents folder is a great place to store your Tracking File, so just click the Save button and you're all set!

If you are working on a public computer, such as one in a school lab, be aware that data stored on the hard disk might be erased or changed by other students unless you have a protected personal storage area. When working on a public computer or when you need to transport your data from one computer to another, a floppy disk or USB flash drive is a better option for storing your Tracking File.

To save your Tracking File in a location other than your computer's Documents folder, click the Computer icon and then double-click a storage location to select it. Click the Save button to finalize your storage selection.

■FAQ How do I navigate through the BookOnCD?

Each onscreen page exactly duplicates a page from the paper book. Use the mouse or the vertical scroll bar to scroll up and down the page.

Tools on the menu bar help you navigate from page to page. If your computer screen does not show an entire page, use the scroll bar.

Click Contents, then click any chapter to jump to the start of a chapter.

Enter a page number here, then click the > button to jump to a specific page.

Click here to go to the previous page.

Click here to go to the next page.

Click File, then click Exit to close the BookOnCD.

Drag the scroll box down or press the Page Down key to scroll down the page.

Drag the scroll box up or press the Page Up key to scroll back up the page.

Click Do It! buttons to view screentours.

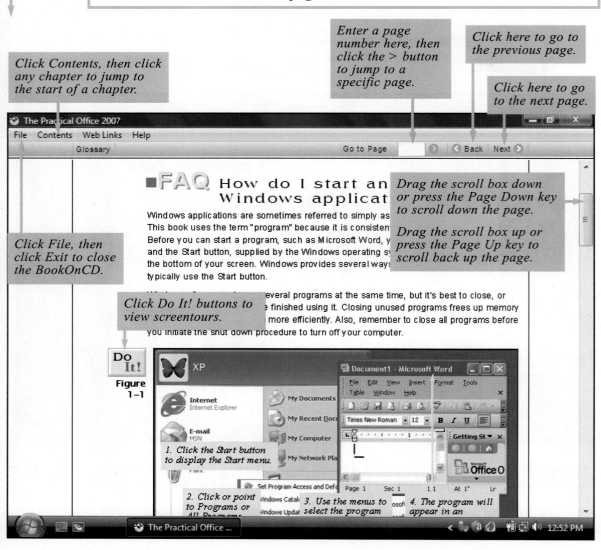

■FAQ How does the interactive assessment page work?

Each chapter ends with an assessment page containing interactive activities. You can use these activities to evaluate how well you've mastered the concepts and skills covered in the chapter. If you do well on the QuickChecks and Skill Sets, then you're ready to move on to the next chapter. If you don't do well, you might want to review the material before going on to the next chapter.

> *QuickChecks and Skill Sets are computer-scored activities that help you assess your understanding of chapter material.*

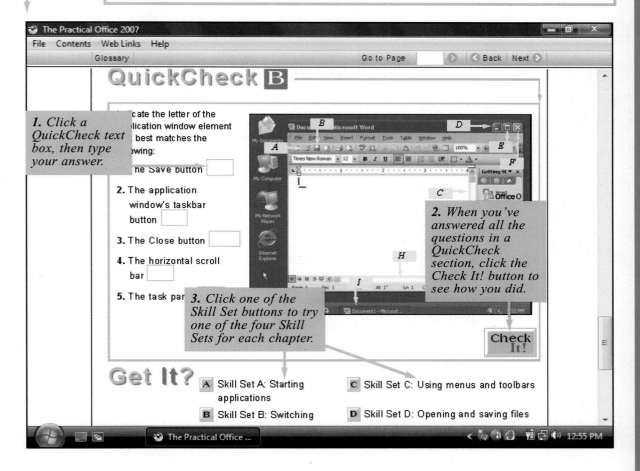

Before You Begin

■FAQ Are all my scores tracked?

Your scores on Skill Sets and QuickChecks are tracked if you have activated tracking with a check mark in the *Save Tracking data* box.

■FAQ How can I change tracking?

You can access the Tracking Options window at any time by clicking File on the menu bar and selecting Change Tracking Options. When the Tracking Options window appears, you can activate or deactivate tracking, create a new Tracking File, or select a different Tracking File.

■FAQ What if the Tracking Options window shows the wrong Tracking File?

When working in a computer lab or using a computer where other students are using the BookOnCD, the Tracking Options window might show the name of a Tracking File that belongs to another person because that person was the last one to use the computer. You can use the Open button on the Tracking Options window to select a different Tracking File.

You can select a different Tracking File if the one displayed is not yours. Tracking files are usually stored in the Documents folder.

Tracking Options

You can save the results of many BookOnCD activities in a Tracking file. If you would like to save your results, make sure the Save Tracking data box contains a check mark and the Tracking file you want to use is listed below.

☑ Save Tracking data

Use Tracking file for: Sarah Smith

Student ID: 12345678   Class Section: CDC101
Location: C:\Users\Sarah Smith\Documents\tracking-12345678.tk3

If you would like to create a new Tracking file, use the Create other than the one listed above, use the Open button.

Create a new Tracking file   [Create...]

Open a different Tracking file   [Open...]

To change the Tracking File, click Open, select a storage device and folder, and then select a Tracking File.

[OK]   [Cancel]

■FAQ How do I submit my Tracking File?

In an academic setting, your instructor might request your Tracking File data to monitor your progress. Your instructor will tell you if you should submit your Tracking File using the WebTrack system, if you should hand in your entire Tracking File, or if you should send the Tracking File as an e-mail attachment.

■ ■ ■

■FAQ How do I end a session?

You'll need to leave the BookOnCD disk in the CD drive while you're using it, or you will encounter an error message. Before you remove the CD from the drive, you must exit the program by clicking File on the BookOnCD menu bar, then clicking Exit. You can also exit by clicking the Close button in the upper-right corner of the window.

■FAQ How do I get the most out of the book and the BookOnCD?

If you have your own computer, you might want to start the CD and do your reading online. You'll then be able to click the Play It! and Do It! buttons as you come to them and click boldface terms to see pop-up definitions. Also, you'll be able to immediately interact with the QuickCheck section at the end of each chapter.

If you do not have a computer, you should read through the chapter in the book. Later, when it is convenient, take your BookOnCD to a computer at school, home, or work and browse through the chapter, clicking each Play It! and Do It! activity. After you try each skill, you can jump to the QuickCheck and Get It? sections to complete those interactive activities.

When you complete a chapter, you might want to try the corresponding projects at the end of the book. Refer to the instructions at the beginning of the Projects section for more information on completing projects.

After you've completed the *Practical Office 2007* chapters, keep the book near your computer as a handy reference. When you have a question about a Microsoft Office 2007 task, find the appropriate page in the Table of Contents, then use the figure captions and bulleted list items to refresh your memory.

■FAQ What about sound?

If your computer is equipped for sound, you should hear audio narrations during the screentours and interactive simulations. If you don't hear anything, check the volume control on your computer by clicking the speaker icon in the lower-right corner of your screen. If you're working in a lab or office where sound would be disruptive, consider using headphones.

Before You Begin

■FAQ Which version of Windows do I need?

Your PC's operating system sets the standard for the way all your software looks and works. Most of today's PCs use a version of the Microsoft Windows operating system—"Windows" for short. The most recent version of Windows is Windows Vista.

The *Practical Office 2007* BookOnCD is optimized for use with Windows Vista, but will also work on most computers running older versions of Windows, such as Windows XP.

If you see a screen similar to this one when you start your PC, your computer is running Windows Vista.

Look for this Start button.

■FAQ Where can I get more information about using the BookOnCD?

Your BookOnCD includes extensive help, which you can access by clicking Help on the menu bar.

Practical Microsoft® Office 2007

Chapter 1

Getting Started with Application Software

What's inside and on the CD?

Application software helps you use your computer to accomplish many useful tasks. Some of today's most popular software is included in the Microsoft Office suite. The suite's flagship software is Microsoft Word—a word processing application that has become a worldwide standard. Microsoft Excel is the spreadsheet software of choice for many computer owners. Microsoft PowerPoint is top-rated presentation software. Microsoft Access is among the most frequently used PC database software packages.

A software program designed for the Windows operating system is often referred to as a **Windows application**. Understanding the features common to most Windows applications makes it easy to learn new software. In this chapter, you'll take a look at features common to many Windows applications. You can use what you learn in this chapter as a foundation for working with Word, Excel, PowerPoint, and Access in later chapters. This material also applies to working with a browser and e-mail.

FAQ How do I start and exit Windows applications?

Windows applications are sometimes referred to simply as "applications" or "programs." This book uses the term "program" because it is consistent with Windows terminology. Before you can start a program, such as Microsoft Word, your computer should be on, and the Start button, supplied by the Windows operating system, should be displayed at the bottom of your screen. Windows provides several ways to start a program, but you'll typically use the Start button.

Windows allows you to run several programs at the same time, but it's best to close, or "exit," a program when you're finished using it. Closing unused programs frees up memory and helps your computer run more efficiently. Also, remember to close all programs before you initiate the shut down procedure to turn off your computer.

Do It!

Figure 1–1

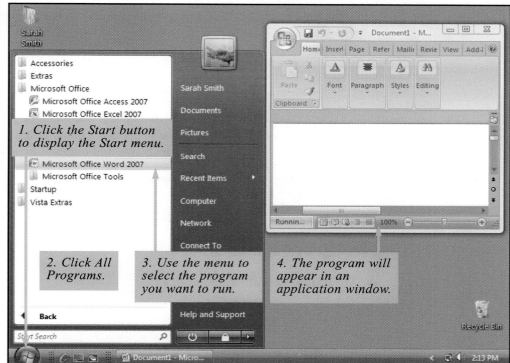

When you install a new program on your computer, it is typically added to the All Programs menu. To start the program, click its name on the All Programs menu.

Some menu options, indicated by a ▇ symbol, represent multiple programs. When you click one of these options, a list of program names is displayed. Click the program you want to start from the list.

In addition to appearing in the All Programs menu, some programs, such as Internet Explorer, are represented by an icon on the Windows desktop. To use one of these icons to start a program, just double-click it.

To close a program, click the ▇X▇ Close button.

■FAQ What are the components of an application window?

An open program is displayed in a rectangular **application window** on the Windows desktop. Application windows contain many similar elements, even when they hold very different kinds of programs.

A window's title bar displays the name of the program, the name of the open file, and a set of sizing buttons for minimizing, maximizing, and closing the window.

Many application windows may include a **menu bar** that provides access to commands for controlling the program. Below the menu bar, you might see one or more **toolbars** containing small pictures. Each picture is a **toolbar button** that provides a shortcut for accomplishing a task.

Microsoft Office 2007 modules include a **ribbon** instead of a menu bar that provides access to commands and options. For example, the ribbon's Insert tab displays options for inserting headers and footers into a document.

A status bar runs across the bottom of most application windows. A **status bar** contains information about the current condition of the program. Depending on the program, the status bar might display the current page number, the zoom level, or a Web page address.

A **scroll bar** on the side of the window helps you move a document or graphic up and down within the window. A horizontal scroll bar might also appear at the bottom of an application window to help you scroll wide documents and graphics from left to right.

Figure 1-2

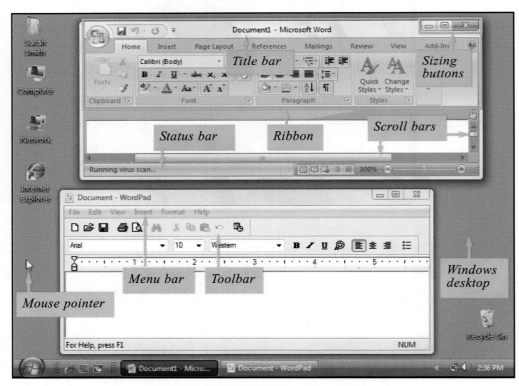

■FAQ How do I switch between application windows?

You can have more than one application window open, or "running," on the desktop. This Windows feature is handy if you want to work on two projects at the same time or if you want to copy a photo from your photo editing software to a document. Open application windows are represented by buttons on the taskbar. Clicking one of these buttons brings the window to the front of the desktop. Although multiple programs can be open at the same time, only one program can be active at a time. The active program is indicated by a depressed taskbar button.

Some programs also allow several data files to be open at the same time. For example, when using Microsoft Word, you could have your To-Do list open at the same time you are working on a term paper. When your desktop contains only a few windows, each data file has its own taskbar button. As you open more windows, the data files are combined into a single button that opens to display a list of files.

Figure
1-3

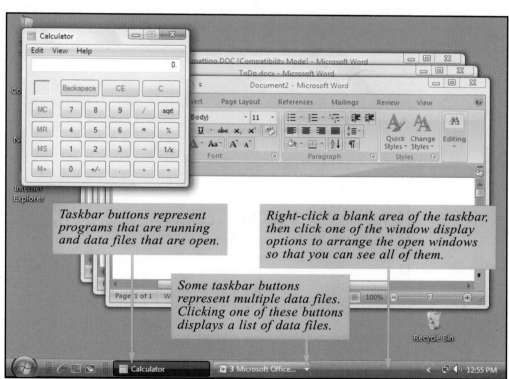

Taskbar buttons represent programs that are running and data files that are open.

Right-click a blank area of the taskbar, then click one of the window display options to arrange the open windows so that you can see all of them.

Some taskbar buttons represent multiple data files. Clicking one of these buttons displays a list of data files.

■ If a program window is open, but hidden underneath another program window, clicking the program's button on the taskbar brings that window to the front, overlapping other windows on the desktop. You can also click any visible part of the hidden window to make it active.

■ If a program window is minimized, clicking the program's button on the taskbar restores the window to its previous size and location.

■ When multiple data files are open in a single program, such as Microsoft Word, you can click the Switch Windows command from the Windows group on the View tab to see a list of files and switch from one to another.

■FAQ How do menus and toolbars work?

Most application windows include a menu bar. Clicking an option from the menu bar displays a menu with a list of choices. For example, clicking Edit on the menu bar displays the Edit menu. You can use this menu to accomplish several tasks. For example, the Copy option allows you to copy a selected item onto the Clipboard.

Typically, a menu bar provides access to all the features of a program. If you don't remember how to access a program feature, you can browse through the menu options to find it.

Most application windows display one or more toolbars, typically located below the menu bar near the top of the window. Toolbars contain several buttons, sometimes called "tools," that provide a single-click shortcut for the most commonly used menu options.

Figure 1-4

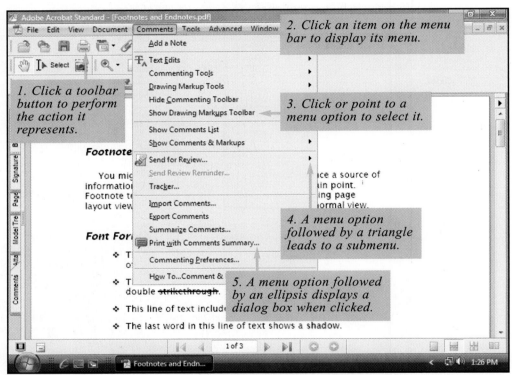

■ If you open a menu, and then decide you don't want to select an option after all, click the menu title again or press the Esc key to close the menu.

■ You can use your keyboard for fast access to frequently used menu items. Hold down the Alt key and press the underlined letter to display a menu. Press the underlined letter to select an option from an open menu.

■FAQ How does the ribbon work?

In Microsoft Office 2007, the ribbon replaces the menu bar and toolbars at the top of the application window. The ribbon has been divided into a hierarchy consisting of **tabs**, **groups**, and **commands**. The tabs are divided into groups. The groups contain the commands to perform an action. For example, in Word to add clip art to a document, you would select the Insert tab and then select the Clip Art command from the Illustrations group.

Figure 1-5

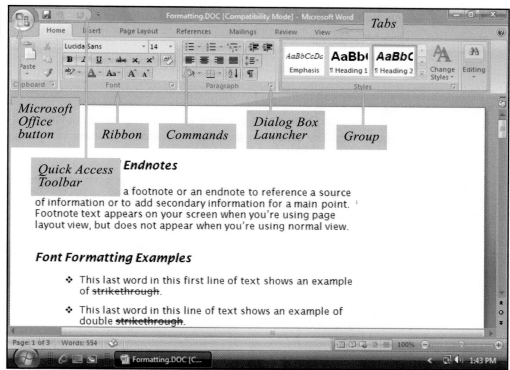

■ The **Microsoft Office button** leads to many of the commands that previously existed on the File menu. You can create new documents, open existing documents, save documents, and print documents from the Microsoft Office button.

■ The **Quick Access Toolbar** contains commands that you use regularly. The Quick Access Toolbar is completely customizable. Commands can be added to the Quick Access Toolbar by right-clicking a command and then selecting Add to Quick Access Toolbar from the shortcut menu.

■ **Contextual tabs**, which contain formatting options for an object, appear when the object is selected. For example, in Word after a table is inserted, the Table Tools tab appears. From this tab, you can change borders, insert or delete columns, and change cell properties.

■ Dialog boxes can be opened from the **Dialog Box Launcher** in the lower-right corner of a group. For example, in Word the Font dialog box can be launched from the Font group on the Home tab.

■FAQ How do I open a file?

Data is stored in files on the disks and CDs in your computer system. Files can be referred to in different ways in different programs. For example, a file created with Microsoft Word is usually called a document, while a Microsoft PowerPoint file is usually called a presentation.

Before you can work with a file, you must open it. There are several ways to open a file. You can:

■ Use the Recent Items option on the Start menu to view a list of recently saved files.

■ Double-click a file shortcut icon if one exists on the Windows desktop.

■ Double-click a file name from within Windows Explorer.

■ Use the Open dialog box provided by an application.

When you use the Open dialog box from within an application window, you'll see a list of files and folders. The dialog box uses file extensions to filter the list of files so that it displays only those files that can be opened with the program.

Figure 1-6

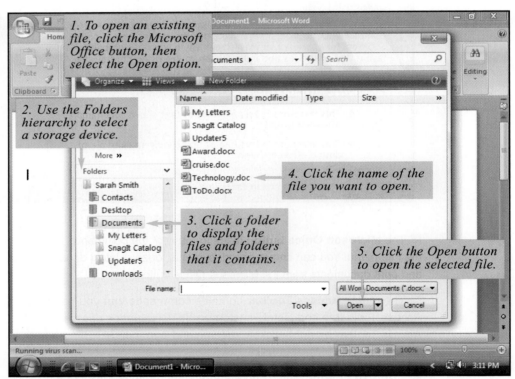

■ Many Windows applications, including Microsoft Office, store files in the Documents folder if no other drive or folder is specified. If you save a file but forget where it went, look in the Documents folder.

■FAQ How do I save a file?

When you create a file on your computer, you must save it if you want to be able to use it again in the future. Make sure you save files before you close their application windows; otherwise, you could lose the work in progress.

Figure 1-7

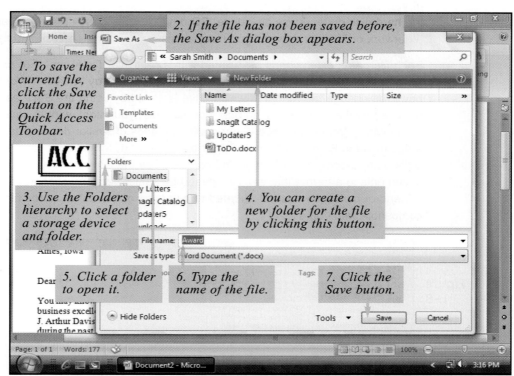

2. *If the file has not been saved before, the Save As dialog box appears.*

1. *To save the current file, click the Save button on the Quick Access Toolbar.*

3. *Use the Folders hierarchy to select a storage device and folder.*

4. *You can create a new folder for the file by clicking this button.*

5. *Click a folder to open it.*

6. *Type the name of the file.*

7. *Click the Save button.*

■ When you first save a file, you must name it. File names can consist of letters, spaces, numbers, and certain punctuation symbols. File names cannot include the characters / ? : = < > | and must not be longer than 255 characters. Each folder can contain only one file with a particular file name. However, different documents with the same name can be stored in different folders.

■ A file extension is a set of up to four characters that indicates the file type. A file extension is separated from the file name by a period. Windows programs add the appropriate file extension automatically, so you don't have to type it when saving a file.

■ The Save button works differently, depending on whether the file was previously saved. Clicking the Save button automatically stores a file using the original name, drive, and folder where it was previously stored. If the file hasn't been saved before, clicking the Save button opens the Save As dialog box. Select the drive and folder where you want to save the file, enter a file name, then click the Save button.

■ If you've modified an existing file and want to save the new version under a different name, click the Microsoft Office button, then click Save As to display the Save As dialog box. Enter a new name and select the drive and folder in which to store the file. The modified version of the file is saved under the new name, leaving the original version of the file unchanged under the original name.

■ How do I save a file? (continued)

Many Windows programs are configured to automatically save files in the Documents folder. Other programs are configured to save files in the same directory used for the last save operation. Regardless of the configuration, you have full control over the destination of your files. You can save to any storage device connected to your computer, including the hard disk drive, floppy disk drive, CD drive, or USB flash drive. You can also save to a network or Internet server if you have access rights and permission to save files.

Each file name extension is associated with a particular file format. For example, the .docx file extension is associated with data files created by Microsoft Word. You can, however, change the format in which a file is saved by using the *Save as type* list provided by the Save As dialog box. For example, you might want to save a document as a template (.dotx) to be used in generating a series of similar documents. You might save a document in Rich Text format (.rtf) or plain text (.txt) format so it can be opened by other word processing software. You can also use the *Save as type* list to save documents in a format that can be opened by earlier versions of Microsoft Word in case a friend or colleague has not updated to a version of Word that stores files in a format compatible with yours.

Figure 1-8

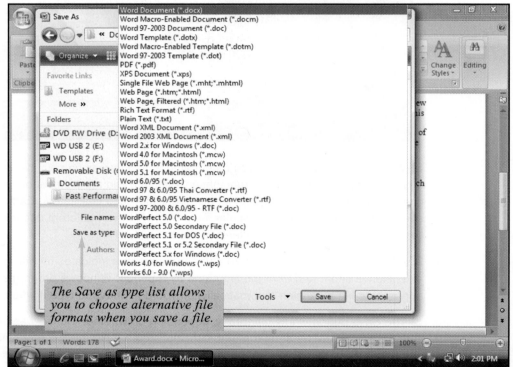

The Save as type list allows you to choose alternative file formats when you save a file.

■FAQ How do I access help for an application?

While using application software, you can access help from a variety of sources. The source you turn to first depends on the type of help you need. Typically, general questions about how to use software features can be best answered by on-screen Help windows that explain features and provide step-by-step instructions for their use. Additional documentation is usually available in a printed user manual, on a CD, or from third-party reference books. If a feature doesn't seem to work as explained in documentation and user manuals, it is a good idea to check online user groups or the publisher's Web site for up-to-date information. If you have questions about work-related procedures, your first source of information should be your organization's help desk. Sometimes, coworkers and friends are willing to answer your questions.

On-screen Help is probably the most frequently used help resource. Different programs offer different ways to access on-screen Help. For example, Microsoft Office modules offer help through a comprehensive electronic user manual that also connects to Office Online.

Figure 1-9

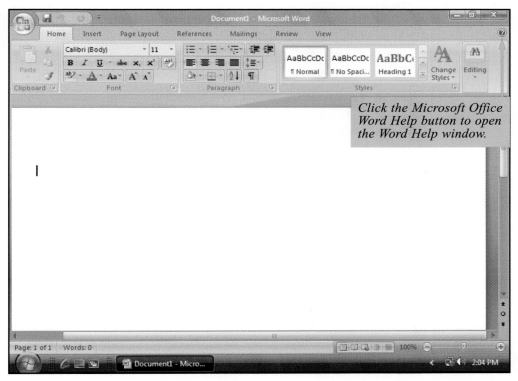

Click the Microsoft Office Word Help button to open the Word Help window.

■How do I access help for an application? (continued)

The Help manual provides tools to scan through its Table of Contents, type a question, or look for keywords in the Help window.

Figure 1-10

The Table of Contents section displays an outline of the Help manual you can use to drill down to the topic about which you have a question.

The Search text box allows you to enter a question and a list of topics is displayed.

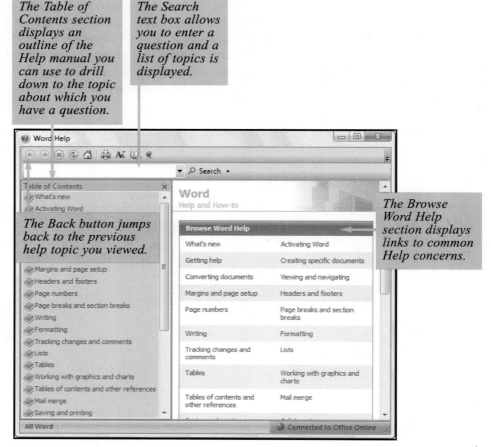

The Browse Word Help section displays links to common Help concerns.

The Back button jumps back to the previous help topic you viewed.

■ You can access Help's electronic user manual by clicking the Microsoft Office Help button in the top-right corner of the application window. You can also access the manual by pressing the F1 function key at the top of your keyboard.

■ The Help window remains open on the desktop until you click its Close button. If the Help window drops back behind other windows, you can use its taskbar button to bring it to the top of the desktop.

QuickCheck A

1. Before you close an application window, you should [＿＿＿＿＿＿＿] any work in progress.

2. When multiple data files are open in a single program, such as Microsoft Word, you can click the [＿＿＿＿＿＿＿] tab to switch from one to another.

3. True or false? When you open a file, you have to know which file name extensions the program can work with. [＿＿＿＿＿]

4. Most applications save files in the [＿＿＿＿＿＿＿] folder.

5. True or false? The first time you save a file, you will use the Save As dialog box to assign the file a name and specify its location. [＿＿＿＿＿]

Check It!

QuickCheck B

Indicate the letter of the application window element that best matches the following:

1. The Save button [＿＿]

2. The application window's taskbar button [＿＿]

3. The Close button [＿＿]

4. The horizontal scroll bar [＿＿]

5. The Home tab [＿＿]

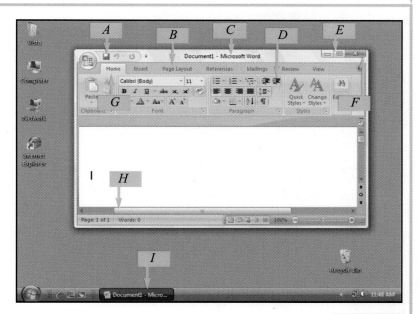

Check It!

Get It?

 **A** Skill Set A: Starting applications

C Skill Set C: Using menus, toolbars, and the ribbon

B Skill Set B: Switching between applications

D Skill Set D: Opening and saving files

Chapter 2
Creating a Document

What's inside and on the CD?

Microsoft Word is the component of Microsoft Office best suited for creating documents such as letters and reports. As word processing software, Microsoft Word provides a set of tools for entering and revising text, adding graphical elements such as color and tables, and then formatting and printing completed documents.

Most people use Microsoft Word more frequently than any other component of Microsoft Office. Microsoft Word is an excellent tool for creating documents of all sorts—from personal letters to business proposals.

In this chapter, you'll learn how to create documents using Microsoft Word. Then you'll learn how to select and edit text. You'll also learn how to use document templates to quickly generate common types of documents.

■FAQ What's in the Word program window?

The Word program window is the window that appears when you start Microsoft Word. To start Word, click Start, point to All Programs, click Microsoft Office, then click Microsoft Office Word 2007. The Word program window contains objects, such as the title bar, the ribbon, status bar, views, and document window. You'll use these objects to create, edit, save, print, and format your documents.

Figure 2-1

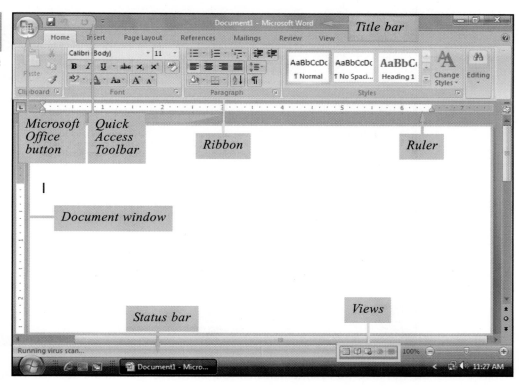

■ The **document window** represents a blank piece of paper. Characters that you type on the keyboard appear in the document window. The title bar indicates the name of the current document. If the current document has never been saved, the title bar displays the generic title "Document1". Word's ribbon contains commands and tools that you can use to create and edit your document.

■ There are different ways to view your document. The **Draft view** allows quick text editing and formatting; header and footers are not visible. The **Web Layout view** shows how your document would look in a Web browser. The **Print Layout view** shows how the content will look on the page, including margins as well as headers and footers. The **Full Screen Reading view** displays your document with minimized toolbars at the top of the window. You can also work in **Outline view** to look at the structure of a document.

■ The status bar provides information about the document displayed in the window. The information can include page numbers, the word count, and the Zoom controls for the document. If you right-click the status bar, you can customize which options you want displayed.

■ You can increase or decrease the zoom level to view the document at various sizes by adjusting the Zoom level on the status bar.

■ ■ ■

■FAQ How do I create a document?

To create a new document, just click the blank document window and start typing. When typing a document, don't worry too much about spelling, formatting, or arranging the document. It is very easy to edit and format a document after you've entered the text.

**Figure
2-2**

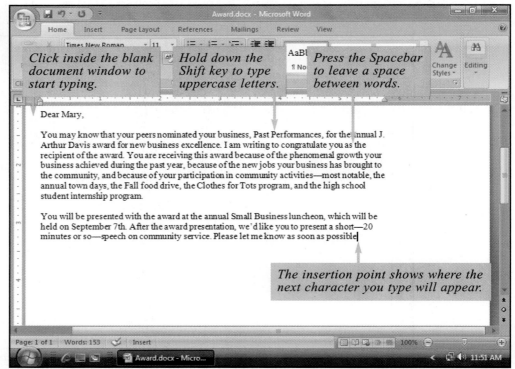

■ The **insertion point** indicates your current location in the document. As you type, the insertion point moves to show where the next character will appear. Click anywhere in the document window to move the insertion point to that location.

■ Through a feature known as **word wrap**, the insertion point automatically jumps down to the beginning of the next line when you reach the right margin of the current line. If the last word you type is too long for the line, it will be moved down to the beginning of the next line. Press the Enter key only when you complete a paragraph. Press the Enter key a second time to create a blank line between paragraphs.

■ Press the Backspace key to delete the character to the *left* of the insertion point. You can also press the Delete key to delete the character to the *right* of the insertion point. These keys also work to erase spaces and blank lines.

■ To add text in the middle of a line or word, use the mouse or arrow keys to move the insertion point to the desired location, then type the text you want to add. To make room for the new text, everything to the right of the insertion point is pushed to the right and down as you type.

■ Use the Insert key to toggle between Overtype and Insert mode. Overtype mode causes new characters to be typed over existing characters. Insert mode causes new characters to be inserted at the current location in the document.

■ Insert special characters, such as the trademark symbol, by clicking the Insert tab, clicking the Symbol command, then clicking More Symbols. Select the symbol you want to insert, click Insert, then click Close to close the Symbols dialog box.

■FAQ How do I select text for editing?

Many word processing features require you to select a section of text before you edit, change, or format it. When you **select text**, you are marking characters, words, phrases, sentences, or paragraphs to modify in some way. Selecting text doesn't do anything useful by itself, but combined with other commands, it enables you to use many of the other important features of Word. Selected text is "highlighted." Word provides several ways to select text.

Figure 2–3

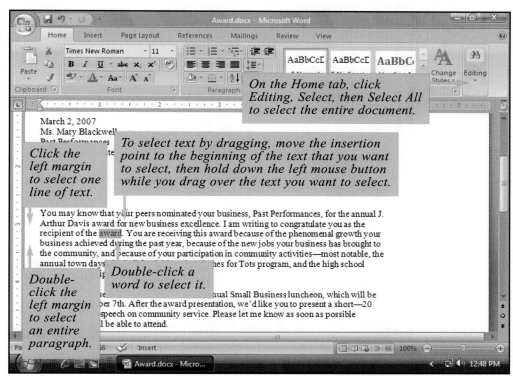

■ Use the drag method to select short sections of text, such as a few characters or several words. Use one of the other selection methods when you need to select a single word, a line, a paragraph, or the entire document.

■ When you point to a word, you can double-click to select only that word. You can triple-click to select the current paragraph.

■ When you point to the left margin, the pointer changes to a white arrow. You can click once to select a line of text or double-click to select a paragraph.

■ If you have trouble using the mouse, you can also use the keyboard to select text. Use the mouse or arrow keys to move the insertion point to the beginning of the text that you want to select. Hold the Shift key down while you use the arrow keys to select text.

■ To deselect text, you should click away from the text that is currently selected. You can also press one of the arrow keys to deselect text.

■ To select a section of text, such as several paragraphs, click at the beginning of the selection, then Shift-click at the end. You can also select non-contiguous text by selecting the first word or section, then using Ctrl-click to select subsequent sections.

■FAQ How do I move, copy, and delete text?

As you create a document, you'll need to move or copy sections of text—words, paragraphs, or even entire pages—from one part of the document to another. To copy or move text, you use the **Clipboard**, a special memory location that temporarily holds sections of your document.

Do It!

Figure 2-4

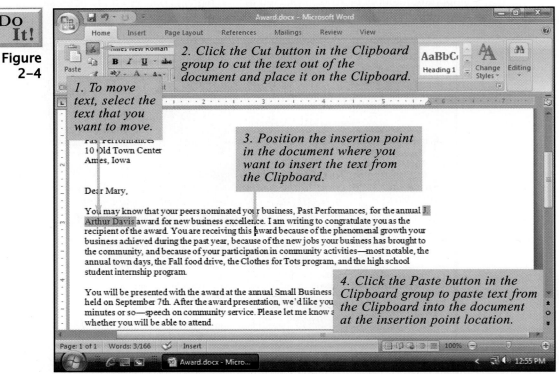

1. To move text, select the text that you want to move.

2. Click the Cut button in the Clipboard group to cut the text out of the document and place it on the Clipboard.

3. Position the insertion point in the document where you want to insert the text from the Clipboard.

4. Click the Paste button in the Clipboard group to paste text from the Clipboard into the document at the insertion point location.

■ To move a section of text from one part of your document to another, first select the text, then click the Cut button. The selected text is cut out of the document and placed on the Clipboard. To paste that text back into the document, move the insertion point to the place where you want to position the text, then click the ▊ Paste button. The text is copied from the Clipboard and placed into the document. This operation is known as **cut and paste**.

■ You can also cut and paste using the drag and drop method. Select the text you wish to cut, and use the mouse to drag it to the new location.

■ **Copy and paste** works much the same way as cut and paste, except that the text is not removed from its original location. Select the text you want to copy, then click the ▊ Copy button. The selected text is copied to the Clipboard, but the original text is not removed from the document. Move the insertion point to the place where you want to place the copy, then click the Paste button.

■ After you cut or copy, the copied text remains on the Clipboard. You can use this feature when you need to put several copies of the same text into your document. Just move the insertion point to the location where you want to place the next copy and click the Paste button. You can paste as many copies of the text as you like.

■ You can cut and paste text, numbers, graphics, tables, and other objects between different applications, such as pasting Excel worksheet data into a Word document.

■FAQ Can I undo a command?

If you perform an action and then change your mind, you may be able to use the Undo button to undo the action. The Undo button has a counterpart—the Redo button—that allows you to repeat an action that you mistakenly undid.

Do It!

Figure 2–5

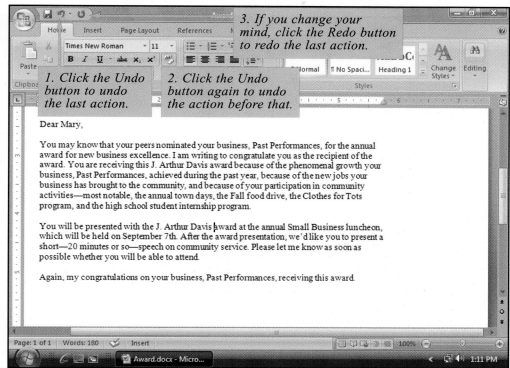

■ If there are no actions that can be undone or redone, the Undo and Redo buttons are disabled—they appear "grayed out" and nothing happens if you click them.

■ The Undo button works best when undoing an editing or formatting command. Actions such as saving and printing files cannot be undone.

■ If you need to undo a series of actions, click the ▾ down-arrow button on the right side of the Undo button to display a list of actions that can be undone. Drag down the list to highlight the actions you want to undo. You can also click a specific action to select it, but all the actions prior to that one will also be performed.

■FAQ How do I use a document template?

You can create a document "from scratch" by entering text in the blank, new document window. As an alternative, you can use a **document template**, which is a pre-formatted document that can be used as the foundation for creating a new document. Word includes templates for many basic document types, including letters, faxes, and resumes.

Figure 2-6

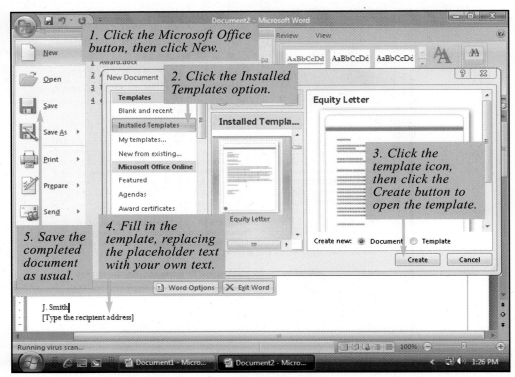

■ A **placeholder** is an element in a document template into which you enter text that personalizes your document. Common placeholders provide entry areas for today's date, your name, or your fax number. To use a placeholder, click inside it and type your own text. The placeholder disappears and your text is displayed.

■ Word allows you to create your own document templates. After you're more familiar with Word, you might want to explore this feature to create templates for documents that you create on a regular basis. You can find more information about creating templates in Word Help and in the program documentation.

■ If you work in a large business or organization, you might be required to use templates created by managers, supervisors, or designers. Some examples of document templates used in businesses are letterheads, fax cover sheets, memos, and reports. Requiring these "official" templates helps businesses maintain professional standards.

■FAQ How do I save a document?

After you have created a document from scratch or personalized a document template, it's important to save the document properly so that you can find and use it again. The first time you save your document, be sure to store it in the correct location with the appropriate file type.

Do It!

Figure 2-7

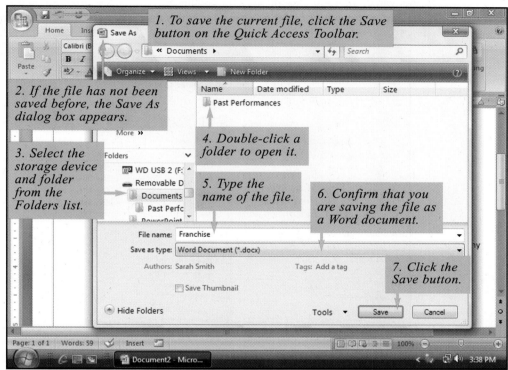

■ The first time you save your document, the Save As dialog box appears. By default, Word saves your file in the Documents folder as a Word document with a .docx extension. You can save the document in another location by selecting a different drive and folder.

■ You can save your document as a different file type if you click the down-arrow button to the right of the *Save as type* text box. For instance, you might want to save the document as an earlier version of Word in order to open the document on another computer that doesn't have Microsoft Office 2007 installed.

■ After you save the document the first time, you can save it more quickly by using the Save button. This action automatically saves the document using the original file name in the drive and folder where it was previously stored. It's a good idea to save frequently as you work on a document. Saving frequently minimizes data loss due to power outages, software bugs, or other unforeseen events.

■FAQ How do I perform a mail merge?

A **mail merge** allows you to create multiple documents from a starting document and a data source. The starting document can be a letter, label template, or envelope template. The starting document usually contains formatted information that you want to be the same for all of the document recipients. The data source, or list, contains the information that will be merged into the starting document. After the information is merged, the final documents can be printed or saved for future use.

Figure 2-8

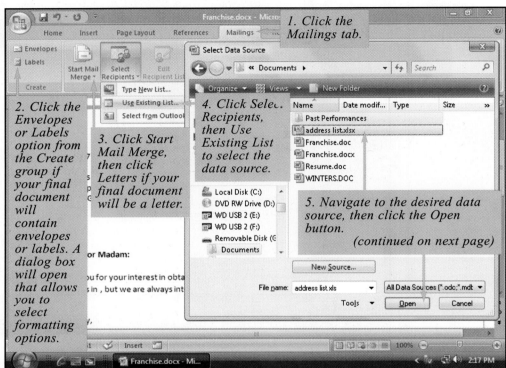

1. Click the Mailings tab.

2. Click the Envelopes or Labels option from the Create group if your final document will contain envelopes or labels. A dialog box will open that allows you to select formatting options.

3. Click Start Mail Merge, then click Letters if your final document will be a letter.

4. Click Select Recipients, then Use Existing List to select the data source.

5. Navigate to the desired data source, then click the Open button.

(continued on next page)

■ You can compose your starting document "from scratch" or from a document template.

■ The data source can come from a database file, Outlook, an Excel spreadsheet, or a Word document.

■How do I perform a mail merge? (continued)

Figure
2-9

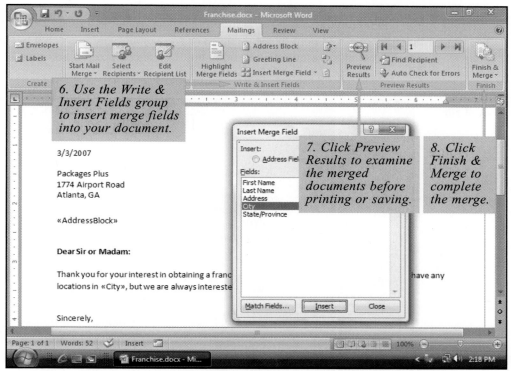

6. Use the Write &
Insert Fields group
to insert merge fields
into your document.

7. Click Preview
Results to examine
the merged
documents before
printing or saving.

8. Click
Finish &
Merge to
complete
the merge.

■ You can insert pre-formatted merge field blocks or individual merge fields from the Write & Insert Fields group. Use the Match Fields button if there are any discrepancies with field names.

■ Preview your final documents to make sure they are exactly what you want before saving or printing them.

■FAQ How do I print a document?

You can print a document using the Print option available through the Microsoft Office button. Options to print multiple copies of a document, print selected pages, or select an alternate printer are available through the Print dialog box. To access the Print dialog box, click the Microsoft Office button and then click Print.

Do It!

Figure 2–10

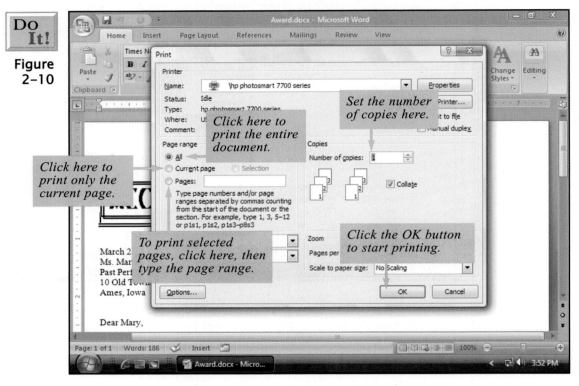

■ You can select a printer by clicking the ▾ down-arrow button at the right side of the Printer list, then clicking the printer you want to use.

■ To print the entire document, make sure the All option button is selected in the *Page range* section. To print only the current page, click the *Current page* option button in the *Page range* section.

■ To print a range of pages, enter the first page, a hyphen, then the last page in the range. For example, to print pages 13 through 28, you would enter 13-28.

■ To print specific pages that are not in a sequence, click the Pages option button, then enter the page numbers, such as 3,7,12, in the Pages text box, separated by commas.

■ To print more than one copy of a document, use the *Number of copies* spin box.

■ If your document doesn't print, make sure the printer is online and you have specified the correct printer in the Print dialog box.

■ Before you print a document, you can use Print Preview to see how it will look when printed. The preview appears when you click the Microsoft Office button, click the arrow next to Print, then click Print Preview. The Print Preview toolbar provides options for adjusting the magnification and number of pages displayed. If the preview is acceptable, click the Print button provided on the preview screen to print the document. To exit Print Preview without printing, click the Close Print Preview button.

■FAQ How can I troubleshoot printing problems?

Suppose you print a document but nothing happens! Printing problems can be caused by the printer, by the software that controls the printer, or by installation glitches. Luckily, most printing problems are easily fixed. Your first step is to check the power light to make sure the printer is turned on. Also, verify that the printer is ready to print by pressing the appropriate buttons on the printer's control panel. You should also make sure the printer is loaded with the correct size and type of paper, and the ribbon, print cartridge, or toner cartridge is properly installed.

If the printer checks out, your next step is to check the print queue. A **print queue** manages multiple documents waiting to be printed. When one document is printed, the next document in the print queue is sent to the printer. Each printer connected to your computer has a separate print queue. You can use a print queue to display information about each print job; to pause, restart, or cancel print jobs; and to move documents higher or lower in the queue.

Figure 2-11

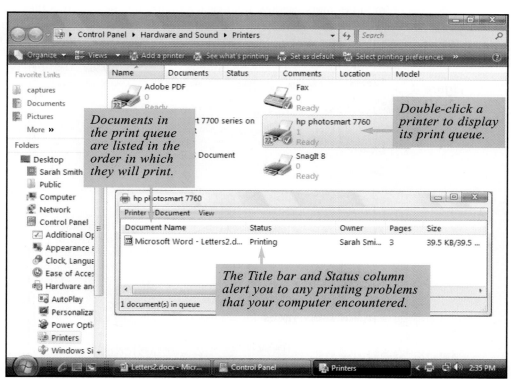

Documents in the print queue are listed in the order in which they will print.

Double-click a printer to display its print queue.

The Title bar and Status column alert you to any printing problems that your computer encountered.

■ You can view the print queue at any time by clicking the Start button, clicking Control Panel, and then clicking Printers under the Hardware and Sound section. Double-click the printer that corresponds to the print queue you want to view.

■ To pause, restart, or cancel a print job, right-click the name of the print job and choose the desired option from the shortcut menu.

■ If the printer is shared, other people might have documents in the print queue ahead of yours. Check the print queue to see if your document is waiting to be printed.

■How can I troubleshoot printing problems? (continued)

If your computer's Printers window contains icons for several printers, only one of those printers can be designated as the default printer. All documents are sent to the default printer unless you specify otherwise. A common printing problem occurs when you connect a different printer to your computer but forget to change the default printer. When a printing problem occurs, make sure the default printer setting is correct.

■ To change the default printer, click the Start button, click Control Panel, and then click Printers under the Hardware and Sound section. Right-click the printer you want to set as the default printer, and choose Set as Default Printer.

The Printer Properties dialog box is another useful tool for troubleshooting printing problems. You can use this dialog box to change print settings, activate printer sharing, check the port used to connect your printer and computer, and even print out a test page. Printing a test page can help you determine if the printer is connected correctly.

■ From the Printers window, right-click a printer and select Properties.

Figure 2-12

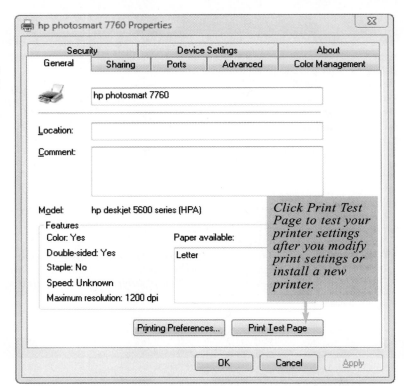

A document might not print if the page settings are not specified correctly on the Page Setup dialog box. Some printers cannot print outside of certain page boundaries, or are limited to certain page sizes. Check your printer documentation for details, and verify that the margins and page size are correct by clicking the Page Layout tab, then clicking the Page Setup Dialog Box Launcher.

Another potential cause of printing problems is the printer driver software used by your computer to control the printer. If you can't find any other solution, check with your printer's manufacturer to see if an updated printer driver is available. Updated printer drivers are typically posted online and can be easily downloaded and installed.

QuickCheck A

1. When creating a document in Microsoft Word, characters you type appear in the [   ] window.

2. Press the [   ] key to delete the character to the right of the insertion point.

3. When you [   ] text, the selected text is removed from the original location and placed on the Clipboard.

4. True or false? If you accidentally delete the wrong text, you can click the Redo button to cancel the deletion and display the original text. [   ]

5. A document [   ] allows you to create a new document from a pre-formatted document.

Check It!

QuickCheck B

Indicate the letter of the desktop element that best matches the following:

1. Selected text [   ]

2. The Copy button [   ]

3. The Paste button [   ]

4. The Cut button [   ]

5. The end of a line of text where the Enter key was pressed [   ]

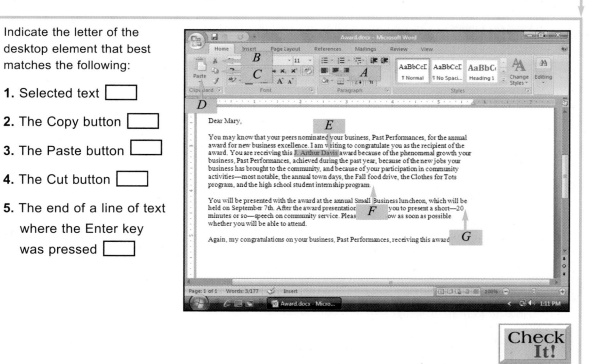

Check It!

Get It?

A Skill Set A: Creating a document

B Skill Set B: Selecting text

C Skill Set C: Moving, copying, pasting, and deleting text

D Skill Set D: Document templates and mail merges

Chapter 3

Formatting a Document

What's inside and on the CD?

In this chapter, you'll learn how to format your documents using features such as bold and italic text, different fonts and font sizes, paragraph alignment, and bulleted and numbered lists.

Experienced word processing users find that it's useful to apply formatting after writing the document. The idea is to focus initially on the content of the document, while adding, deleting, and moving text as needed. After you're satisfied with the content and order of the document, you can go back and format the document as needed.

Appropriate formatting can greatly increase the attractiveness and readability of your documents. However, it's important not to get carried away with formatting. Use different fonts, font sizes, and colors only where they add to the appearance or readability of the document. After all, you wouldn't want your documents to look like a ransom note pasted together with letters from a variety of newspaper stories!

■FAQ How do I select different fonts, font sizes, and text colors?

You can use the commands on the Home tab to select different text attributes for letters, words, sentences, or paragraphs. The term **font** refers to the design or typeface of each character. Don't use too many fonts—documents look more professional when limited to one or two basic fonts.

Figure 3-1

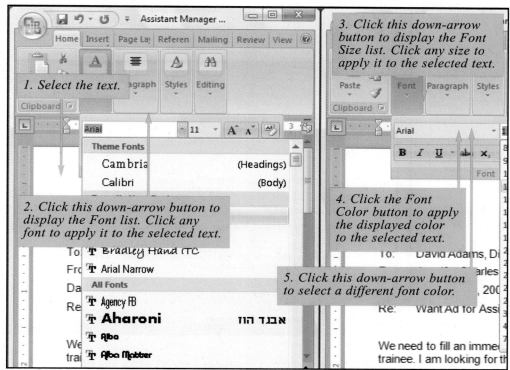

1. Select the text.

2. Click this down-arrow button to display the Font list. Click any font to apply it to the selected text.

3. Click this down-arrow button to display the Font Size list. Click any size to apply it to the selected text.

4. Click the Font Color button to apply the displayed color to the selected text.

5. Click this down-arrow button to select a different font color.

■ **Text attributes** include font, font size, bold, italic, underline, and text color. Font size is normally 9–12 points, but you can select any font size up to 72 points, which is equal to one inch. You can make text even larger by typing in a number larger than 72 up to 1638. This feature is useful for making signs and posters.

■ Once you've selected text, you can change the font, font size, and color without reselecting the text. As long as the text remains selected, you can apply additional formatting options to it. After you've formatted the text, click anywhere outside of the highlighted area to deselect it.

■ Font effects include shadow, outline, and emboss. To apply font effects, select the text, then click the Font Dialog Box Launcher in the Font group. Choose the effects you want to apply, and click OK.

■ If you want to change the font or font size for an entire document, click Editing, Select, then Select All on the Home tab to select the entire document. Using Select All, you can apply any text attributes to all the text in a document, even to multiple pages.

■FAQ How do I apply bold, italic, and underlining attributes?

You can use the commands in the Font group to apply text attributes such as bold, italic, and underlining to text within your document.

Figure 3-2

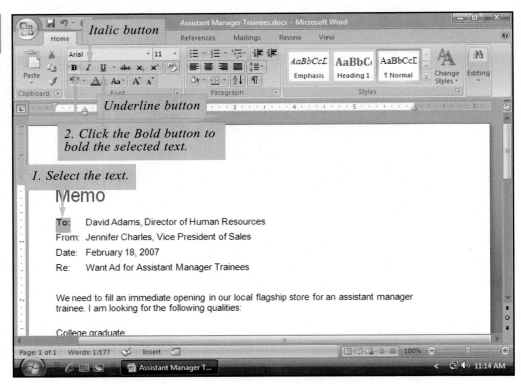

■ Typically, you'll apply text attributes to text you've already typed. Just select the text, then use the desired command button in the Font group to apply the text attribute.

■ You can apply the bold text attribute before typing new text. Click the Bold button, then type the text. Click the Bold button again to discontinue bold and continue typing normal text.

■ Command buttons both apply and remove attributes. For instance, if you applied the bold attribute, but then changed your mind and wanted to display the text as normal, you would select the text, and then click the Bold button to remove the bold attribute. The selected text is displayed as normal text.

■ The Italic button and the Underline button work the same way as the Bold button, but they apply different text attributes.

■ You can combine the bold, italic, and underline text attributes by clicking any combination of buttons. To display bold, underlined text, select the text, click the Bold button, then click the Underline button. You can freely mix and match bold, underlined, and italic text.

■ If you select a section of text that includes both normal and bold text, the first time you click the Bold button, all the selected text is displayed as bold. Click the Bold button again to display all of the selected text as normal text.

■FAQ How do I use the Font dialog box?

As you've already learned, you can apply some text attributes—such as bold, italic, and underlining—using the Font group on the Home tab. But other text attribute options, such as character-spacing options, are only available from the Font dialog box.

You can also use the Font dialog box if you want to apply multiple formatting options to selected text. It's faster to use the Font dialog box to apply all the attributes in one operation than to apply the attributes one at a time using the command buttons.

Figure 3-3

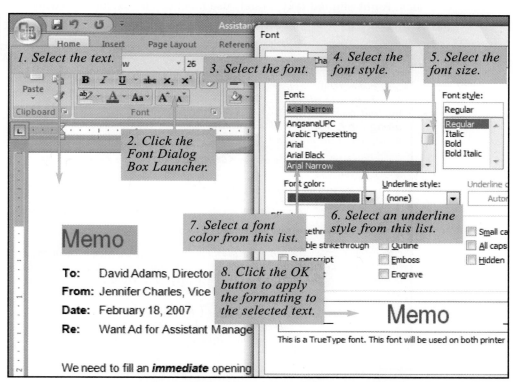

■ Use the Character Spacing tab in the Font dialog box if you need to change the scale, spacing, vertical position, or kerning of selected text. Changing the **kerning**—the space between each letter—can be particularly useful when you need to make text fit into a limited space.

■ The Preview area of the Font dialog box shows how your formatting affects the selected text. You'll see the selected font, font styles, colors, and effects before you click the OK button to accept your changes. If you don't like what you see in the Preview area, you can adjust the format settings or click the Cancel button to close the Font dialog box without applying the formatting options.

■FAQ How do I center and align text?

The Paragraph group on the Home tab provides options for centering, right aligning, left aligning, and justifying text.

Left-aligned text is positioned straight against the left margin, but appears uneven, or "ragged," on the right margin. **Centered text** is positioned between the margins and is typically used for titles. **Justified text** has both left and right margins aligned. You might want to use justified text in the body of a formal document to give it a more professional look. **Right-aligned text** is rarely used, but can be useful for headings in a paper, for example, or for the return address in a letter.

Figure 3-4

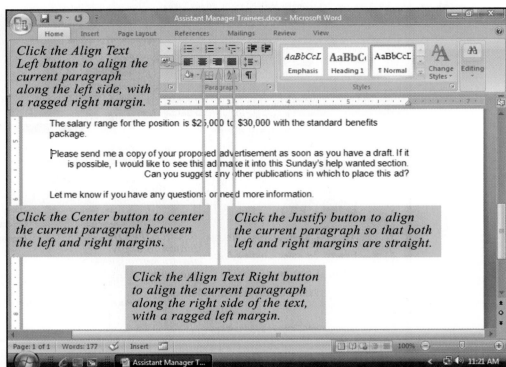

Click the Align Text Left button to align the current paragraph along the left side, with a ragged right margin.

Click the Center button to center the current paragraph between the left and right margins.

Click the Justify button to align the current paragraph so that both left and right margins are straight.

Click the Align Text Right button to align the current paragraph along the right side of the text, with a ragged left margin.

■ Unlike bold, italic, and underlining, alignment options apply to an entire paragraph. You don't have to select the text to align it—just click in the paragraph you want to align, then click the appropriate alignment button.

■ To center a title, press the Enter key at the end of the title so it becomes a separate paragraph. Click anywhere in the title, then click the Center button. Single lines, such as titles, are centered between the left and right margins. If the paragraph consists of multiple lines, every line in the paragraph is centered.

■ To return a centered paragraph to left alignment, click in the paragraph, then click the Align Text Left button.

■FAQ How do I use styles?

A **style** consists of predefined formatting that you can apply to selected text. Word comes with several predefined styles, such as Heading 1 and Subtitle. You can use Word's predefined styles or create your own styles.

One advantage of using styles is that they allow you to be consistent in formatting text throughout a document. If you find yourself regularly applying multiple format settings to sections of text, you can save time by defining your own style, then applying it as needed. Another advantage of styles is that they are recognized by many desktop publishing programs and Web authoring tools. Consequently, a document retains its formats and styles even if you import it into a different software package.

Figure 3-5

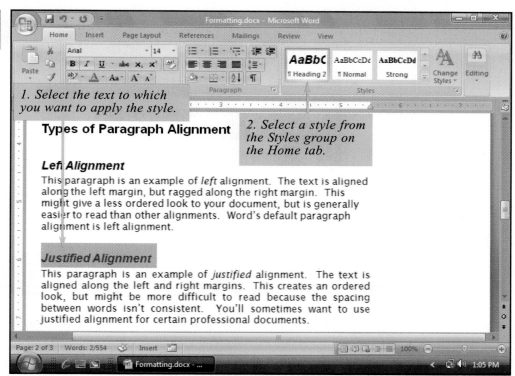

■ To create a style, format a section of text using the desired font, font size, and font styles. Click the Styles Dialog Box Launcher to display the Styles dialog box. Click the New Style button to display the Create New Style from Formatting dialog box. Click the Name text box, then type the name for your new style. Click the OK button to close the Create New Style from Formatting dialog box. Click the Close button to close the Styles dialog box. Your new style is added to the Styles list. To apply the style to other text, select the text, then select your style from the Styles list.

■ To remove a style from a section of text, select the text, then select the Normal style from the Styles list.

■ To delete a style so that it no longer appears in the Styles list, click the Styles Dialog Box Launcher to display the Styles dialog box. Right-click the style you want to delete, then select Delete. Click Yes, then click the Close button to close the Styles dialog box.

■FAQ How do I add numbering and bullets to a list?

Word's Paragraph group on the Home tab contains buttons to format a list with bullets or numbers. A **bullet** is a symbol placed before each item in a list. You can use bullets when you want to set off the items in a list but don't want to imply a specific order. A numbered list is a list with a number in front of each item on the list, which implies the items are listed in order.

Figure 3-6

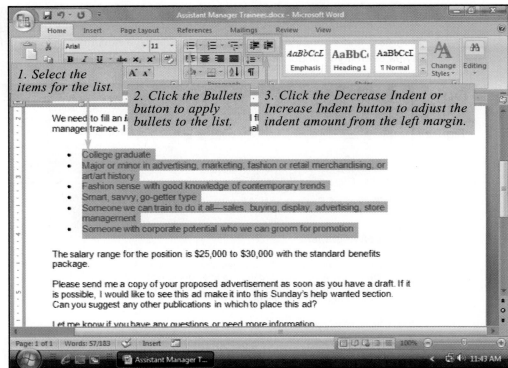

1. Select the items for the list.

2. Click the Bullets button to apply bullets to the list.

3. Click the Decrease Indent or Increase Indent button to adjust the indent amount from the left margin.

■ Numbered lists work the same as bulleted lists. Select the items on the list, then click the ▤ Numbering button to add numbers to the list.

■ If you haven't typed the list yet, click the Numbering or Bullets button, then type the items on the list. Each time you press the Enter key, a new number or bullet is inserted before the next list item. At the end of the list, press the Enter key and click the Numbering or Bullets button to discontinue the numbering for the next line of text.

■ To remove numbering or bullets from a list, select the list, then click the Numbering or Bullets button.

■ If you add, delete, or move the items on a numbered list, Word renumbers the list for you. If the numbering is incorrect, select the list, then click the Numbering button twice. This procedure removes and then reapplies the numbering, which usually corrects any problem with the numbers on the list.

■ To change the numbered or bulleted list style, select the list, then right-click the list to display the shortcut menu. Point to Bullets or Numbering, then select a format.

■FAQ How do I adjust line spacing?

Your Word document is single-spaced unless you specify another spacing option, such as double- or triple-spacing. You can apply line-spacing options to a single paragraph, to a group of paragraphs, or to the entire document. You can also adjust the space between paragraphs.

Figure 3–7

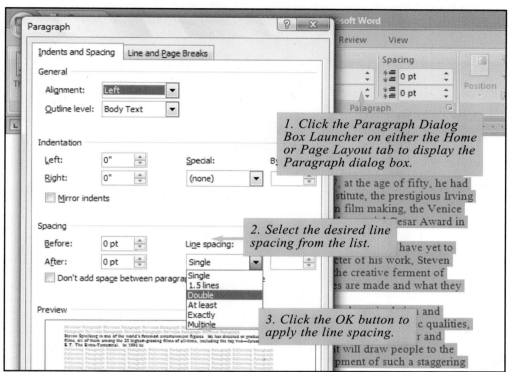

■ Do not press the Enter key at the end of each line to create double-spaced text. This makes it difficult to edit your document because words won't wrap from one line to the next. The preferred way to double-space a document is to type the document as regular single-spaced text, then set the line spacing to double.

■ To adjust the line spacing for one paragraph of text, position the insertion point in the paragraph, then click the Paragraph Dialog Box Launcher on the Home or Page Layout tab to display the Paragraph dialog box. Select the desired spacing from the Line spacing drop-down list on the Indents and Spacing tab. Single- and double-spacing are the most commonly used spacing settings.

■ To adjust the line spacing for more than one paragraph, select the paragraphs, then adjust the line spacing as described above.

■ To adjust the space between paragraphs, click the Paragraph Dialog Box Launcher on the Home or Page Layout tab to display the Paragraph dialog box. Select the desired paragraph spacing from the Before and After boxes on the Indents and Spacing tab.

■ You can set the line spacing for the entire document before you begin typing. Click Editing, Select, then Select All on the Home tab. Click the Paragraph Dialog Box Launcher on the Home or Page Layout tab. Select the desired line spacing, then click the OK button. As you type, the text appears on the screen with the selected line spacing.

■FAQ How do I use tabs?

Setting a **tab** provides an easy way to align text in columns. Word provides default tab stops every 1/2", but you can change the default tab settings and add your own tab stops. The position of a tab stop is measured from the left margin.

Figure 3-8

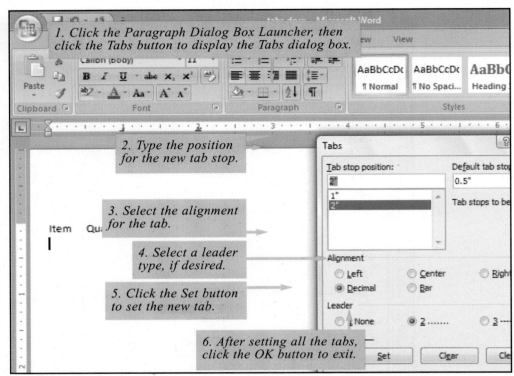

1. Click the Paragraph Dialog Box Launcher, then click the Tabs button to display the Tabs dialog box.

2. Type the position for the new tab stop.

3. Select the alignment for the tab.

4. Select a leader type, if desired.

5. Click the Set button to set the new tab.

6. After setting all the tabs, click the OK button to exit.

■ There are many types of tab stops. A left tab stop means that text will be aligned on the left side of the tab. A right tab stop means that text will be aligned on the right side of the tab. A center tab stop centers text at that location, while a decimal tab stop aligns numbers with the decimal at the tab location. A bar tab stop places a vertical bar at the tab location.

■ A **leader** is a line of punctuation characters, such as periods, that fills the area between text and a tab stop. Leaders are typically used in a table of contents to associate a page number with the appropriate chapter or heading. To add a leader to a tab stop, click the option button to select the leader type. When you tab to that tab stop, the leader character—usually a series of periods—fills the area to the tab stop.

■ To clear one tab stop, click that tab stop in the Tab stop position box, then click the Clear button. To clear all tab stops, click the Clear All button in the Tabs dialog box.

■ On the Word ruler bar, tab stops are represented by these small icons:

∟	Left tab	⊥	Decimal tab
⅃	Right tab	I	Bar tab
⊥	Center tab		

To set tabs using the ruler, select the type of tab stop by clicking the icon at the left end of the ruler. Click a location on the ruler to set the tab stop. You can move a tab stop by selecting it, then sliding it right or left on the ruler bar.

■FAQ How do I indent text?

You can indent text from the left margin, from the right margin, or from both margins. You can also indent the first line of text differently from the rest of a paragraph. Normally, the first line is indented farther to the right than the rest of the paragraph, but you can use a **hanging indent** to move the first line of text more to the left than the rest of the paragraph. Word's Paragraph dialog box provides several options for indenting text.

Figure 3-9

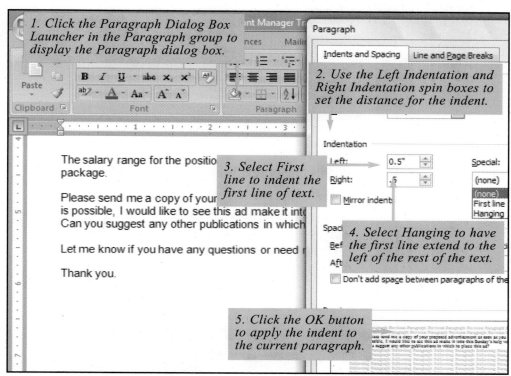

1. Click the Paragraph Dialog Box Launcher in the Paragraph group to display the Paragraph dialog box.

2. Use the Left Indentation and Right Indentation spin boxes to set the distance for the indent.

3. Select First line to indent the first line of text.

4. Select Hanging to have the first line extend to the left of the rest of the text.

5. Click the OK button to apply the indent to the current paragraph.

■ To indent an entire paragraph from the left, click the spin box buttons in the Left Indentation box to increase or decrease the indent distance. Use the same process with the Right Indentation box to increase or decrease the right indentation.

■ The Preview section shows how the paragraph will look after it is indented. As you change your selections, the Preview is updated.

■ To indent the first line of text, select First line from the Special pull-down list. Select the amount of indentation for the first line of the paragraph from the By spin box.

■ To create a hanging indent in which the first line of text extends more to the left than the rest of the text, select Hanging from the Special pull-down list. Select the amount of negative indent for the first line of the paragraph from the By spin box.

■ The indent settings apply to the paragraph that contains the insertion point. To apply an indent to more than one paragraph, select the paragraphs, then use the Paragraph dialog box to set the indent.

■FAQ How do I add footnotes or endnotes to a document?

Footnotes and endnotes are typically used to add comments to blocks of text or cite references to other documents. An asterisk or superscript number appearing in the main text of a document indicates a footnote or endnote. A **footnote** appears at the bottom of the page that contains the corresponding superscript number. An **endnote** appears at the end of a section or chapter.

Figure 3-10

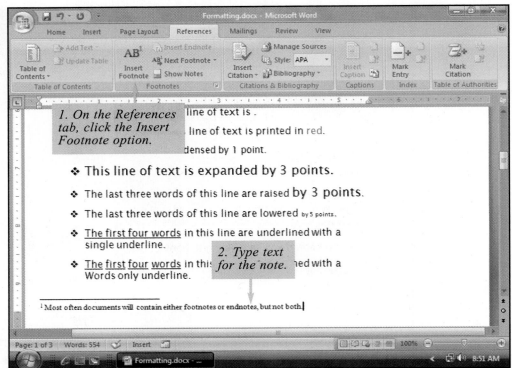

■ To insert a footnote or endnote, click the References tab. Click the Insert Footnote or Insert Endnote button. A text area appears on the bottom of your screen that allows you to type the note text.

■ You can open the Footnote and Endnote dialog box with the Footnote & Endnote Dialog Box Launcher. To modify the format of a footnote or endnote, use the Format options in the Footnote and Endnote dialog box.

■ To delete a footnote or endnote, select the number that corresponds to the note in the text, and press the Delete key.

■FAQ How do I work with outlines and other document views?

Word provides several ways to view a document. You can display **format marks** to reveal hidden symbols that indicate paragraph breaks ¶ , spaces · , and tab stops →. To display hidden formatting marks, click the ¶ Show/Hide button in the Paragraph group on the Home tab.

You can also change the document view to see how it will look when printed (Print Layout view), as a Web page (Web Layout view), or as an outline (Outline view). To change the document view, click one of the view buttons in the lower-right corner of the document window. You can also change the view by clicking the View tab, then clicking one of the views listed.

Outline view is handy for organizing the content of a document. You can assign outline levels to each title, heading, and paragraph, and view any level of the outline to get an overview or include all details. In Outline view, it is easy to rearrange sections of a document to streamline its organization.

Do It!

Figure 3-11

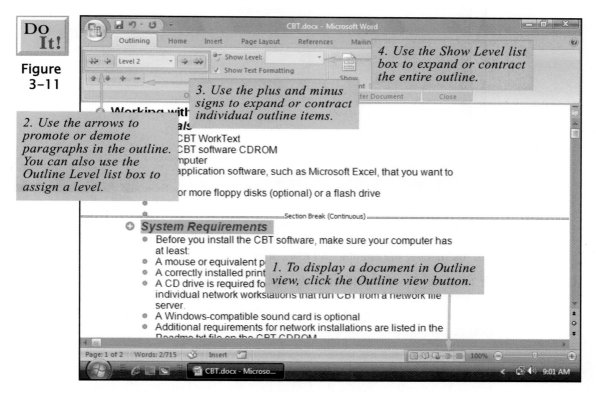

■ Microsoft Word uses the following conventions to indicate outline levels:

A plus sign 🔂 indicates a heading with subtext.

A small solid circle ● indicates body text at the lowest level of the outline.

A gray line under a heading indicates subordinate text that is not displayed.

A dash ⊖ indicates a heading without subordinate text.

■FAQ How do I create a table?

A **table** is a grid consisting of rows and columns. The intersection of each row and column is called a **cell**. Each cell can hold text, numbers, or a graphic. You can format an entire table or individual cells.

Figure 3–12

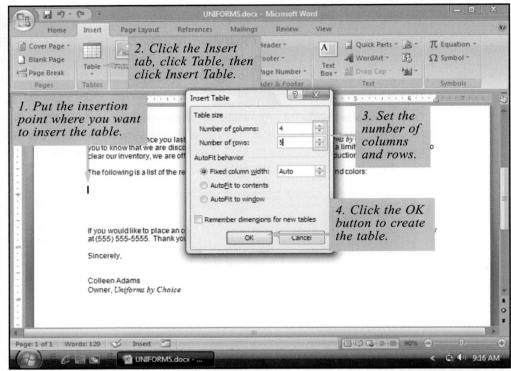

2. Click the Insert tab, click Table, then click Insert Table.

1. Put the insertion point where you want to insert the table.

3. Set the number of columns and rows.

4. Click the OK button to create the table.

■ To create a table, place the insertion point where you want to insert the table. Click the Insert tab, click Table, then click Insert Table to display the Insert Table dialog box. Set the number of columns and rows, then click the OK button to create the table.

■ To add text to the table, click any cell, then type text in that cell. The word wrap feature moves text down while you type and expands the size of the cell to make room for all of your text. To move to another cell, press the arrow keys, press the Tab key, or click the desired cell.

■ To quickly format the table, make sure the insertion point is in the table, then click the Design tab under the Table Tools contextual tab. Select a table style from the Table Styles group. You can then modify the format to change, for instance, the font.

■ To insert a new row or column, place the insertion point in the cell closest to where you want the new row or column to appear. Click the Layout tab under the Table Tools contextual tab, then choose from among the options to specify the placement of the new row or column from the Rows & Columns group.

■ To delete unused rows or columns, position the insertion point in the column or row you want to delete. Click the Layout tab under the Table Tools contextual tab, then click the Delete command in the Rows & Columns group. Select from among the options to specify what you want to delete.

■ To adjust the width of a column, position the pointer over the dividing line between the columns. When the pointer changes to a +‖+ shape, press the left mouse button and drag the column to the correct width.

QuickCheck A

1. To select an entire document for editing from the Editing group, click Select, then click [_____] on the Home tab. Whatever text attribute you then select will be applied to the entire document.

2. Centering and alignment formats apply to an entire [_____] of text.

3. You should use the [_____] dialog box to apply multiple formatting options in a single operation.

4. A(n) [_____] is a symbol, such as a square or circle, placed before an item in a list.

5. True or false? To double-space a document, you should press the Enter key two times at the end of every line of text. [_____]

Check It!

QuickCheck B

Indicate the letter of the desktop element that best matches the following:

1. The Underline button [____]

2. The Font list [____]

3. The Center button [____]

4. The Bullets button [____]

5. A paragraph containing a hanging indent [____]

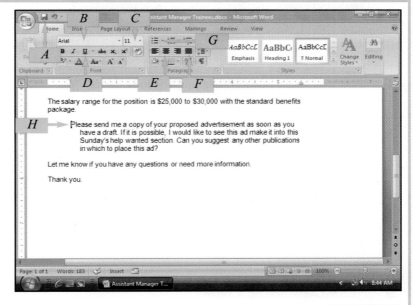

Check It!

Get It?

A Skill Set A: Using text attributes and fonts

B Skill Set B: Centering and aligning text

C Skill Set C: Creating lists and setting line spacing

D Skill Set D: Setting tabs and indenting text

.Chapter 4

Finalizing a Document

What's inside and on the CD?

Writing a document is only half the battle. Once the first draft is done, you'll typically want to check spelling and grammar, apply some formatting, and maybe even change a few words here and there. In this chapter, you'll learn how to add the finishing touches to prepare your document for printing or posting as a Web page.

Important features covered in this chapter include spelling and grammar checking, using the thesaurus to find more suitable words, adding headers and footers, and setting margins. You'll learn how to save your document as a Web page so it can be posted on the World Wide Web. Also, you'll find out how adding comments and tracking changes make it easy for multiple people to collaborate on a single document.

■ ■ ■ ■

■FAQ How do I check spelling, grammar, and readability?

Microsoft Word provides tools to help you check spelling and grammar in your documents. You should use these tools for all documents before printing them—it only takes a few minutes and can help you catch embarrassing mistakes. However, you should also proofread your documents by reading them carefully. You can't depend on the spelling and grammar checker to identify all mistakes or to make sure your document says what you really mean it to say.

In addition to spelling and grammar, you can check the readability of a document by displaying **readability statistics** based on your document's average number of syllables per word and words per sentence. Readability statistics are summarized as a score between 1 and 100 (aim for a score of 60–70) or a grade level (aim for 7th or 8th grade).

Do It!

Figure 4-1

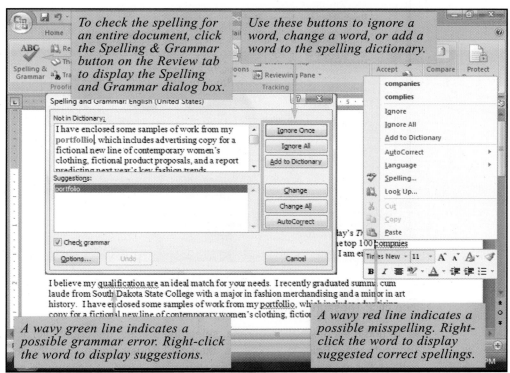

To check the spelling for an entire document, click the Spelling & Grammar button on the Review tab to display the Spelling and Grammar dialog box.

Use these buttons to ignore a word, change a word, or add a word to the spelling dictionary.

A wavy green line indicates a possible grammar error. Right-click the word to display suggestions.

A wavy red line indicates a possible misspelling. Right-click the word to display suggested correct spellings.

■ If you don't see any wavy lines, spelling and grammar checking might be turned off. Click the Microsoft Office button, then click the Word Options button. On the Proofing tab, select *Check spelling as you type*.

■ You can also check the spelling and grammar of a complete document by clicking the Spelling & Grammar button on the Review tab. Words that might be misspelled are shown in red. Possible grammar mistakes are shown in green. You can click the appropriate buttons to ignore or replace each word or phrase.

■ Readability statistics are shown at the end of a spelling and grammar check if the statistics feature is turned on. To turn on this feature, click the Microsoft Office button, then click the Word Options button. On the Proofing tab, select *Show readability statistics*.

■FAQ How do I use the thesaurus?

A thesaurus contains synonyms for words and some common phrases. When you are composing a document and can't think of just the "right" word, you can type the closest word that comes to mind, and then use Word's thesaurus to search for words with a similar meaning.

Figure 4–2

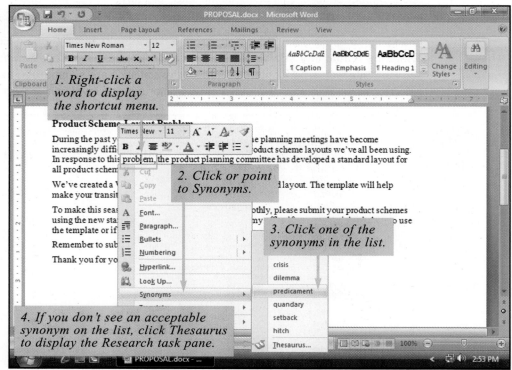

■ You can also access Word's thesaurus through the Review tab. Click the Review tab, then click Thesaurus.

■ To find a synonym for a phrase, select the phrase, then right-click it to display the shortcut menu. Point to Synonyms, then click Thesaurus to open the Research task pane. A list of phrases appears. Sometimes you'll find an acceptable alternate phrase, but beware—some of the phrases listed might not be appropriate substitutes.

■FAQ How do I create headers and footers?

A **header** is text that appears at the top of every page of a document. A **footer** is text that appears at the bottom of every page. Headers and footers typically contain information such as the title of the document, the date, the name of the author, and the current page number.

Do It!

Figure 4-3

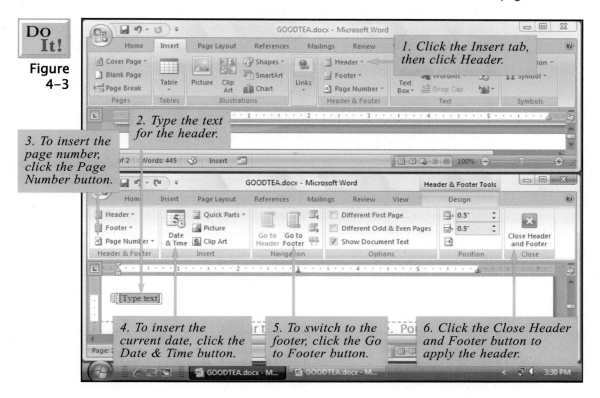

1. Click the Insert tab, then click Header.

2. Type the text for the header.

3. To insert the page number, click the Page Number button.

4. To insert the current date, click the Date & Time button.

5. To switch to the footer, click the Go to Footer button.

6. Click the Close Header and Footer button to apply the header.

■ Headers and footers are displayed only in Print Layout view, in Full Screen Reading view, in a print preview, and on printed pages.

■ The header and footer have preset tabs—a center tab in the middle of the page, and a right tab near the right margin. Press the Tab key to move the insertion point to the next tab to enter text at that location.

■ If you want to include text such as "Page 6" in your header or footer, click the ⬛ Page Number ▾ Page Number button in the Header & Footer group, then select the desired format. Page numbers are automatically updated when page content changes during editing.

■ To insert the current date and time, click the Date & Time button in the Insert group, select the desired format from the Date and Time dialog box, then click OK. The date and time are automatically updated each time you open the document.

■ Click the Go to Header or Go to Footer button to switch between the header and footer. You can edit the header or the footer, but not both at the same time.

■FAQ How do I insert page breaks and section breaks?

A **page break** occurs within a document where one page ends and the next page begins. When a page is filled with text or graphics, Word automatically inserts a page break. In Draft view, a horizontal dotted line indicates an automatic page break. You can also insert a manual, or "forced," page break at any point in the document. In Print Layout view, both automatic and manual page breaks are displayed as the end of a sheet, or page, within the document.

A **section break**, displayed as a double dotted line in Draft view, divides a document into sections. You can apply different formatting to each section of a document. For example, you might define the title page of a term paper as a section, and format it as a single column with no headers. You could then define the body of the document as a separate section formatted with two columns and headers that contain page numbers.

■ Use sections when parts of a document require different page-based format settings for margins, borders, vertical alignment, columns, headers and footers, footnotes and endnotes, page numbering, and line numbers. Paragraph and text-based formatting— such as paragraph spacing, line spacing, font, size, and color—are typically applied to selected text, rather than to sections.

■ To insert a break, click the Page Layout tab, then click Breaks to open the Break dialog box. Select the type of break you want, then click OK. You can also insert a page break with the Page Break button in the Pages group on the Insert tab or by using the keyboard shortcut Ctrl+Enter.

Do It!

Figure 4–4

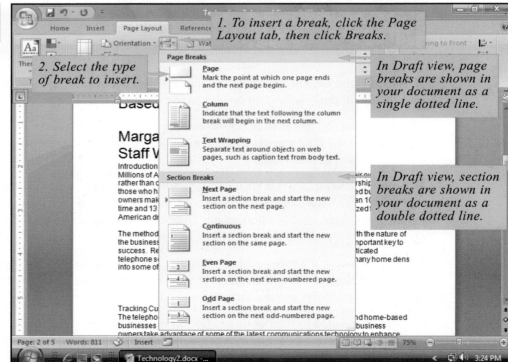

■FAQ Can I insert graphics into a document?

You can use two types of graphics to enhance documents created with Microsoft Word: vector graphics and bitmap graphics. Both types of graphics can be used to add pizzazz to a page, draw interest to certain text selections, or illustrate important points. Don't overuse pictures, however. Too many can cause a page to look cluttered and confusing.

A **bitmap graphic**, referred to in Word as a "picture," is composed of a grid of colored dots. Digital photos and scanned images are typically stored as bitmap graphics with extensions such as .bmp, .png, .jpg, .tif, or .gif. Word does not provide a feature to create bitmap graphics, but you can insert photos and other bitmaps stored in files on your computer. Word provides a Picture Tools contextual tab to help you adjust the color, contrast, and brightness of inserted bitmap graphics. You can also use this tab to crop or rotate a picture.

■ To insert a bitmap graphic into a document, click the Insert tab, then click Picture from the Illustrations group. Use the Open dialog box to navigate to the folder that contains the picture you want to insert, and then click Insert.

■ To crop a picture, select the picture, click the Crop button from the Size group, then drag the edges of the picture to frame the part of the image you want to display.

■ Adjust the brightness, contrast, and color of a picture by selecting the graphic, and then clicking the Brightness, Contrast, or Recolor buttons in the Adjust group.

■ You can control the way text flows around a picture in a document. To wrap text around a picture, select the picture. From the Arrange group, click the Text Wrapping button, and then select a text flow option from the list.

■ To delete a picture, click it, and then press the Delete key.

Do It!

Figure 4-5

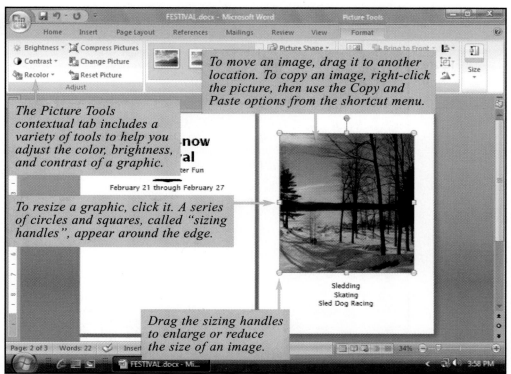

The Picture Tools contextual tab includes a variety of tools to help you adjust the color, brightness, and contrast of a graphic.

To move an image, drag it to another location. To copy an image, right-click the picture, then use the Copy and Paste options from the shortcut menu.

To resize a graphic, click it. A series of circles and squares, called "sizing handles", appear around the edge.

Drag the sizing handles to enlarge or reduce the size of an image.

■Can I insert graphics into a document? (continued)

A **vector graphic**, sometimes called a "drawing," is created with basic shapes, such as lines, curves, and rectangles. Clip art, logos, and organizational charts are often created using vector graphics, and have extensions such as .wmf and .ai. Microsoft Office includes a clip art collection you can access by clicking the Insert tab, then clicking Clip Art in the Illustrations group.

You can use Word's Shapes to create your own simple vector graphics within a document. You can also use it to enhance vector graphics you've obtained from other sources and inserted into a document.

■ You can create vector drawings by combining several shapes within a rectangular area called a "canvas." To open a blank canvas, click the Insert tab, click the Shapes button in the Illustrations group, then click New Drawing Canvas. When the canvas is selected, you can use the Insert Shapes group on the Drawing Tools contextual tab to add shapes to the canvas.

■ Multiple shapes can be grouped together so that they can be moved and resized as a single unit. To group objects, hold down the Ctrl key and select the shapes you want to group. Right-click the shapes, point to Grouping, and then click Group. Shapes can be ungrouped using a similar procedure, but clicking Ungroup instead of Group.

■ You can use layers to make shapes appear to be stacked on top of one another or to appear in front of or behind text. To move a shape from one layer to another, right-click the shape, and then click Order. Choose an order from the list.

■ To control the way text flows around a vector graphic, click Text Wrapping from the Arrange group, and then select an option from the list.

Figure 4–6

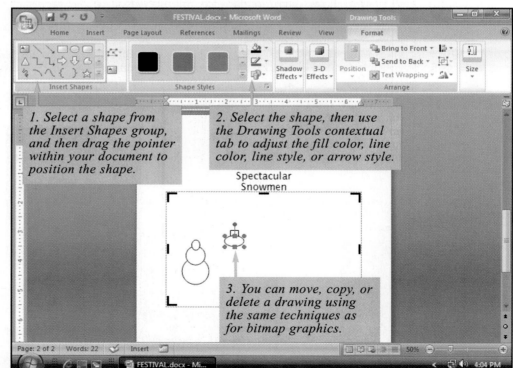

■FAQ How do I set margins?

Margin settings typically apply to an entire document and are changed using the Page Setup group on the Page Layout tab.

In a Word document, the default margins are 1" for all the margins. The margin setting affects the amount of text that you can fit on a page. Smaller margins allow for more text, whereas larger margins reduce the amount of text that fits on a page.

Figure 4-7

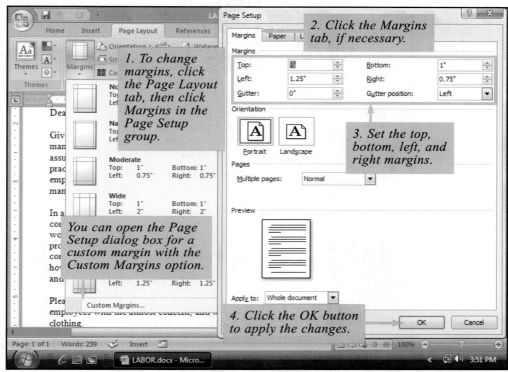

■ Don't set the top and bottom margins too small if you're using headers and footers. The header and footer will not print correctly if there isn't enough room in the top or bottom margin.

■ Select Portrait orientation to print the page vertically. If you have a wide document, select Landscape orientation to print the page sideways.

■ You can use the Paper tab in the Page Setup dialog box to set the paper size and control how paper feeds into your default printer. Select the appropriate paper size from the Paper size list. You can find more information about your printer options in the printer documentation.

■ The Layout tab in the Page Setup dialog box is useful for creating different headers and footers for odd and even pages. Other layout options allow you to center text vertically on the page, insert line numbers, and add graphical elements, such as borders, to the document.

■ All these formatting options can apply to the whole document, to selected sections of the document, or to the rest of the document that follows the current location of the insertion point. You can find more information about page setup options in Word Help.

■FAQ How do I save a document as a Web page?

Instead of printing a document, you might want to post it on the Internet as a Web page. As with other Web pages, your document must be in HTML (Hypertext Markup Language) format to be accessible to Web browsers, such as Internet Explorer or Mozilla Firefox. You can use the *Save As* option through the Microsoft Office button to save a document in HTML format.

Figure 4–8

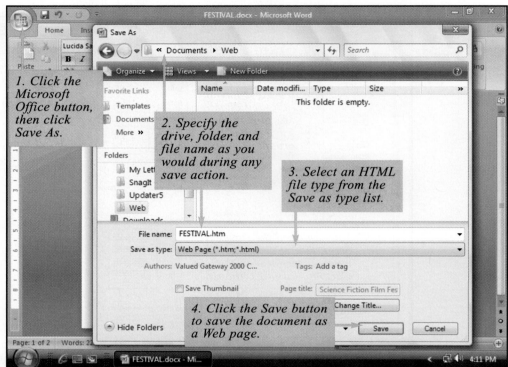

1. Click the Microsoft Office button, then click Save As.

2. Specify the drive, folder, and file name as you would during any save action.

3. Select an HTML file type from the Save as type list.

4. Click the Save button to save the document as a Web page.

■ Word does a fairly good job of converting a document to HTML, but several formatting options available in Word cannot be duplicated in HTML documents. If a document contains formatting that cannot be duplicated in HTML, Word displays a message during the conversion process that describes the problem areas. You then have the option of canceling or continuing with the save.

■ To see how the document will look when viewed in a Web browser, locate the file with Windows Explorer, then double-click the file to open it in a Web browser.

■ When you save a long document as a Web page, it will be displayed as a single long page—sort of like a papyrus scroll—even though it might have been divided into separate pages as a Word document. When you view it in a Web browser, you'll use the vertical scroll bar to move through the document.

■ Contact your Internet Service Provider (ISP) or technical support person if you need instructions for posting your Web pages on the Internet.

■FAQ Can I track changes and insert comments in a document?

As a document is revised, you might want to maintain a record of the original wording. This capability is especially important in the development of legal documents and when multiple people collaborate on a single document. Microsoft Word provides several features for such situations.

The Track Changes feature maintains all deleted, changed, and inserted text for a document and displays it in a contrasting font color. You can hide or display these "changes" and integrate them in the document by "accepting" them. Word's comment feature allows you to insert the electronic version of "sticky notes" in your document. Comments are displayed as balloons in the margins and can be displayed or hidden as needed.

Figure 4-9

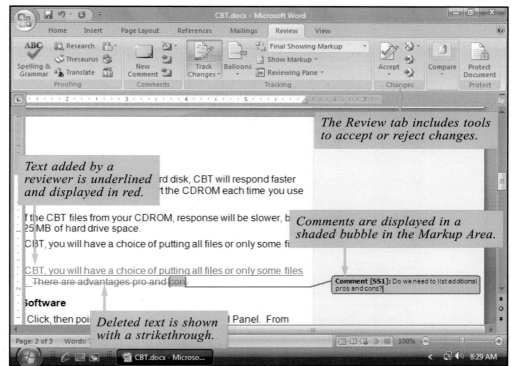

The Review tab includes tools to accept or reject changes.

Text added by a reviewer is underlined and displayed in red.

Comments are displayed in a shaded bubble in the Markup Area.

Deleted text is shown with a strikethrough.

■ To track changes, click the Review tab, then click Track Changes in the Tracking group. As you edit the document, changes are indicated in a contrasting font color.

■ To accept a change in an edited document, click the changed text, click Accept in the Changes group, then click *Accept Change*. To reject a change, use the Reject options in the Changes group.

■ To accept all changes in a document, click Accept in the Changes group, then click *Accept All Changes in Document*.

■ To reject all changes in a document, click Reject in the Changes group, then click *Reject All Changes in Document*.

■ To insert a comment, click New Comment in the Comments group on the Review tab. Type your comment in the comment bubble that appears in the Markup Area.

■FAQ What other features can I use to finalize my documents?

Use the following tips and tricks to create more professional-looking documents, automate document formatting, or simply "spruce up" your existing documents.

■ Borders and shading allow you to emphasize certain sections of text or parts of a table. A **border** is a line or graphic drawn around a page or section of text. Borders can be customized by width, color, number of lines, and type of graphic. **Shading** is grayscale or color background applied to text or table cells. Borders and shading are often used together to highlight sections of text, differentiate cells and titles in a table, or create an eye-catching page or document. To apply borders and shading to a section of a document, click the down-arrow button on the Borders and Shading button in the Paragraph group on the Home tab.

■ Themes make it easy to create professional-looking documents without having to customize the style of every element in the document. A **theme** is a predefined set of coordinated styles, colors, and text options designed to be applied to an existing document. Word includes themes such as Apex, Metro, and Office. To choose a theme for your document, click Themes in the Themes group on the Page Layout tab.

■ **AutoFormat** allows Word to automatically format your document as you type. AutoFormat performs tasks such as replacing fractions (1/4 with ¼) and formatting Internet addresses as hyperlinks. To modify AutoFormat options, click the Microsoft Office button, then click the Word Options button. Click the Proofing tab, then click the AutoCorrect Options button to open the AutoCorrect dialog box.

■ The Format Painter feature makes it easy to replicate formats from one text selection to another. Click any text that has the format you would like to replicate, click the Format Painter button in the Clipboard group on the Home tab to capture the format, then click the text where you would like the format applied. If you double-click the Format Painter button, you can copy the format to several locations. When you are finished copying the format to the desired locations, simply click the Format Painter button to stop the paste process.

Do It!

Figure 4-10

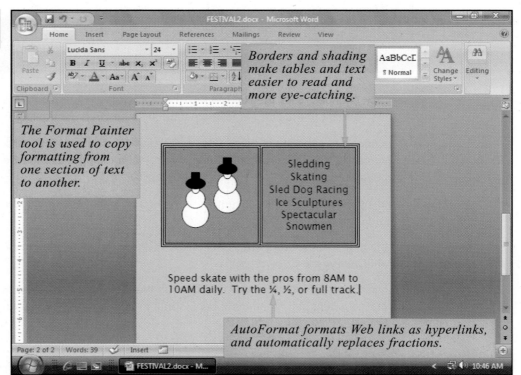

QuickCheck A

1. You can use Word's [_____] feature to find synonyms.

2. Word's [_____] feature allows you to insert electronic "sticky notes" in your document.

3. A(n) [_____] is text placed at the bottom of every page of a Word document.

4. When you save a Word document as a Web page, it is converted to [_____] markup language format.

5. You can use Word's Shapes options to create your own simple [_____] graphics consisting of shapes and lines.

Check It!

QuickCheck B

Indicate the letter of the desktop element that best matches the following:

1. A possible spelling error [____]

2. A possible grammatical error [____]

3. The Go to Footer button [____]

4. The Insert Page Number button [____]

5. The Insert Date & Time button [____]

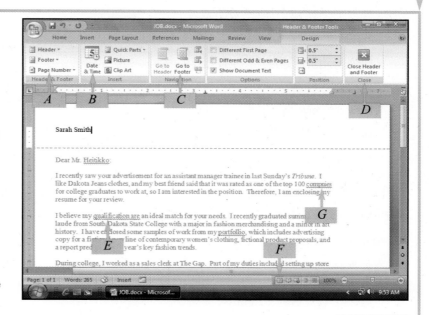

Check It!

Get It?

[A] Skill Set A: Checking spelling and grammar

[B] Skill Set B: Headers and footers

[C] Skill Set C: Breaks and graphics

[D] Skill Set D: Margins and Web pages

Chapter 5

Creating a Worksheet

What's inside and on the CD?

In this chapter, you'll learn the essentials of creating a worksheet with Microsoft Excel. **Microsoft Excel** is the component of the Microsoft Office suite best suited for working with numbers and formulas. As **spreadsheet software**, Microsoft Excel provides a set of tools for simple or complex calculations, such as creating a budget, estimating expenses, and creating an income and expense projection.

An electronic spreadsheet, often referred to as a worksheet, functions much like a visual calculator. You place each number needed for a calculation into a cell of the grid. You then enter formulas to add, subtract, or otherwise manipulate these numbers. The spreadsheet software automatically performs the calculations and displays the results.

■FAQ What's in the Excel window?

To start Excel, click Start, point to All Programs, click Microsoft Office, then click Microsoft Excel 2007. You should notice that the ribbon is displayed and contains tabs, groups, and commands similar to those you learned to use in Microsoft Word. In this chapter, you will learn some of the important features of Excel that are different from the features of Word.

Play It!

Figure 5-1

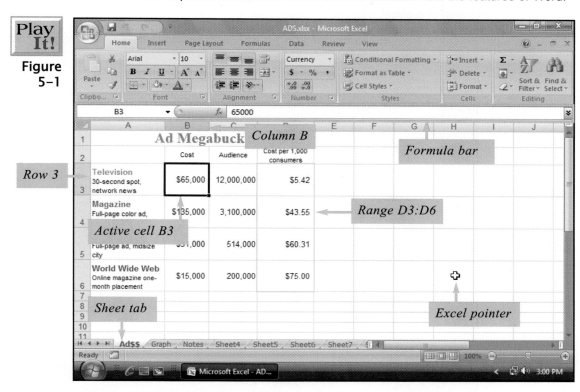

■ A **worksheet** consists of a grid of columns and rows. The columns are typically labeled with letters, starting with A as the column farthest to the left. The rows are typically labeled with numbers, starting with 1 as the top row.

■ Excel worksheets are saved in a **workbook**. A workbook contains one or more worksheets, each represented by a tab at the bottom of the Excel window. When you save or open a workbook, all worksheets in that workbook are automatically saved or opened. To switch to a different worksheet in the current workbook, click its sheet tab. Right-click a sheet tab to rename, insert, or delete a worksheet.

■ A **worksheet cell** (or "cell" for short) is the rectangle formed by the intersection of a column and row. Each cell has a unique name consisting of the column letter and row number. For example, cell B3 is located in the second column of the third row.

■ The **active cell** is the cell you can currently edit or modify, and it is marked with a black outline. You can change the active cell by clicking any other cell. You can also change the active cell by pressing the arrow keys to move the black outline up, down, left, or right.

■ A **range** is a series of cells. For example, D3:D6 is a range that contains all cells from D3 through D6, inclusive. When specifying a range, use a colon to separate the first and last cells. To select a range of cells, click the cell in the top-left corner of the range, then drag the mouse to the bottom-right cell in the range.

■ ■ ■

■FAQ How do I enter labels?

A **label** is any text entered into a cell of the worksheet. You can use labels for a worksheet title, to describe the numbers you've entered in other cells, and for text data, such as the names of people or cities. Any "number" data you do not intend to use in a calculation should be entered as a label. This data might be a telephone number, a social security number, or a street address.

Figure 5-2

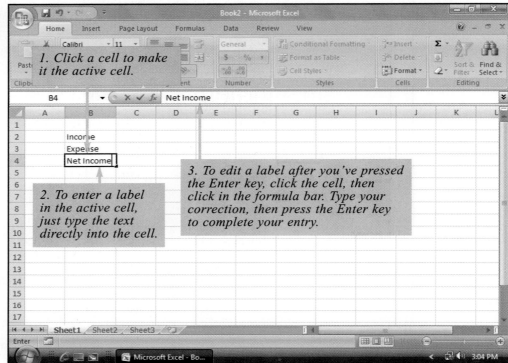

1. Click a cell to make it the active cell.

2. To enter a label in the active cell, just type the text directly into the cell.

3. To edit a label after you've pressed the Enter key, click the cell, then click in the formula bar. Type your correction, then press the Enter key to complete your entry.

■ If a label is too long to fit in the current cell, it extends into the cells to the right if they are empty. If the cells on the right are not empty, part of the label will be truncated, which means it will be hidden behind the adjacent cell's content.

■ It's possible to make a long label "wrap" so that it is displayed in two or more lines of text inside the same cell. Select the cell or cells. From the Home tab, click the Wrap Text button in the Alignment group.

■ To edit a label after you've pressed the Enter key, click the cell, then click in the formula bar. Use the left and right arrow keys to move the insertion point in the formula bar, and use the Backspace and Delete keys to delete characters. Press the Enter key when you finish editing the label. You can also press the ✓ Enter button on the formula bar to complete your entry. Press the ✕ Cancel button to exit the formula bar without keeping any changes.

■ It's possible to edit a label inside a cell. Double-click the cell to activate it, then edit the contents using the arrow, Backspace, and Delete keys. Press the Enter key when you finish editing the label.

■FAQ How do I enter values?

A **value** is a number that you intend to use in a calculation and that is entered into a cell of a worksheet. Cells containing values can be used in formulas to calculate results. It is important for you to recognize when a number should be entered as a value and when a number should be entered as a label.

Figure 5–3

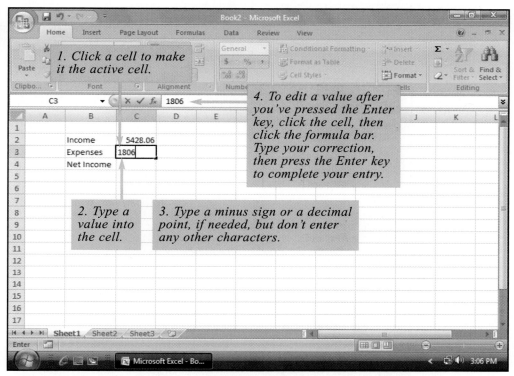

■ Type a minus sign (-) before a number to enter a negative value. Although you can include the dollar sign and comma in values, it's best to just enter the unformatted number into a cell. You will learn how to format values in another chapter.

■ After you've pressed the Enter key, you can edit a value just as you would edit a label—in the cell or in the formula bar.

■ Excel makes assumptions about your entry while you are typing, and recognizes common combinations of numbers and punctuation as label data rather than as value data. If you want to specifically enter a number as a label, you can type an apostrophe (') before the number. For instance, type '555-1234 to enter 555-1234 as a telephone number.

■ Values can be entered automatically using the fill handle and a technique called **drag-and-fill**. Enter a number in a cell and then point to the bottom-right corner of the cell. The pointer changes to a black cross ✚ shape when you are in the right spot. Drag that pointer across or down several other cells. After the cell selection is made, the 🔲 Auto Fill Options button is displayed. With the Auto Fill Options button, you can fill the selection with a series of numbers, the value of the initial cell with or without cell formatting, or cell formatting without a value.

■ There are several other ways to drag-and-fill data, and you can use the Fill button in the Editing group on the Home tab. You can find more information about automatically filling cells in Excel Help.

■FAQ How do I enter formulas?

A **formula** specifies how to add, subtract, multiply, divide, or otherwise calculate the values in worksheet cells. A formula always begins with an equal sign (=) and can use cell references that point to the contents of other cells. A **cell reference** is the column and row location of a cell. In the example below, the formula =C2-C3 would subtract the contents of cell C3 from the contents of cell C2 and display the results in cell C4.

Figure 5-4

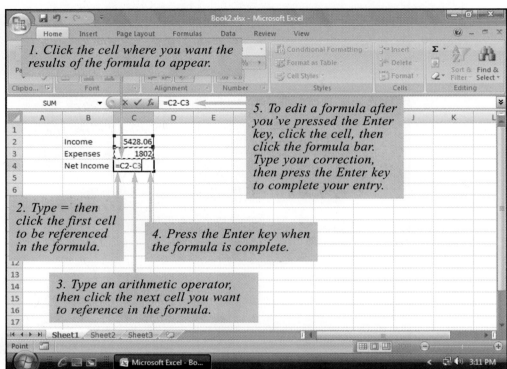

■ The most common arithmetic operators are - (subtraction), + (addition), * (multiplication), / (division), % (percent), and ^ (exponent). Note that an asterisk (*) instead of the letter X is used for multiplication.

■ The easiest way to create a formula is to use the "pointer method." Basically, this means that you click the cell where the results of the formula should appear, type the equal sign (=), and click the cell that contains the first number you want to reference in the formula. A rectangle of dashes appears around the cell you just clicked. This is a **marquee**, which indicates the cell you selected. If it is not the correct cell, click another cell to place the correct cell reference into your formula. To continue creating your formula, type an arithmetic operator (+, -, *, /), then click the next cell you want to reference. Continue until the formula is complete, then press the Enter key to end the formula.

■ You can also type a formula directly into a cell. For example, you could type =B2*B3 and then press the Enter key to complete the formula. The problem with this method is that it's easy to make a mistake and type an incorrect cell reference.

■ You can edit a formula after you've pressed the Enter key in the same way you would edit labels or values—in the cell or in the formula bar.

∎FAQ How do I create complex formulas?

A worksheet can be used for more than simple calculations. You can build complex formulas to calculate statistical, financial, and mathematical equations by using the usual arithmetic operators, parentheses, and a mixture of both values and cell references.

Figure 5-5

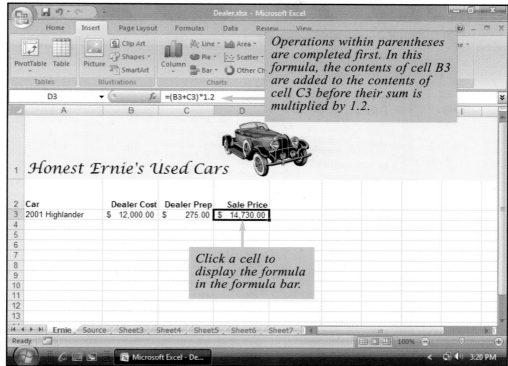

Operations within parentheses are completed first. In this formula, the contents of cell B3 are added to the contents of cell C3 before their sum is multiplied by 1.2.

Click a cell to display the formula in the formula bar.

∎ Use parentheses to make sure that arithmetic operations in a complex formula are executed in the correct order. If you don't use parentheses, Excel calculates the result using the standard mathematical order of operations—multiplication and division, then addition and subtraction. For example, if you enter the formula =B3+C3*1.2, Excel first multiplies the contents of cell C3 by 1.2, then adds the result of the calculation to the value in cell B3. By using parentheses, you can specify a different order for a calculation. For example, if you would like to add the contents of B3 and C3 before multiplying by 1.2, you would enter this formula: =(B3+C3)*1.2.

∎ Formulas can include values, cell references, or both. For example, if the total price of an item is displayed in cell C18, you could calculate a 6% sales tax using the formula =C18*.06. Or, you could put the sales tax percentage in cell C19, then calculate the sales tax using the formula =C18*C19. The result would be the same either way.

∎ You should be aware that cell references in formulas can lead to unexpected results when you copy or move the formulas. You'll learn more about this topic in another chapter.

■FAQ How do I use functions?

In addition to writing your own formula, you can use a predefined formula called a **function**. Excel includes many financial functions such as payments and net present value, mathematical and trigonometric functions such as absolute value and arctangent, and statistical functions such as average and normal distribution.

Avoid common errors when using formulas and functions by verifying that your formulas and functions reference the correct cells and data. A **circular reference**—a formula that references the cell in which the formula resides—can produce erroneous results and should be avoided.

Figure 5–6

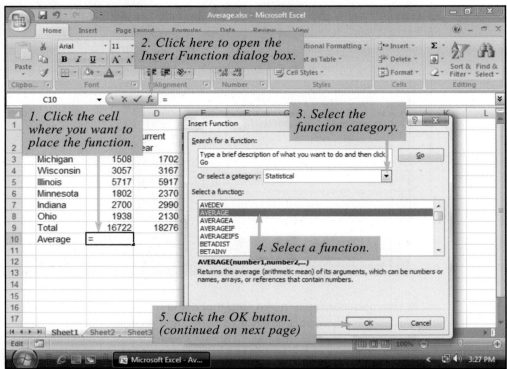

1. Click the cell where you want to place the function.

2. Click here to open the Insert Function dialog box.

3. Select the function category.

4. Select a function.

5. Click the OK button. (continued on next page)

■ You can use the Insert Function button to select a function from a list. Excel includes more than 250 functions from which you can choose. Aside from the Sum function, other commonly used functions, such as Average, Minimum, and Maximum, are located in the Statistical category.

■ Another useful function is the Payment, or PMT, function, which calculates the payments for a loan. You can use the PMT function to calculate all types of loan payments, such as those for a car or for a house. Unfortunately, the PMT function is one of the more difficult functions to use, which is why it's covered in the Do It! on this page.

■ Formulas can include multiple functions. For example, you could create a formula that uses both the Sum and the Average functions to get a total of the average values of a group of cells.

■How do I use functions? (continued)

After you select a function, you'll have to specify the arguments. An **argument** consists of values or cell references used to calculate the result of the function. For example, the Average function requires an argument consisting of a series of numbers or a series of cells. When you complete the Average function, the result is calculated as an average of the values in the cells you specified.

Figure 5-7

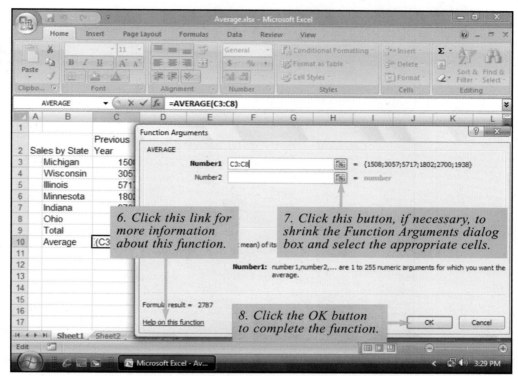

■ To select a range of cells for use as arguments in a function, click the top-left cell that contains data you want to use in the function, then drag down to the bottom-right cell. When you release the mouse button, the selected range of cells is displayed in the dialog box. Click the OK button to calculate the function.

■ Some functions use more than one argument and those arguments can be required or optional. The Payment (or PMT) function, for example, has three required arguments (Rate, Nper, and Pv) and two optional arguments (Fv and Type).

■ It can be difficult to determine how to enter the arguments for a function. For the PMT function, you have to divide the annual interest rate by 12 if you're using monthly payments. If you need help with the arguments for a function, click the *Help on this function* link.

■ Be careful when using functions you don't fully understand. If you're not sure how a function works, use the Excel Help window to find out more about it. When you use a new function, you should check the results with a calculator to make sure the function is working as you expected.

■FAQ How do I use the AutoSum button?

Use the AutoSum button to quickly create a function to calculate the total of a column or row of cells. Excel examines the cells to the left of and above the current cell to determine which cells should be included in the total.

Figure 5-8

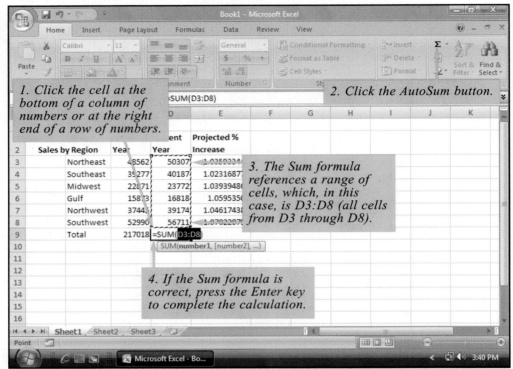

1. Click the cell at the bottom of a column of numbers or at the right end of a row of numbers.

2. Click the AutoSum button.

3. The Sum formula references a range of cells, which, in this case, is D3:D8 (all cells from D3 through D8).

4. If the Sum formula is correct, press the Enter key to complete the calculation.

■ The cells included in the Sum function are displayed as a range or as a series of adjacent cells.

■ The AutoSum button usually does a good job of selecting the cells to be included in the function, but a blank cell or a cell containing a label can produce an incorrect answer. AutoSum works best if every cell in the row or column of cells contains a value.

■ Be careful if you use the AutoSum button to calculate the sum of a column of cells with a number—such as 2007—as a column heading. If the heading has not been specifically formatted as a date, Excel includes it in the sum. Watch the marquee to be sure the correct range of cells is selected before you press the Enter key.

■ If the AutoSum button does not automatically select the correct cells, press the Esc key to remove the function and create the Sum function manually. You can also drag across the correct range of cells, or hold down the Shift key while you use the arrow keys to select the correct range of cells. When the correct cells are selected, press the Enter key to complete the function.

QuickCheck A

1. The [_____] cell is the cell you can currently edit or modify.

2. B3:B12 is an example of a(n) [_____] of cells.

3. To edit a label, value, or formula after you've pressed the Enter key, click the cell, then click the [_____] bar.

4. The formula to subtract the contents of cell C3 from the contents of cell C2 is [_____] .

5. A(n) [_____] is a value or cell reference used to calculate the result of a function.

Check It!

QuickCheck B

Indicate the letter of the desktop element that best matches the following:

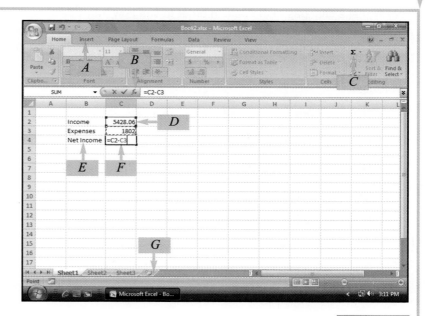

1. A cell containing a label [____]

2. A cell containing a value [____]

3. A cell containing a formula [____]

4. The AutoSum button [____]

5. The Insert Function button [____]

Check It!

Get It?

A	Skill Set A: The Excel window
C	Skill Set C: Formulas
B	Skill Set B: Labels and values
D	Skill Set D: Functions

Chapter 6

Formatting a Worksheet

What's inside and on the CD?

In this chapter, you'll learn how to format worksheets created with Microsoft Excel. Formatting is not just for looks—an effectively formatted worksheet is more approachable and helps readers understand the meaning of values and formulas presented in the worksheet. For example, an accountant might use a red font for negative values in a large worksheet so that possible losses are easier to spot. A quarterly banking statement might use a different colored border for each month to help readers recognize which transactions were made in a particular month.

In this chapter, you will learn that each type of data has special formatting characteristics, which help to identify its purpose. Rather than typing in dollar signs to identify financial values, for example, you will learn to format the values as currency data.

One of the most powerful advantages of using spreadsheet software for calculations is that you can easily make changes to the data in order to see how they affect results. You will learn how to copy and move data in a worksheet, and how the new location might change formulas and produce different results. Most importantly, this chapter explains how to avoid making incorrect modifications to values in a worksheet.

■FAQ How do I add borders and background colors?

Borders and background colors define areas of a worksheet and call attention to important information. You can use the Font group on the Home tab and Format Cells dialog box to add borders and a colored background to one or more cells.

Figure
6–1

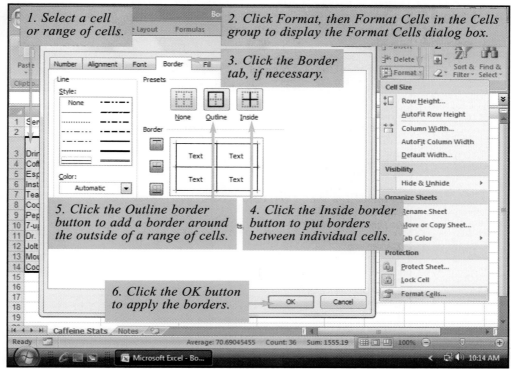

■ To add borders around the outside and inside edges of selected cells, click both the Outline and Inside border buttons in the Presets section, as shown in the above figure. The Outline button puts a border around the outside edges of selected cells. The Inside button adds borders between individual cells.

■ You can add and remove border lines by selecting border option buttons in the Border section of the dialog box. These buttons control all the lines in the selected range of cells:

	Top of range		Left of range
	Inside horizontal lines		Inside vertical lines
	Bottom of range		Right of range

■ The Line area allows you to select a decorative line style or to make all the border lines appear in a selected color.

■ To add a colored background to the selected cell or cells, click the Fill tab. Select a color, then click the OK button to apply the background color.

■ You can quickly add borders using the Borders button in the Font group on the Home tab. However, this shortcut doesn't allow you to use options that are only available in the Format Cells dialog box.

■FAQ How do I format worksheet data?

You can use buttons in the Font group on the Home tab to select different font attributes for any data in worksheet cells. Values and formula results can be formatted with the same font attributes used to enhance the appearance of labels.

Figure 6-2

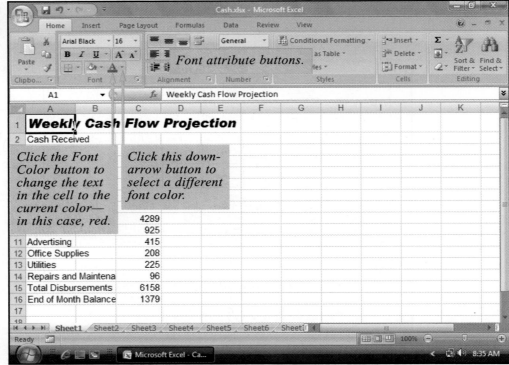

■ You can apply font attributes to any worksheet data—a single character, a single cell, a range of cells, or the entire worksheet. Click in the cell you want to format, then click as many font attribute buttons as you want. Click outside the cell to complete the process.

■ To change the font for a range of cells, click the top-left cell, then drag the mouse to select the cells. Release the mouse button, then apply the font formatting option to the selected cells.

■ Font attributes are typically applied to the entire contents of a cell, but it is possible to change the font attributes for selected text inside a cell. For example, to display one of the words in a cell in bold text, type the contents of the cell, then click the formula bar. Use the mouse or the arrow keys to select one word within the cell, then click the Bold button. You can use the same process to apply different fonts and attributes such as italics, underlines, and font sizes.

■ For more formatting options, select a cell to format. Click Format, then click Format Cells from the Cells group or click the Format Cells Dialog Box Launcher from the Font group to display the Format Cells dialog box. Click the Font tab, if necessary. Select the formatting options, such as superscript or subscript, then click the OK button to apply them.

■FAQ How do I use the Format Cells dialog box?

In addition to font attributes, you can also apply number formats—currency, percent, commas, and decimals—to cells that contain values. The most commonly used number formats are available as buttons in the Number group on the Home tab. In addition, the Format Cells dialog box provides some special format options for number data to improve the readability of a worksheet.

Figure 6-3

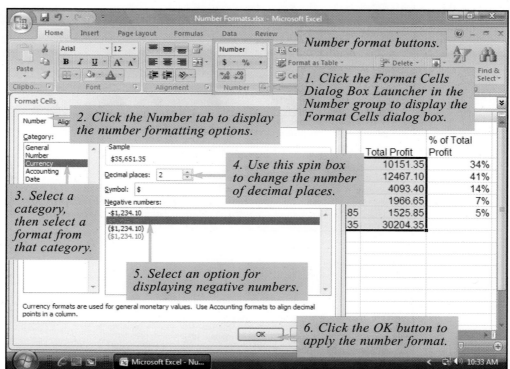

■ The $ Accounting Number Format button displays cell contents in your local currency format. For example, if your copy of Windows is configured for use in the U.S., the currency button displays the cell contents as dollars and cents with a leading dollar sign ($) and two digits to the right of the decimal point.

■ The % Percent Style button displays cell contents as a percentage, which means .35 is displayed as 35%.

■ The , Comma Style button adds a comma to the values displayed in the cell. If your computer is configured for use in the U.S., the Comma Style button adds a comma every three digits to the left of the decimal place and displays two digits to the right of the decimal point.

■ When you click the .00 →.0 Decrease Decimal button, one less digit is displayed after the decimal point. When you click the ←.0 .00 Increase Decimal button, one more digit is displayed after the decimal point.

■ To apply number formats to more than one cell, select a range of cells before you click any of the number format buttons or before you open the Format Cells dialog box.

■FAQ How do I adjust column and row size?

If a column is too narrow, labels might be cut off and numbers might be displayed as #####. Narrow columns allow you to fit more information on the screen or on the printed page, but you might need to adjust the width of columns in your worksheet to make all of your worksheet data visible.

Figure 6-4

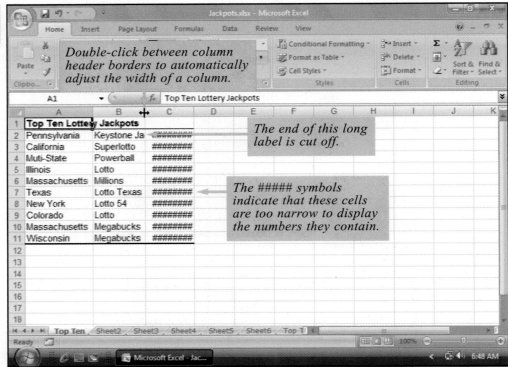

Double-click between column header borders to automatically adjust the width of a column.

The end of this long label is cut off.

The ##### symbols indicate that these cells are too narrow to display the numbers they contain.

■ To change the width of a cell, you must increase the width of the entire column. You can't make one cell in a column wider without affecting the other cells in that column.

■ To manually adjust the width of a column, position the pointer over the vertical line between two column headings so that the pointer changes to a ✛ shape. Press and hold the left mouse button while you drag the vertical line left or right to manually adjust the width of the column.

■ If a label is too long to fit into a cell, it extends into the next cell on the right, if that cell is empty. If the cell on the right contains data, the end of the label is cut off.

■ If a value is too long to fit into a cell, Excel displays a series of # characters in the cell. This is a signal that the cell contains a value that cannot fit within the current cell width. To see the number, simply increase the width of its cell.

■FAQ How do I center and align cell contents?

By default, labels are aligned on the left edge of the cell while values and formulas are aligned on the right edge of the cell. Unfortunately, this means that a label at the top of a column of numbers is not aligned with numbers in the rest of the column. Typically, you'll want to center or right-align the headings for columns of numbers.

Do It!

Figure 6-5

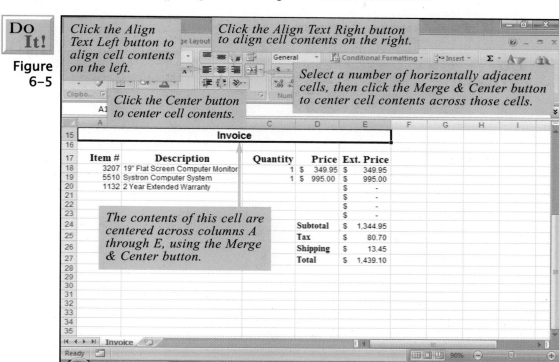

Click the Align Text Left button to align cell contents on the left.

Click the Align Text Right button to align cell contents on the right.

Select a number of horizontally adjacent cells, then click the Merge & Center button to center cell contents across those cells.

Click the Center button to center cell contents.

The contents of this cell are centered across columns A through E, using the Merge & Center button.

■ If a cell containing label data is a column heading, select the cell and click the Align Text Right button in the Alignment group on the Home tab to move the label to the right side of the cell so that it aligns with the column of numbers.

■ To change the alignment of a range of cells at one time, select the range of cells, then click the desired alignment button from the Alignment group on the Home tab.

■ To quickly select all cells in a column, click the column header at the top of the column. To quickly select all cells in a row, click the row header on the left side of the row.

■ Sometimes you'll need to center a label across a number of columns. In the figure above, the title "Invoice" is centered across columns A through E. To center text across columns, select the range of cells to be merged, then click the Merge & Center button in the Alignment group on the Home tab.

■ To merge a range of cells in a column, select the range of cells, then click the Merge & Center button in the Alignment group on the Home tab. The down-arrow button next to the Merge & Center button allows you to unmerge cells as well as merge without centering.

■FAQ What happens when I copy and move cells?

You can use the Cut, Copy, and Paste buttons in the Clipboard group on the Home tab to copy and move cell contents to a different worksheet location. Label data is copied or moved without changing. If you copy and paste cells that contain a formula, the copied formula is modified to work in the new location. A cell reference that changes when a formula is copied or moved is called a **relative reference**. Excel treats all cell references as relative references unless you specify otherwise.

Figure 6-6

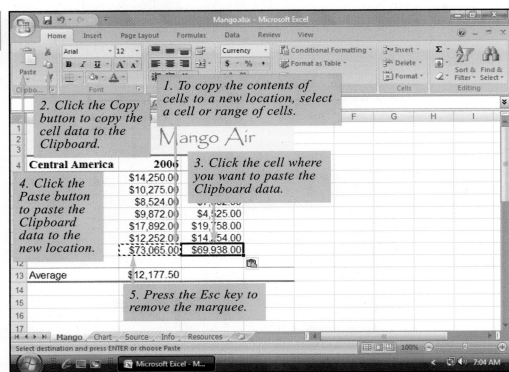

■ To move the data in cells, select the cells, then click the Cut button. Click the cell where you want to paste the data, then click the Paste button. The data is moved from the original location to the new location.

■ If you copy or move the data in a range of cells, the pasted data is positioned below and to the right of the active cell. In other words, click the cell in the top-left corner of where you want the data to be pasted.

■ A formula that contains a relative reference changes when the formula is copied or moved. For example, assume cell C4 contains the formula =C2+C3. You then copy and paste that formula to cell F4. The formula will be changed to =F2+F3. The references C2 and C3 in the original formula were relative references. When the formula was originally located in cell C4, it actually meant =(the contents of the cell two rows up)+(the contents of the cell one row up). When you copied the formula to cell F4, Excel adjusted the formula so that it retained the same relative references. When you pasted the formula into cell F4, it became =F2+F3.

■FAQ When should I use absolute references?

Most of the time, you want Excel to use relative references, but in some situations, cell references should not be modified when moved to a new location. An **absolute reference** does not change, and will always refer to the same cell, even after the formula is copied or moved.

Figure 6-7

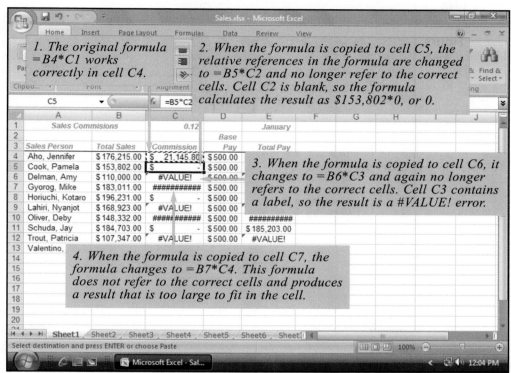

1. The original formula =B4*C1 works correctly in cell C4.

2. When the formula is copied to cell C5, the relative references in the formula are changed to =B5*C2 and no longer refer to the correct cells. Cell C2 is blank, so the formula calculates the result as $153,802*0, or 0.

3. When the formula is copied to cell C6, it changes to =B6*C3 and again no longer refers to the correct cells. Cell C3 contains a label, so the result is a #VALUE! error.

4. When the formula is copied to cell C7, the formula changes to =B7*C4. This formula does not refer to the correct cells and produces a result that is too large to fit in the cell.

■ In the example above, cell C1 contains a commission rate. When you copy the formula in cell C4 to cell C5, the original formula =B4*C1 is changed to =B5*C2. The B5 part is fine, but C2 is an empty cell. The formula should still refer to the commission rate in cell C1.

■ To create an absolute reference, insert a dollar sign ($) before the column reference and another dollar sign before the row reference. In the example above, you would modify the original formula to read =B4*C1. Now, no matter what you do to the worksheet, Excel must always refer to the contents of cell C1 for the second part of the formula. When you copy the formula =B4*C1 to cell C5, the formula is changed to =B5*C1. The absolute cell reference is "protected" by the $ sign and will not be modified or adjusted.

■ If you want to use an absolute reference in a formula, you can start typing, then press the F4 key after you click a cell to add it to the formula. Pressing the F4 key changes the current reference to an absolute reference.

■ You can also create mixed references by combining references so that only one of the column or row references is absolute. For example, $C1 creates an absolute column and a relative row reference. C$1 creates a relative column and an absolute row reference. The absolute identifier will not change, but the relative identifier will.

■FAQ How do I delete and insert rows and columns?

It is easy to delete a row, or insert a blank row between rows that already contain data. You can also insert and delete columns. Excel even modifies your formulas as needed to make sure they refer to the correct cells each time you insert a new row.

Figure 6-8

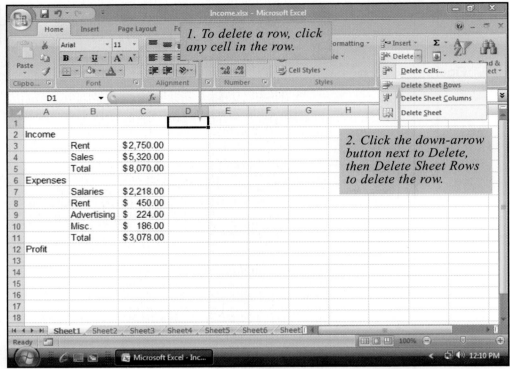

■ To insert a row, click any cell. You can also select a row by clicking the row identifier button on the left side of the window. Click the down-arrow button next to Insert in the Cells group, then click Insert Sheet Rows. The new row is inserted above the selected row.

■ To insert more than one row at a time, drag down over the number of rows you want to insert. Click the down-arrow button next to Insert in the Cells group, then click Insert Sheet Rows to insert the new rows.

■ To delete more than one row at a time, drag down over the rows you want to delete. Click the down-arrow button next to Delete in the Cells group, then click Delete Sheet Rows to delete the rows.

■ Use the same procedures to insert and delete columns. To insert one or more columns, select the column or columns, click the down-arrow button next to Insert in the Cells group, then click Insert Sheet Columns. To delete one or more columns, select the column or columns, click the down-arrow button next to Delete in the Cells group, then click Delete Sheet Columns.

■ As you insert and delete rows and columns, Excel adjusts the relative cell references in formulas to keep them accurate. For example, the formula =C8+E8 changes to =C8+D8 if the original column D is deleted. In the same way, the formula =C8+E8 changes to =C7+E7 if row 6 is deleted.

■FAQ Can I use styles?

As with Microsoft Word, Excel allows you to work with styles. You can use predefined styles or create custom styles. Predefined styles are built into the software, and include formats for displaying currency, percentages, and general numbers. You can also create your own styles to enhance the appearance of your worksheet.

■ The $, % , and • buttons in the Number group automatically format a cell or group of cells with a predefined style. Click Cell Styles in the Styles group, right-click the desired style from the Number Format section, then click Modify to redefine the default setting.

■ Styles include text formatting, such as font, size, and color, as well as numeric formatting, such as comma placement, number of decimal points, and the currency symbol.

■ You can create your own styles for numbers or text. Click Cell Styles in the Styles group, then click New Cell Style. Type the new style name. If you want to modify the characteristics of the new style, click the Format button to open the Format Cells dialog box. Click the OK button to accept the changes in the Format Cells dialog box, then click the OK button in the Style dialog box to create the style.

■ The 🖌 Format Painter button allows you to copy and paste formats from one cell to another. Click the cell containing the formats you want to copy, then click the Format Painter button in the Clipboard group. Click the cell where you want to apply the formats.

■ The Styles group includes a variety of predefined formats designed to format entire worksheets or sections of worksheets. Click either the Cell Styles or Format as Table button in the Styles group to view available formats.

■ The Hide function can be used to hide rows or columns you don't want displayed. To hide a block of rows or columns, first select the rows or columns to be hidden. Right-click the highlighted area, then select Hide.

■ To display rows or columns that were previously hidden, select the rows or columns that border the hidden section. Right-click, then choose Unhide.

Figure
6–9

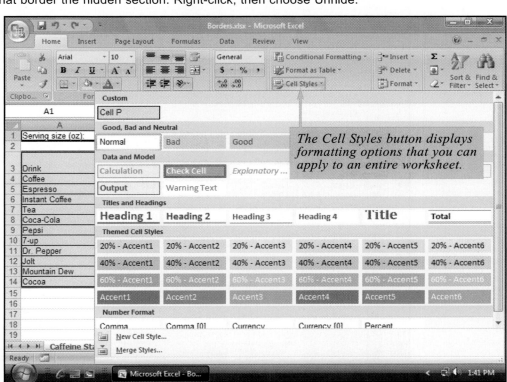

The Cell Styles button displays formatting options that you can apply to an entire worksheet.

■FAQ How do I manage multiple worksheets?

A workbook—sometimes called a "3D workbook"—is a collection of worksheets. Workbooks allow you to group related worksheets together in one file, and easily navigate from one worksheet to another. Worksheets in a workbook can access data from other worksheets in the workbook; for example, a workbook might contain a Quarterly Report worksheet, which accesses totals calculated from January, February, and March worksheets.

■ The default workbook contains three worksheets, titled Sheet1, Sheet2, and Sheet3. Click the tabs at the bottom of the screen to navigate through the worksheets.

■ You can rename worksheets, change the color of the tabs, or change the order of the worksheets by right-clicking a worksheet tab and making a selection from the shortcut menu.

■ Insert a new worksheet by right-clicking the tab for the worksheet that should immediately follow the new worksheet. Select Insert from the shortcut menu, then make a selection from the Insert dialog box. You can insert a new worksheet at the end of the worksheet tabs by clicking the Insert Worksheet button after the final worksheet.

■ Delete an existing worksheet by right-clicking the worksheet's tab and clicking Delete.

■ The Move/Copy option allows you to change the order of worksheets. For example, if you want to insert a new worksheet in front of Sheet1, simply insert the sheet after any tab, then use the Move/Copy option to position it as the first worksheet.

■ To reference data from other worksheets, include the tab name before the row letter and column number. For example, the reference Sheet3!A1 indicates Column A, Row 1, on the worksheet called Sheet3. You can also reference data in other worksheets by navigating to the worksheet and clicking the desired cell while entering a formula or function.

Do It!

Figure 6–10

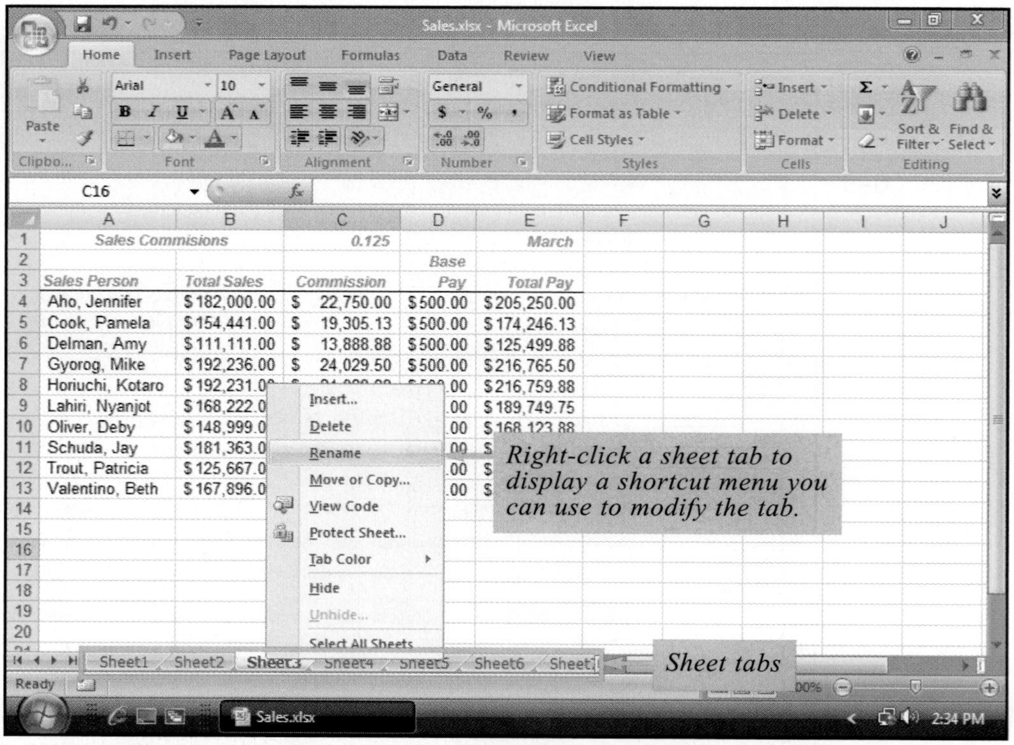

Right-click a sheet tab to display a shortcut menu you can use to modify the tab.

Sheet tabs

QuickCheck A

1. True or false? When the contents of a cell are displayed as #####, that cell contains a number that is too long to display in the cell. [_____]

2. To center a label across several cells, select the horizontally adjacent cells, then click the [_____] & Center button.

3. A(n) [_____] reference is a cell reference that will be modified if the formula is copied or moved to a new cell.

4. A(n) [_____] reference is a cell reference that will not be modified if the formula is copied or moved to a new cell.

5. To write the formula =B2*D6 so that it always refers to cell D6, even when moved or copied, you would change the formula to [_____] .

Check It!

QuickCheck B

Indicate the letter of the desktop element that best matches the following:

1. The Accounting Number Format button [____]

2. The Merge & Center button [____]

3. A cell formatted in the Currency style [____]

4. A cell formatted in the Percent style [____]

5. The Decrease Decimal button [____]

	A	B	C	D	E	F	G	H
1								
2	Product	Price	Cost	Units Bought	Units Sold	Total $ Sales	Total Profit	% of Total Profit
3	12 oz Mug	$ 12.95	$ 8.50	3,000	2,753	$35,651.35	$10,151.35	36%
4	16 oz Mug	$ 14.95	$ 9.50	3,500	3,058	$45,717.10	$12,467.10	44%
5	12 oz Glass	$ 8.95	$ 6.50	1,700	1,692	$15,143.40	$4,093.40	14%
6	16 oz Glass	$ 10.95	$ 7.50	1,500	1,207	$13,216.65	$1,966.65	7%
7	Pitcher	$ 16.95	$ 10.00	700	400	$6,780.00	$220.00	-1%
8				10,400	9,110	$116,508.50	$28,458.50	

Check It!

Get It?

| A | Skill Set A: Borders and background colors |
| C | Skill Set C: Column width and aligning cell contents |

| B | Skill Set B: Fonts and number formatting |
| D | Skill Set D: Copying cells and inserting, deleting, and hiding rows |

Chapter 7

Finalizing a Worksheet

What's inside and on the CD?

In this chapter, you'll learn how to finalize your worksheets by sorting data, creating charts, adding graphics, checking spelling, and testing formulas. You'll also learn how to prepare your worksheets for printing by adding page breaks, headers and footers, and gridlines. As an added bonus, you'll find out how to turn your worksheets into Web pages.

■FAQ Can I sort data in a worksheet?

Excel provides tools that allow you to sort data in ascending or descending order. Data sorted in ascending order will be arranged in alphabetical order—labels that start with A will be positioned above those that start with B. Data sorted in descending order will be arranged in reverse alphabetical order—labels that start with Z will be positioned above those that start with Y.

Do It!

Figure 7-1

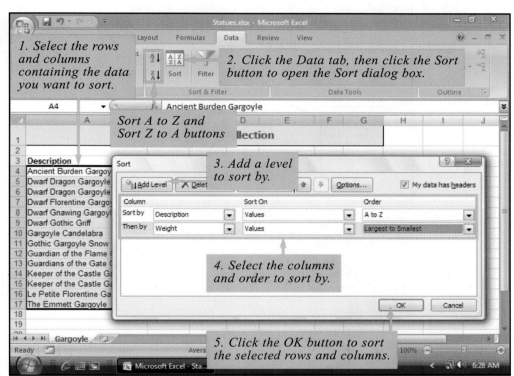

1. Select the rows and columns containing the data you want to sort.

2. Click the Data tab, then click the Sort button to open the Sort dialog box.

Sort A to Z and Sort Z to A buttons

3. Add a level to sort by.

4. Select the columns and order to sort by.

5. Click the OK button to sort the selected rows and columns.

■ It's a good idea to save your worksheet before performing a sort, just in case you forget to select all the necessary columns and end up scrambling your data.

■ It is essential that you select all columns of related data. For example, if column A contains the names of salespeople and column B contains the year-to-date sales for each person, you must select all cells in columns A and B before performing the sort. If you don't, your data will become scrambled, and the names will no longer be associated with the correct year-to-date sales numbers.

■ If you forget to select all columns before sorting, click the Undo button to undo the sort. Check the data carefully to make sure each row still contains the correct data, then select all columns of data and try the sort again.

■ If you just want to sort by the data in the first column, you can use the ⧦↓ Sort A to Z or ⧦↓ Sort Z to A buttons in the Sort & Filter group on the Data tab.

■ If you want to sort by a column other than the first column, or if you want to sort by several columns, use the procedure shown in Figure 7-1. If you need to perform a multilevel sort, designate the first column in the *Sort by* box. Add additional levels with the *Add Level* button and designate the columns from the *Then by* list. You can set each level of the sort for either ascending or descending order. Click the OK button to apply the sort.

■FAQ How do I create a chart?

You can use the Charts group on the Insert tab to chart or graph data in your worksheet. You should pick a chart type that suits the data. A **line chart** is used to show data that changes over time. A **pie chart** illustrates the proportion of parts to a whole. A **bar chart** (sometimes called a "column chart") is used to show comparisons.

Figure 7–2

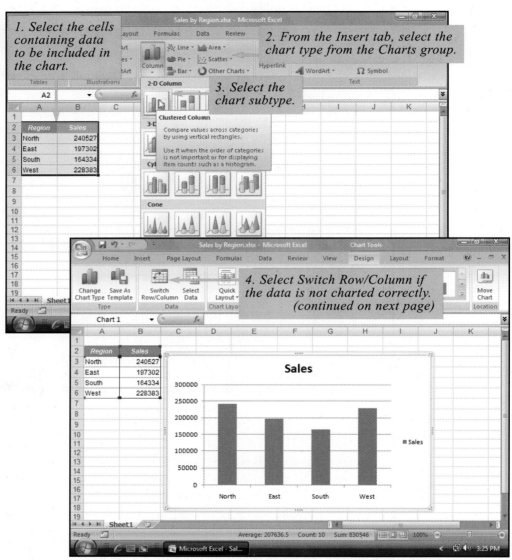

■ To create a chart, select the range of cells that contain data you want to chart. If the selected cells consist of a column of labels followed by one or more columns of data, the labels will be used to identify the data series.

■ Click the Insert tab. Select the type of chart from the Charts group. Select the chart subtype. A description of the chart will be displayed if you hold the cursor over the chart subtype.

■ If the data is not charted correctly, click the Switch Row/Column button in the Data group on the Chart Tools Design contextual tab. Data charted in rows has related cells positioned in a row next to each other. Data charted in columns has related cells positioned in a column above or below each other.

■How do I create a chart? (continued)

Figure 7-3

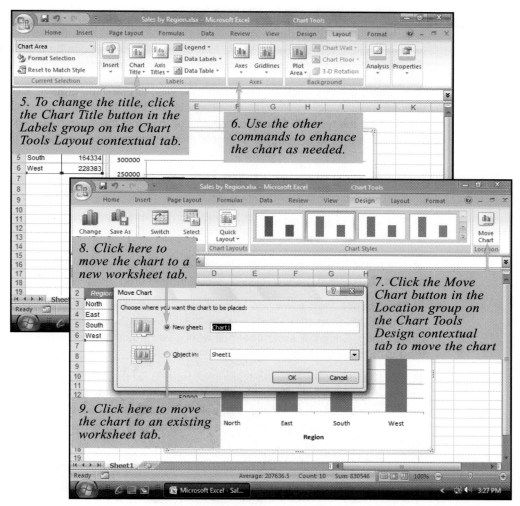

5. To change the title, click the Chart Title button in the Labels group on the Chart Tools Layout contextual tab.

6. Use the other commands to enhance the chart as needed.

7. Click the Move Chart button in the Location group on the Chart Tools Design contextual tab to move the chart

8. Click here to move the chart to a new worksheet tab.

9. Click here to move the chart to an existing worksheet tab.

■ Click the Chart Title button on the Chart Tools Layout contextual tab to add a chart title. Select the desired option, then enter the text for the title.

■ If you'd like to include labels for the X (horizontal) axis or the Y (vertical) axis, click the Axis Titles button on the Chart Tools Layout contextual tab. Select the desired options, then enter the text for the labels.

■ You can use the other commands on the Chart Tools Layout contextual tab to modify titles, add or remove axes and gridlines, move or remove the legend, add or remove data labels, and add or remove a data table that displays the values for each data series.

■ By default, the chart is inserted into the current worksheet. You can move the chart with the Move Chart button in the Location group on the Chart Tools Design contextual tab.

■ To edit a completed chart, click the chart border. When the chart is selected, you can see the small, square sizing handles on its border. Use options from the Chart Tools contextual tabs to change the chart type, modify the chart's appearance, adjust the chart's data range, and change other chart elements such as title, axes, gridlines, and data labels.

■ When a chart is selected, you can move it or resize it by dragging the sizing handles.

■FAQ Can I add graphics to a worksheet?

Worksheet graphics can be used to highlight important sections, add interest or pizzazz to otherwise dull pages, or graphically illustrate spreadsheet data. Vector drawings can be created using Excel's drawing tools. Photographs or clip art can be inserted from a file or imported directly from imaging devices, such as scanners and digital cameras.

■ To insert Clip Art, click the cell where you wish to place the graphic. Click the Insert tab, then click Clip Art in the Illustrations group. When the Clip Art task pane appears, enter a keyword for the type of clip art you would like to use in the Search for text box, then click Go. Choose an image from the available pictures, then close the Clip Art task pane.

■ Graphics can be resized using the round "handles" that appear on the edges of a selected graphic. For example, to enlarge a graphic, first select it by clicking anywhere on the graphic. Drag the handle in the bottom-right corner down and to the right.

■ To move a graphic, click the graphic to select it, then hold the mouse button down while dragging it to the new location.

■ The round, green handle that appears at the top of a graphic allows you to rotate the graphic. To rotate a graphic, click to select it, then drag the green rotate handle right or left.

■ The Shapes tools allow you to draw simple lines and shapes. To draw an arrow, click the Insert tab, then click Shapes in the Illustrations group. Select ↘ Arrow from the Lines group. Click the worksheet cell where you would like the arrow to start, and then drag to "draw" the arrow.

■ The SmartArt button in the Illustrations group on the Insert tab allows you to insert SmartArt into your worksheet. To insert SmartArt, click the SmartArt button from the Illustrations group on the Insert tab, select the shape you want to insert, and then click the OK button. Drag the shape to the location on the worksheet where you would like the shape to be positioned.

Figure 7–4

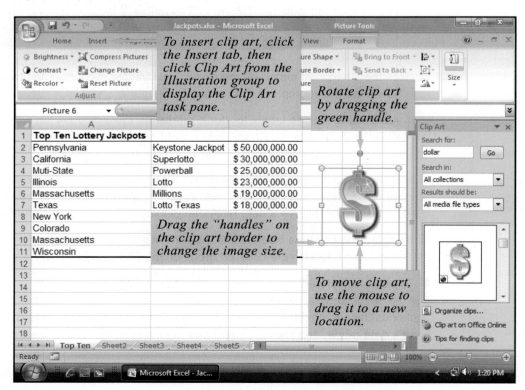

■FAQ How do I check spelling in a worksheet?

Excel can check the spelling of all labels in a worksheet. Unlike Word, however, Excel doesn't show misspelled words with wavy red underlines. Excel also doesn't provide a grammar checker. So it is important for you to proofread your worksheets for grammar errors and spelling errors not caught by the spelling checker.

Figure 7-5

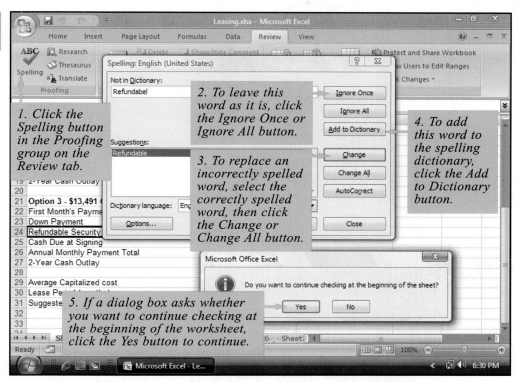

1. Click the Spelling button in the Proofing group on the Review tab.

2. To leave this word as it is, click the Ignore Once or Ignore All button.

3. To replace an incorrectly spelled word, select the correctly spelled word, then click the Change or Change All button.

4. To add this word to the spelling dictionary, click the Add to Dictionary button.

5. If a dialog box asks whether you want to continue checking at the beginning of the worksheet, click the Yes button to continue.

■ You can begin to check the spelling with any cell selected. However, if you make cell A1 the active cell, you will avoid the question displayed in Step 5 above.

■ If the correct spelling appears in the Suggestions list, click to select it, then click the Change button to correct the misspelled word.

■ If no suggested spellings are displayed, click the *Not in Dictionary* text box, then type the correct word. Click the Change button to replace the misspelled word.

■ If you're sure the word is spelled correctly, click the Ignore Once button to ignore this occurrence of the word. Sometimes a word—for example, a person's name—is not recognized by Excel. Click the Ignore All button if you want to ignore all other occurrences of this word throughout the entire worksheet.

■ If the word is one you use frequently, click the Add to Dictionary button to add the current word to the spelling dictionary. For example, adding the city name *Ishpeming* to the Excel dictionary stops the spelling tool from identifying it as a misspelled word.

■FAQ How do I test my worksheet?

You should always test your worksheets before relying on the results. Don't assume the result is correct just because it's generated by a computer. Your computer is almost certainly returning the correct results for the formulas and data you've entered, but it is possible you might have entered the wrong value in a cell, used the wrong cell reference in a formula, or made some other mistake in a formula.

Figure 7–6

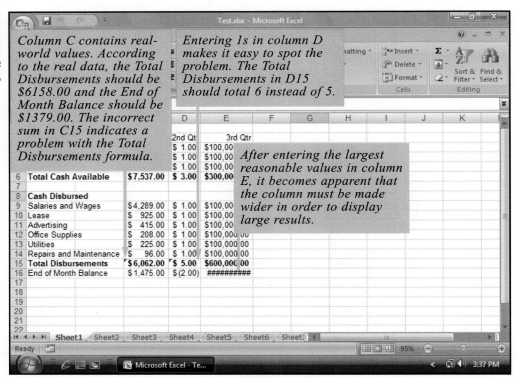

Column C contains real-world values. According to the real data, the Total Disbursements should be $6158.00 and the End of Month Balance should be $1379.00. The incorrect sum in C15 indicates a problem with the Total Disbursements formula.

Entering 1s in column D makes it easy to spot the problem. The Total Disbursements in D15 should total 6 instead of 5.

After entering the largest reasonable values in column E, it becomes apparent that the column must be made wider in order to display large results.

■ It's a good idea to use the Save As option to rename and save an extra copy of your worksheet before testing, just in case your test significantly changes the worksheet.

■ One way to test your worksheet is to enter a series of consistent and easily verified values, such as 1 or 10, into the data cells. If you enter 1s, you can quickly check the calculated results "in your head" and spot potential formula errors.

■ Another way to test your worksheet is to enter a set of real-world values for which you already know the results. Compare the calculated result from the worksheet with the real-world result to make sure the worksheet is returning correct results. Testing with real data also helps identify problems such as columns that are too narrow to hold calculated results.

■ It is also a good idea to test your worksheet by entering the largest and smallest values that would reasonably be expected in normal use of your worksheet. Small values, including zero, can lead to errors such as division by zero. The use of large values can lead to results that do not fit into the cell where the answer is to be displayed. In such a case, you'll need to make those columns wider.

■FAQ How do I use Print Preview and Page Setup?

Excel's Print Preview window allows you to see how a worksheet will look when it is printed. To display the Print Preview window, click the Microsoft Office button, point to Print, then click Print Preview. You can also open the Print Preview window by clicking the Preview button on the Print dialog box. Most experienced worksheet designers use the Print Preview window in the final stages of worksheet development. They look at the default print format, and then refine it by adjusting margins, adding headers, and specifying whether to fit the worksheet on a single page or distribute it over multiple pages.

Figure 7-7

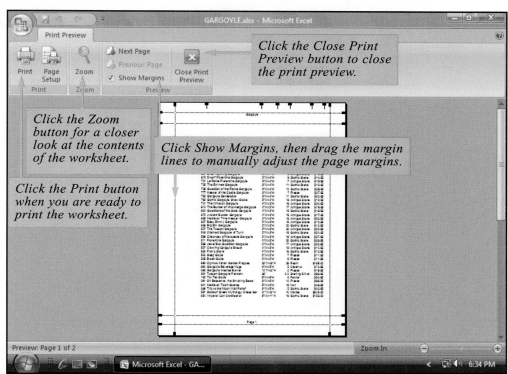

■ The Zoom button switches between a close-up and a normal view. Just click the Zoom button again to switch back to the previous view. It's a good idea to zoom in to look for cells that contain #####, indicating a column that needs to be wider.

■ To adjust the margins, click the Show Margins check box. Position the pointer over a margin line until it changes to a ✛ shape or a ✚ shape, drag that margin line to its new position, then release the mouse button. You can also set the margins using the Page Setup dialog box.

■ Notice that there are two margin lines at the top and bottom of the page. The outside top and bottom lines control the location of the header and footer. The inside lines control the placement of worksheet data.

■ If you're not satisfied with the appearance of the worksheet in the Print Preview window, click the Page Setup button to display the Page Setup dialog box. You will find more options there for controlling the worksheet's printed format.

■ How do I use Print Preview and Page Setup?   (continued)

Excel's Page Setup dialog box allows you to control the orientation and structure for printed worksheet pages. Use this feature along with the Print Preview feature before you print a worksheet. You can access the Page Setup dialog box by clicking the Page Setup button from the Print Preview window. You can also click the Page Layout tab, then click the Page Setup Dialog Box Launcher in the Page Setup group. Settings you make with the Page Setup dialog box are saved when you save the worksheet.

Figure 7-8

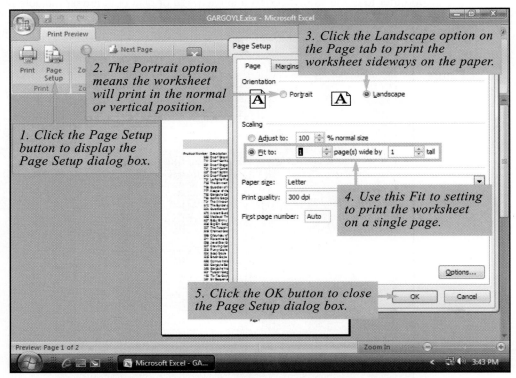

The Page tab in the Page Setup dialog box contains handy settings for worksheet orientation and scaling. **Portrait orientation** prints a worksheet on a vertically oriented page. **Landscape orientation** prints a worksheet on the page sideways. You can use the Scaling options to adjust a worksheet's overall size or force it to fit the width of a single page. Printing a large worksheet on a single page makes it easier to read, as long as the font is legible. To cancel scaling, click the *Adjust to* option button and change the corresponding value to 100% normal size.

■ The Margins tab in the Page Setup dialog box provides an alternative to the Print Preview window for specifying margin settings.

■ The Header/Footer tab in the Page Setup dialog box allows you to work with headers and footers.

■ The Sheet tab in the Page Setup dialog box allows you to specify a section of a worksheet to print—useful for printing a selected section of a large worksheet. The Sheet tab also allows you to specify whether you want to print gridlines or row and column headings. **Gridlines**—the lines that separate one cell from another—can be added to create visual boundaries for rows and columns. Row and column headings are the column letters and row numbers. Printouts that include gridlines and row/column headings can be useful when you want to show the structure of a worksheet.

■FAQ How do I add headers and footers to a worksheet?

As in Microsoft Word, Excel worksheets can contain headers and footers. A header is text that appears at the top of every page. A footer is text that appears at the bottom of every page. Excel includes predefined headers and footers that contain information such as the title of the worksheet, the date, and the page number. You can also create your own headers and footers.

Figure 7–9

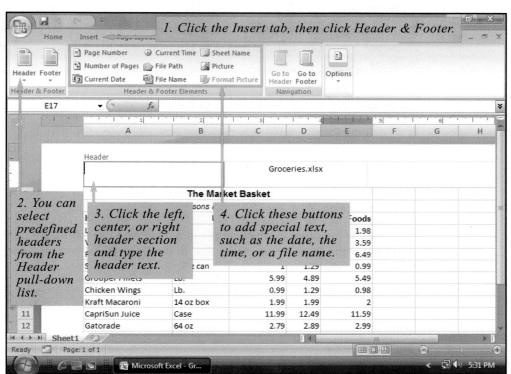

■ Footers work just like headers—simply select the appropriate footer option.

■ Header and footer options are available on the Header/Footer tab in the Page Setup dialog box. The custom Header and Footer dialog boxes contain buttons that insert commonly used elements in the header or footer. To use these buttons:

A Select the text, then click this button to display the Font dialog box to format the header text.

Click this button to insert page numbers.

Click this button to insert the total number of pages.

Click this button to insert the current date.

Click this button to insert the current time.

Click this button to insert the file path (drive letter and folders).

Click this button to insert the name of the file.

Click this button to insert the name of the worksheet tab.

Click this button to insert a picture.

Click this button to format the picture you inserted.

▪FAQ How do I set up a multipage worksheet?

Large worksheets sometimes require additional setup so that they print correctly on multiple pages. Before printing a multipage worksheet, use the Page Break Preview to examine page breaks and modify them to arrange data logically on each page. It is also good practice to include row and column labels on every printed page to help readers identify data in rows and columns after they read past page 1. To save time collating, you can use the Page Setup dialog box to specify the order in which multipage worksheets print.

■ To view page breaks, click the View tab, then click Page Break Preview in the Workbook Views group. Click and drag the blue page break lines to change their locations.

■ To insert a new page break, click a location for the new page break. Click the Page Layout tab, click Breaks in the Page Setup group, then click Insert Page Break.

■ To exit the Page Break View, click the View tab, then click Normal.

■ To include column or row labels on every page, open the Page Setup dialog box with the Page Setup Dialog Box Launcher from the Page Setup group on the Page Layout tab. On the Sheet tab, use the *Print titles* text boxes to specify the row and column that contain headings.

■ To specify the order in which pages of a multipage worksheet are printed, use the Sheet tab of the Page Setup dialog box. In the Page Order section, choose *Down, then over* or *Over, then down*.

Figure 7-10

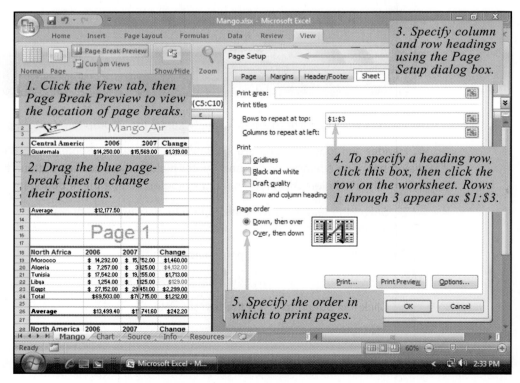

■FAQ How do I print a worksheet?

Use the Print dialog box to print a single copy of the current worksheet, to print multiple copies, print selected pages, or use advanced print options. For example, you can print all the worksheets that make up a workbook. The default setting prints only the current worksheet.

Figure 7-11

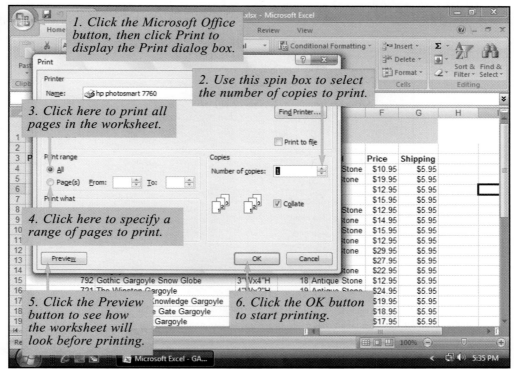

1. Click the Microsoft Office button, then click Print to display the Print dialog box.

2. Use this spin box to select the number of copies to print.

3. Click here to print all pages in the worksheet.

4. Click here to specify a range of pages to print.

5. Click the Preview button to see how the worksheet will look before printing.

6. Click the OK button to start printing.

■ Determine what you want to print before opening the Print dialog box. By default, Excel prints the entire active worksheet. If you want to print only a section of the worksheet, select the range of cells before you click the Microsoft Office button and select Print. You can then simply click the *Selection* option in the *Print what* section of the dialog box.

■ To print only the current worksheet, click the *Active sheet(s)* option in the *Print what* section of the dialog box.

■ To print all worksheets in the current workbook, click the *Entire workbook* option in the *Print what* section of the dialog box.

■ Click the Preview button to see how the worksheet or workbook will look when printed.

■ If your worksheet doesn't print, check that the printer is online, and make sure you have specified the correct printer in the Print dialog box.

■FAQ How do I save a worksheet as a Web page?

You can save your worksheet as a Web page that you can post on the Internet. This Excel feature provides an easy way to make your worksheet data accessible to a large number of people without having to send each person a printed copy of the worksheet.

Do It!

Figure 7-12

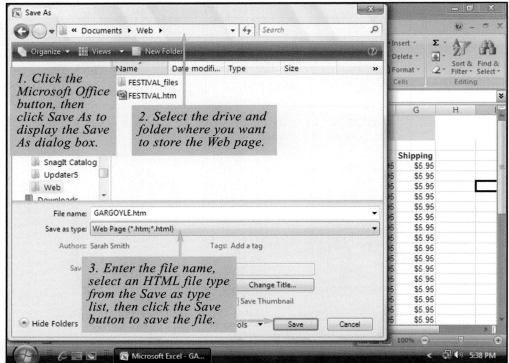

1. Click the Microsoft Office button, then click Save As to display the Save As dialog box.

2. Select the drive and folder where you want to store the Web page.

3. Enter the file name, select an HTML file type from the Save as type list, then click the Save button to save the file.

■ Before you save a worksheet as a Web page, it's a good idea to save it as a normal worksheet.

■ Tables are a valuable formatting tool for creating Web pages. You can use Excel to create a table for this purpose. First, select the range of cells you want to include in the table, then follow the same steps to save as a Web page. In the Save As dialog box, click the Selection option, choose the HTML file type, name your file, and click Save.

■ Some formatting options available in Excel cannot be duplicated in a Web page. If a worksheet contains formatting that isn't available in HTML, you'll be notified of the problem areas and will have the option of canceling or continuing with the save.

■ Not all worksheets convert successfully to Web pages, so you should preview your worksheet in a Web browser to make sure the conversion is acceptable before you post your worksheet Web pages on the Internet.

QuickCheck A

1. True or false? Excel displays a wavy red underline under words that might be misspelled.

   [   ]

2. If the words apple, banana, and peach are sorted in descending order, which word would be at the top of the sorted list? [   ]

3. True or false? Spreadsheet software always calculates correctly, so it's not necessary to test your worksheets before using them. [   ]

4. Use a(n) [   ] chart to show proportions of a part to a whole.

5. True or false? Excel includes a feature that fits a worksheet onto a single page of paper when printed. [   ]

Check It!

QuickCheck B

Indicate the letter of the desktop element that best matches the following:

1. The Spelling button [   ]

2. The Sort Ascending button [   ]

3. The Clip Art button [   ]

4. The Header & Footer button [   ]

5. A column that is good for testing data because it contains easily verified values [   ]

Check It!

Get It?

[A] Skill Set A: Sorting data and creating charts

[C] Skill Set C: Print Preview, Page Setup, and headers and footers

[B] Skill Set B: Checking spelling and testing worksheets

[D] Skill Set D: Printing and saving as a Web page

Chapter 8

Creating a Presentation

What's inside and on the CD?

In this chapter, you'll learn the essentials of creating presentations with Microsoft PowerPoint.

Microsoft PowerPoint is the component of the Microsoft Office suite best suited for creating visual backdrops for speeches and oral presentations. As presentation software, Microsoft PowerPoint provides a set of tools to help you script, organize, and display a presentation.

A **PowerPoint presentation** consists of a number of slides. Each **slide** contains objects such as titles, items in a bulleted list, graphics, and charts. Typically, slides are presented with a computer and a projection device. PowerPoint presentations can also be printed on transparent sheets for use with an overhead projector, printed on paper for handouts, or converted to Web pages for display on the Internet.

Good graphic design makes slides visually compelling and presentations easy to understand. A few simple bullets can be used to list key concepts. Numbered lists can present the steps in a process. Tables, charts, and graphics can simplify complex ideas and present numerical or statistical data creatively. To design effective slides, avoid clutter and unnecessary graphical elements. Put common elements, such as the title of the presentation or the name of the author, on each slide to create consistency from slide to slide.

■FAQ What's in the PowerPoint window?

Microsoft PowerPoint creates a slide show that can be presented with a computer and a projection device, printed on transparency film, or converted to HTML and viewed through a Web browser. To create useful handouts for distribution to an audience, the slides can be printed on paper in a variety of layouts.

To start PowerPoint, click Start, point to All Programs, click Microsoft Office, then click Microsoft Office PowerPoint 2007. The PowerPoint window includes several work areas, called "panes," as shown in Figure 8-1.

Figure 8-1

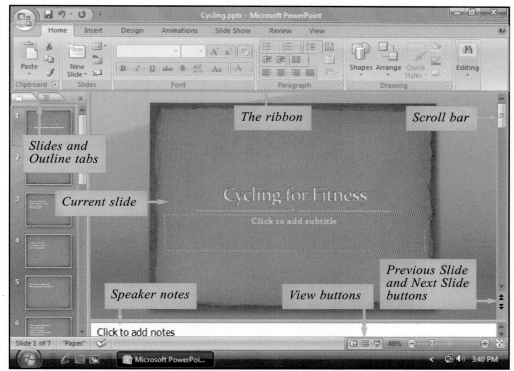

■ When a presentation is open in Normal view, the current slide is displayed in the right pane of the PowerPoint window, the Slides and Outline tabs are shown in the left pane, and a pane near the bottom of the window provides a place to type speaker notes.

■ Use the scroll bar or the ▲ Previous Slide and ▼ Next Slide buttons to move from one slide to another in Normal view.

■FAQ How do I create a presentation?

You can create a presentation by selecting a theme or template. You can also create a blank presentation, which allows you to fully customize the slide components.

A **theme** is a collection of professionally selected slide color schemes, fonts, graphic accents, and background colors. All the slides in a presentation should have a similar "look," or design. Once you select a theme, PowerPoint automatically applies it to every slide in your presentation.

Figure
8–2

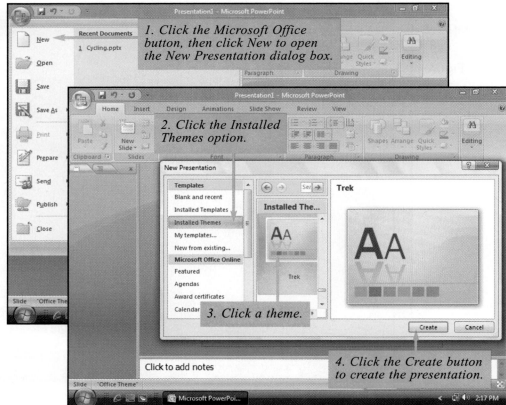

■ When you create a new presentation, a Title Slide is generated for you. You can select other layouts from the Layout button in the Slides group on the Home tab.

■ It's a good idea to save your presentation as soon as you have created the first slide. PowerPoint presentations are saved with a .pptx extension. As you are building the presentation, you should save frequently. When you save a presentation, all slides in the presentation are saved in the same file.

■ If you change your mind about the theme you selected for a presentation, you can change it by clicking the Design tab. Click any theme from the Themes group to apply the new theme to all slides in the presentation. You can also apply a theme to just one slide or to a group of slides by selecting the slide(s), right-clicking the theme in the Themes group, then selecting Apply to Selected Slides. All formatting applied before you change the theme is replaced with the new design.

■ Change the background color of a slide by clicking the Design tab, selecting Background Styles from the Background group, then selecting a style from the drop-down list. Additional background formatting is available from the Format Background option in the drop-down list.

■FAQ How do I add a slide?

The New Slide button adds a slide to your presentation. When you add a slide, PowerPoint gives you a choice of slide layouts. Most slide layouts include at least one placeholder, in which you can enter text or graphics. You'll typically use the Title Slide layout for the first slide in your presentation.

Figure 8-3

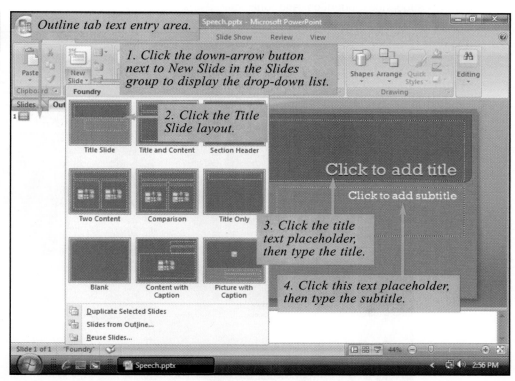

■ The New Slide drop-down list includes thumbnail sketches of each slide type. Hold your mouse over a slide layout to see its name.

■ Each theme has its own Title Slide layout. There is usually a graphic element, which you can delete or modify to customize your presentation.

■ If you don't like the Title Slide layout, you can use the Title Only layout or Blank layout for the first slide of your presentation. Use the buttons on the Insert tab to add new placeholders. For example, click the ▣ Text Box button in the Text group, then drag across a section of the slide to create a text placeholder. Click inside the placeholder, then type your text.

■ You can resize any placeholder or any slide object by using its sizing handles—the small squares that appear on the object's borders.

■ In addition to entering text into placeholders, you can enter text for slides in the Outline tab entry area whenever the slide show is displayed in Normal view. You can edit this text, much like working with a word processor, using the editing keys. You can also rearrange items by dragging them to new locations in the outline.

■FAQ How do I add a bulleted list?

When you want to present a list of bulleted or numbered points, use one of PowerPoint's title and content layouts, such as *Title and Content*, *Two Content*, or *Comparison*. Bulleted lists focus the audience's attention on each point you are making. Each bullet should be a brief summary of what you are saying. Numbered lists help the audience to focus on sequences, priorities, and rankings.

Figure 8-4

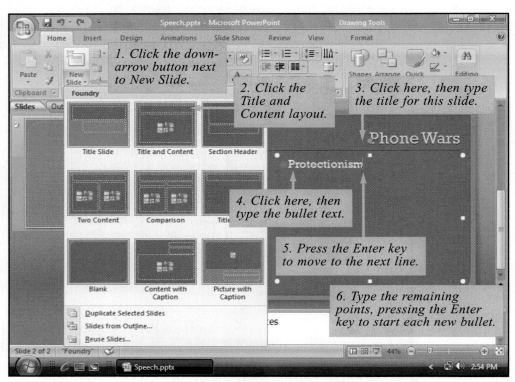

■ When you use the Title and Content layout, the text is formatted as a bulleted list in the Content area. If you do not want the text bulleted, you can click the 🔢 Bullets button in the Paragraph group on the Home tab to remove them.

■ If you would like the list numbered, use the 🔢 Numbering button.

■ Press the Enter key after typing each item in a list. Each time you press the Enter key, PowerPoint generates a new bullet or number. After you type the last item in the list, press the Enter key. Click the Bullets button in the Paragraph group to stop generating bullets. Or, click the Numbering button to stop generating numbers.

■ You can press the Backspace key to remove a bullet or number.

■ To create sub-bullets, use the 🔢 Increase List Level button in the Paragraph group on the Home tab.

■ You can add animation effects to a bulleted list to make the bulleted items appear one by one. You'll learn how to do this in the next chapter.

■FAQ How do I add a graphic?

You can add visual interest to your slides with graphics. The easiest way to add a slide with a graphic is to select a slide layout with content in the New Slide drop-down list. After adding the slide, you'll replace the content placeholder with the graphic you want to use.

Do It!

Figure 8–5

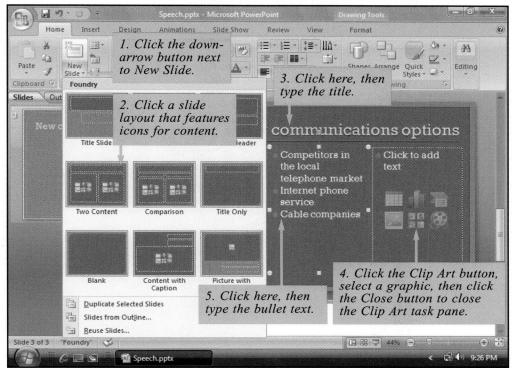

■ To add clip art, click the Clip Art button. The Clip Art task pane opens. Click any graphic to select it. The graphic is inserted in the slide, replacing the placeholder.

■ The Clip Art task pane includes a search tool to look for clip art. Enter a search specification in the Search for text box, then click the Go button.

■ To add a photo or scanned image instead of clip art, click the Insert Picture from File button displayed in the slide's placeholder. When the Insert Picture dialog box appears, use it to specify the picture's disk location, folder, and file name.

■ To delete a graphic, select it, then press the Delete key.

■ You can insert pictures or clip art into any slide layout, even if it doesn't contain a graphic placeholder. Click the Insert tab, click Picture or Clip Art from the Illustrations group, then select a graphic. Use the sizing handles to position and size the graphic.

■FAQ How do I add a chart?

PowerPoint provides several slide layouts containing chart placeholders. You can use the placeholder's Insert Chart button to add a bar chart, line chart, or pie chart. The chart comes complete with sample data in a datasheet, which you'll change to reflect the data you want to display on your chart. Some slide layouts provide an area for a large chart, while others are designed to accommodate a smaller chart plus bullets or other text.

**Figure
8–6**

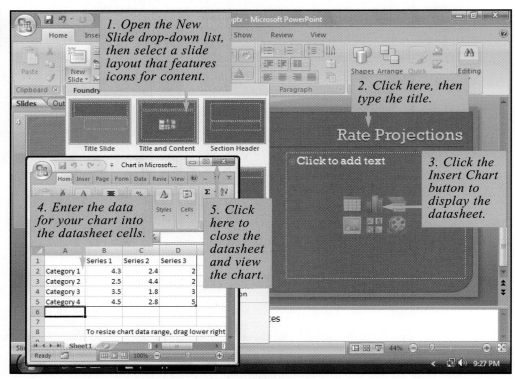

■ You'll need to change the table of sample data by entering your own column headings, row labels, and data values. Click each cell containing sample data and replace it with your own labels or numbers.

■ If you want to delete sample data in the datasheet's columns or rows, select the cells, then press the Delete key.

■ Use the scroll bars to view additional rows and columns.

■ If you want to move data, select the cells, then right-click to display the shortcut menu. Click Cut, then right-click the cell where you want to move the data. Click Paste on the shortcut menu.

■ To insert a row, right-click the cell where you want the row inserted. Click Insert on the shortcut menu, then select Table Rows Above. The steps to insert a column are similar to inserting a row. The steps to delete a row or column are similar to the steps to insert them, except you use the Delete option on the shortcut menu.

■**FAQ** How do I add a table?

You can add a table to a slide if you want to display text or graphics arranged in columns and rows. Use the New Slide drop-down list to select a slide layout that includes a placeholder for a table. You can then enter your own data into the rows and columns of the table.

Figure 8-7

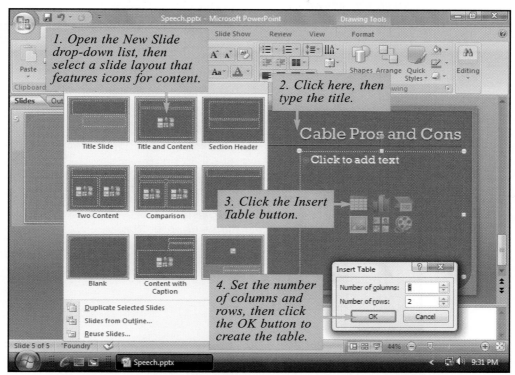

■ When a table is inserted into a slide, the Table Tools Design and Layout contextual tabs appear. Using the buttons on these tabs, you can format the table borders, add color shading to the cells, and adjust the alignment of text in the cells.

■ To add text to a cell, click inside the cell, then type the text. You can edit and format text inside the table just as you do outside the table. You will learn more about formatting text in the next chapter.

■ To add a graphic to a cell, click the cell, then click the Insert tab. Select Picture or Clip Art from the Illustrations group, depending on the type of graphic you want to insert.

■ To adjust the height or width of the cells, position the pointer over the dividing lines so that it changes to a ✛ or ✛ shape. Drag the dividing line to the correct position.

■ To insert rows, click the cell where you want to insert a row, then click either Insert Above or Insert Below from the Rows & Columns group on the Table Tools Layout contextual tab. The steps to insert a column are similar to the steps for inserting a row, except you click either Insert Left or Insert Right. The steps to delete a row or column are similar to the steps to insert them, except you use the Delete option from the Rows & Columns group on the Table Tools Layout contextual tab.

■FAQ How do I view a slide show?

When you build a presentation, your screen contains the ribbon, and other objects that should not be displayed when you deliver your presentation before an audience. In this chapter, you have seen how to create and modify a presentation in the Normal view. When you are ready to see how your slides will look to your audience, switch to the **Slide Show view**.

Figure 8-8

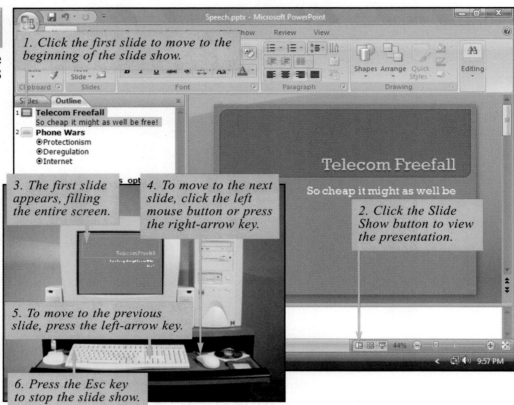

1. Click the first slide to move to the beginning of the slide show.

3. The first slide appears, filling the entire screen.

4. To move to the next slide, click the left mouse button or press the right-arrow key.

2. Click the Slide Show button to view the presentation.

5. To move to the previous slide, press the left-arrow key.

6. Press the Esc key to stop the slide show.

■ The slide show starts with the current slide, so it's important to move to the first slide before starting your presentation.

■ You can use the buttons in the bottom-left corner of the slide during the slide presentation to navigate through the slides as well as add or view Speaker notes, write on the slide with a pen or highlighter, or switch to another program during the slide presentation.

■ You can navigate through the slides during your presentation in several ways. For instance, you can press the left mouse button or the right-arrow key to display the next slide or the next bullet. Press the left-arrow key or the P key to move to the previous slide or the previous bullet.

■ Right-click a slide to display a shortcut menu that allows you to select a specific slide to display. Click Previous on the shortcut menu to go back one slide.

■ Press the Esc key to cancel the slide show and return to the PowerPoint application.

■ Before presenting to an audience, be sure to familiarize yourself with the content of each slide. Then, practice the timing of your presentation.

QuickCheck A

1. Microsoft PowerPoint is an example of [   ] software.

2. After adding a slide, you click the title text [   ] to replace it with your own title.

3. To add a new bullet to a bulleted list, press the [   ] key at the end of the previous bullet.

4. When you add a(n) [   ] to a presentation, you specify the number of rows and columns that will be displayed on the slide.

5. Before displaying a presentation, you should move to the [   ] slide in the presentation.

Check It!

QuickCheck B

Indicate the letter of the desktop element that best matches the following:

1. The New Slide button [   ]

2. The Title Slide layout [   ]

3. The Normal view button [   ]

4. The Slide Show button [   ]

5. The Insert Chart button [   ]

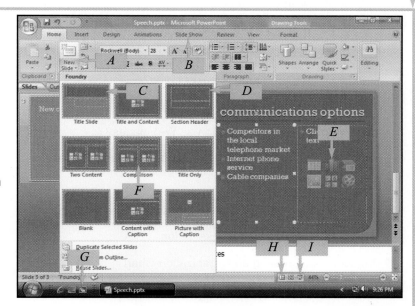

Check It!

Get It?

 Skill Set A: Creating a new presentation

 Skill Set B: Adding titles and bulleted lists

 Skill Set C: Adding graphics and charts

 Skill Set D: Adding tables and viewing your presentation

Chapter 9

Finalizing a Presentation

What's inside and on the CD?

In this chapter, you'll learn how to use the different views included with Microsoft PowerPoint. In addition, you'll learn formatting techniques, as well as how to add animation and other visual effects to your slides. To finalize presentations, you'll learn how to print notes for yourself, create handouts for your audience, save your presentation as Web pages, and use an overhead projector if a computer projection device is not available.

■FAQ How do I use the Normal view?

Microsoft PowerPoint provides different views you can use to build, modify, and view your presentation. Most of the time, you will work in Normal view. To change views, click the View buttons in the lower-right corner of the PowerPoint window.

Figure 9-1

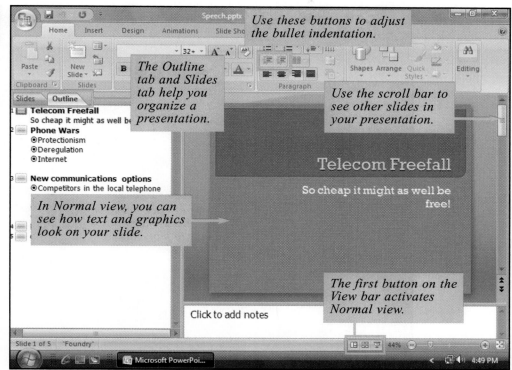

■ In Normal view, you can work in any of the three panes—the Slide pane, the Notes pane, or the Outline/Slides tab pane. Normal view is convenient for building the basic structure of your presentation and for adding speaker notes.

■ To work effectively on all the slides' contents, use the Outline tab. After you create most of the slides in a presentation, the Outline tab is useful for revising and rearranging the contents of your presentation. Use the Increase List Level button to indent a bullet, or use the Decrease List Level button to return a bullet to its previous level.

■ When you are satisfied with the order of the content in your presentation, use the Slides tab to add graphics and visual effects to one slide at a time. You can navigate to and work on other slides by clicking the slide icons in the Slides tab or by using the scroll bar on the right side of the PowerPoint window.

■FAQ How do I use the Slide Sorter view?

Slide Sorter view allows you to view miniaturized versions of all the slides in a presentation. In this view, it is easy to rearrange slides as needed. You can add special effects to your presentation by using the Animations tab on the ribbon.

Figure 9-2

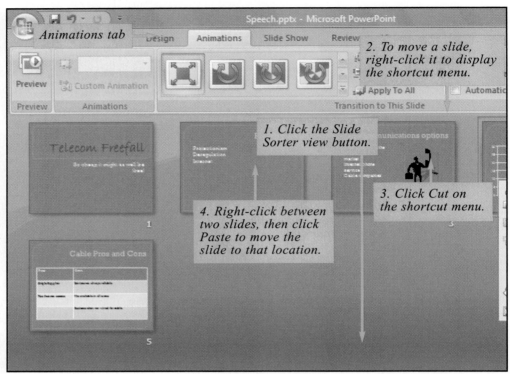

■ You can use the drag-and-drop method to move a slide. Select the slide, then drag it to a new location. PowerPoint displays a vertical line between slides to indicate the proposed position before you release the mouse button.

■ To delete a slide, right-click the slide to display the shortcut menu, then click Delete Slide. You can also select the slide, then press the Delete key on your keyboard.

■ You can duplicate a slide in several ways. You can use the Copy and Paste buttons on the Home tab. You can right-click a slide and use the shortcut menu's Copy and Paste options. You can also click the down-arrow button next to the New Slide button on the Home tab, then select Duplicate Selected Slides. Before using any of these methods, click the slide you want to duplicate.

■ You can hide a slide so that it won't appear when you show the presentation. While in Slide Sorter or Normal view, right-click the slide, and then click Hide Slide on the shortcut menu. Repeat this procedure when you want to make the slide visible again. Hiding slides can be handy when you would like to give a shortened version of your presentation. Rather than showing slides without commenting on them, you can just hide the slides you won't have time to discuss.

■FAQ How do I add transitions?

A **transition** is an effect that specifies how a slide replaces the previous slide during a presentation. Transitions include fades, wipes, and other effects. You can also select sound effects to go along with each transition. If you do not specify a transition, a new slide replaces the entire current slide all at once. Carefully selected transitions can make a presentation more interesting and help the audience pay attention, but overuse of transitions can become irritating and distract attention from the content of your presentation.

Figure 9-3

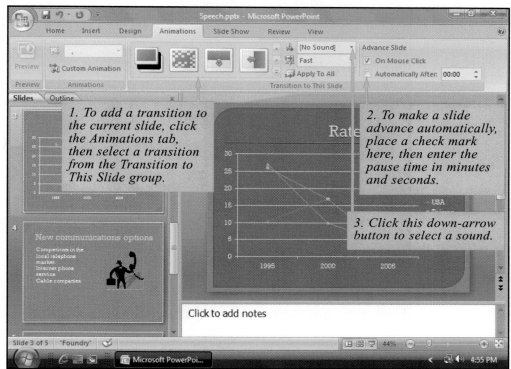

1. To add a transition to the current slide, click the Animations tab, then select a transition from the Transition to This Slide group.

2. To make a slide advance automatically, place a check mark here, then enter the pause time in minutes and seconds.

3. Click this down-arrow button to select a sound.

■ After you apply a transition, it is indicated by an 🟦 Animation icon. You can see the icon on the Slides tab (Normal view) or in Slide Sorter view. While developing your slide show, you can click the icon any time you want to see how the transition looks.

■ You can change a transition by selecting the slide, clicking the Animations tab, then selecting a different transition from the Transition to This Slide group.

■ In Slide Show view, a presentation advances from one slide to the next when you click the mouse or press a key. If you want the slide to advance automatically after a specified period of time, click the *Automatically After* check box in the Transition to This Slide group on the Animations tab. Use the spin box to set the display time. The time is displayed as mm:ss, where the first two digits represent the number of minutes and the last two digits represent the number of seconds. To force the slide to advance after 1 minute and 30 seconds, for example, enter 01:30 in the *Automatically After* spin box.

■FAQ How do I format text on a slide?

PowerPoint includes themes pre-formatted with fonts and font sizes specially selected to complement the background design. In most cases, these fonts work well, but sometimes, you'll find it necessary to modify font attributes.

Figure
9-4

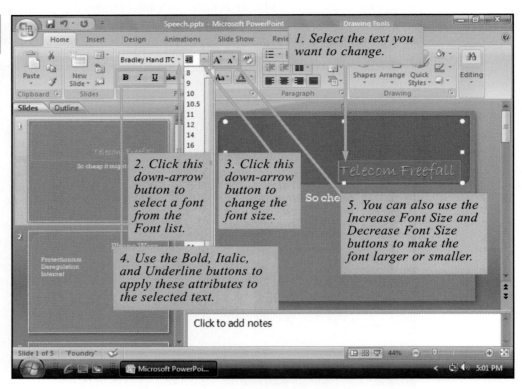

■ For more font options, select the text, then click the Font Dialog Box Launcher in the Font group on the Home tab to display the Font dialog box. Select the desired font, font style, size, color, and effect, then click the OK button to apply the font changes.

■ When you select font sizes, you should consider the number of people in the audience. If the presentation will be given in a large room, you should use a large font that is visible even from the back of the room. In order to do so, you might have to use fewer words on each slide.

■ You also should consider the lighting in the room in which your presentation will be given. In a brightly lit room, slides are easier to read if you use a dark font color on a light background. In a dark room, you should use a dark background with light font colors. You can experiment with font colors to find the combination that works best in the room in which you deliver the presentation.

■ You can change the font attributes for all the slides in your presentation at the same time by using the slide master. The **slide master** is a template you can modify to create a consistent look for your presentation. Click the View tab, then click Slide Master from the Presentation Views group. Select the text styles you want to modify, then change the font attributes using the Font dialog box. To close the slide master, click Close Master View on the Slide Master tab. Use the Slide Sorter view to verify that the new font attributes are applied to the text on all the slides in your presentation.

■FAQ How do I add animation effects to a bulleted list?

The Animations tab provides options for adding animation effects and sounds to items on a slide. **Animation effects** are typically used to draw attention to bullets as they appear on the slide during a presentation. For example, each bulleted item can "fly" in from the side when you click the mouse button. Animation effects can also be accompanied by sound effects to draw attention to each new bullet. You can use the Custom Animation task pane to add effects to bullets.

Do It!

Figure 9–5

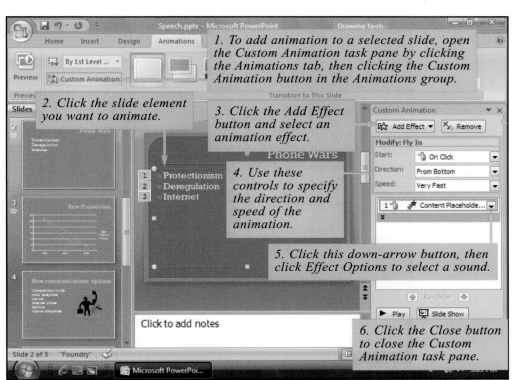

1. To add animation to a selected slide, open the Custom Animation task pane by clicking the Animations tab, then clicking the Custom Animation button in the Animations group.

2. Click the slide element you want to animate.

3. Click the Add Effect button and select an animation effect.

4. Use these controls to specify the direction and speed of the animation.

5. Click this down-arrow button, then click Effect Options to select a sound.

6. Click the Close button to close the Custom Animation task pane.

■ You can apply animation effects to any slide element, including text, graphics, charts, and tables. After you apply an animation effect, you can test it by clicking the 🌠 Animation icon next to the slide. You can also select the slide and then switch to Slide Show view.

■ After selecting Effect Options, you can use the *After animation* option to indicate whether the object should change to a different color or disappear after animation. For example, you can change a bullet to a light font color just before the next bullet appears. The new bullet in a darker font will then become the focus.

■ Use sounds sparingly—a sound effect can be humorous and effective the first time it's used, but the effect can become less amusing after ten or twenty slides. If you use sounds for a presentation, make sure your presentation equipment includes a sound system with adequate volume for your audience.

■ ■ ■

■FAQ How do I check spelling in a presentation?

PowerPoint's spelling checker is very similar to the one you use in Word. It provides an inline spelling checker that automatically indicates possible spelling errors with a wavy red line. As with Word, you simply right-click a word marked with a wavy red line to view a list of correctly spelled alternatives. You can also use the Spelling button on the Review tab to manually initiate a spelling check of an entire presentation.

Do It!

Figure 9–6

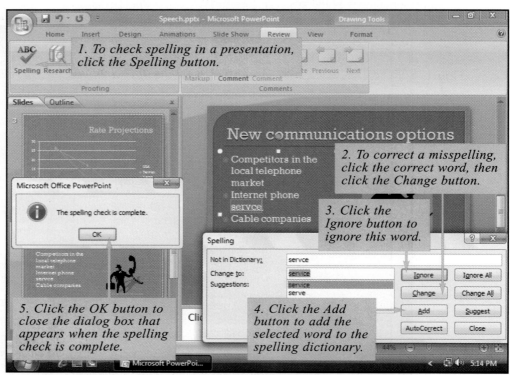

1. To check spelling in a presentation, click the Spelling button.

2. To correct a misspelling, click the correct word, then click the Change button.

3. Click the Ignore button to ignore this word.

4. Click the Add button to add the selected word to the spelling dictionary.

5. Click the OK button to close the dialog box that appears when the spelling check is complete.

■ Don't worry—the wavy red lines do not appear in Slide Show view when you display a presentation.

■ You should always check spelling in a presentation before you save the final version. Misspellings can make your audience doubt the accuracy and validity of your statements.

■ PowerPoint does not include a grammar checker, so make sure you proofread your presentation to eliminate grammar errors. Bulleted items are usually sentence fragments, but sometimes, complete sentences are more appropriate. You should try to be consistent on each slide, using either complete sentences or only phrases.

■ PowerPoint's AutoCorrect feature can automatically correct common typing errors as you work. Click the Microsoft Office button, the PowerPoint Options button, the Proofing tab, then click the AutoCorrect Options button. In the AutoCorrect dialog box, select any options that are useful to you. Options include automatically capitalizing the first word in a sentence and the names of days, changing two capital letters at the beginning of a word to a single capital letter, and correcting capitalization errors caused by accidental use of the Caps Lock key.

■FAQ How do I add and print - speaker notes?

You can prepare and print **speaker notes** that remind you what to say about each slide. Because speaker notes also contain printed versions of each slide, you won't have to keep looking back at the projected slides. This feature allows you to maintain better eye contact and rapport with the audience.

Do It!

Figure 9-7

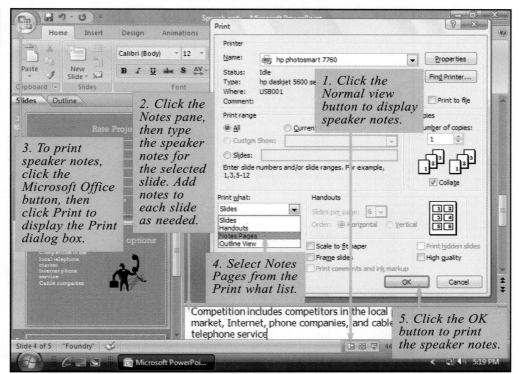

■ Speaker notes shouldn't include the exact text that appears on the slide. Use speaker notes for any additional comments you want to make.

■ To print speaker notes, click the Microsoft Office button, then click Print. Select Notes Pages from the *Print what* section of the Print dialog box. Click the OK button to print the speaker notes.

■ When you print speaker notes, each slide and its notes are printed on a page. You can use the printed slide and notes during your presentation so that you don't have to keep looking back at the projected slide.

■ Speaker notes can be included as part of a presentation viewed in a Web browser. This feature can be useful for sharing your presentation and comments with others who could not attend the actual presentation. You will learn how to save the slides in your presentation as Web pages later in this chapter.

■FAQ How do I print handouts?

Handouts help your audience remember the content of your presentation. Microsoft PowerPoint offers several print layouts for handouts. Choose the one that best fits the content and number of slides in your presentation.

Figure 9-8

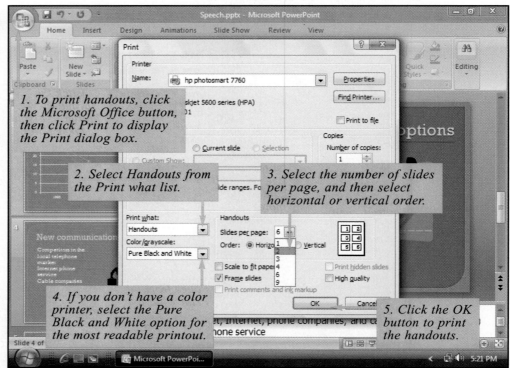

1. To print handouts, click the Microsoft Office button, then click Print to display the Print dialog box.

2. Select Handouts from the Print what list.

3. Select the number of slides per page, and then select horizontal or vertical order.

4. If you don't have a color printer, select the Pure Black and White option for the most readable printout.

5. Click the OK button to print the handouts.

■ If your presentation is brief, you can print two or three slides per page for handouts. The two-slide layout prints each slide on one-half of the page. It is appropriate to use this layout when the graphics and bullets on the slides include most of the details of your presentation content. The three-slide layout prints blank lines to the right of each slide. It is appropriate to use this layout when you expect your audience to write notes about each slide.

■ You can save paper by printing four to nine slides per page. You can select either horizontal or vertical order for all of these print layouts. Horizontal order prints multiple slides (in order) across the page; vertical order prints the slides (in order) down the page. The Handouts section of the Print dialog box provides a preview of the selected order.

■ The biggest advantage of using a PowerPoint presentation is the variety of colors and graphics you can use to enhance your slides. Your handouts can be printed in black and white, or in color, depending on your printer. Select the Pure Black and White option to convert the colors in your slides to the most readable grayscales for a black and white printer.

■ The Frame slides option gives your handouts a professional look by drawing a thin black line around each slide.

■ You can print a text-only version of your presentation by selecting Outline View from the Print what list. This handout is useful for very long presentations that include a number of bulleted items. Graphics do not print in the Outline View version.

■FAQ How do I save a presentation as Web pages?

If you convert your presentation to Web pages, people who missed it or didn't take notes can later view it on the Web.

It's easy to save your presentation as Web pages. The converted presentation can be viewed over the Internet using a standard Web browser. Each slide appears as a separate Web page with navigation tools to move from slide to slide.

Figure 9-9

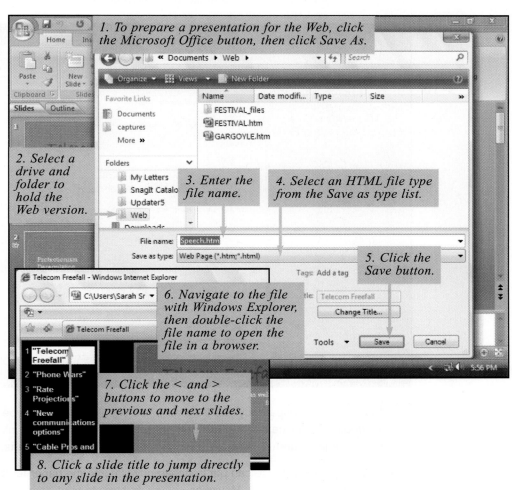

1. To prepare a presentation for the Web, click the Microsoft Office button, then click Save As.

2. Select a drive and folder to hold the Web version.

3. Enter the file name.

4. Select an HTML file type from the Save as type list.

5. Click the Save button.

6. Navigate to the file with Windows Explorer, then double-click the file name to open the file in a browser.

7. Click the < and > buttons to move to the previous and next slides.

8. Click a slide title to jump directly to any slide in the presentation.

■ If your slides are posted on the Web, during your presentation you might display a slide with the Web site URL so that interested audience members can later review the presentation on the Web.

■ In the Save as type box, use Microsoft's Single File Web Page (*.mht, *.mhtml) format or select the Web page (*.htm, *.html) format.

■ PowerPoint is useful for converting a presentation to Web pages, but some slide features cannot be duplicated. For instance, a viewer who is looking at the Web presentation might not see transitions and animation effects. If a presentation contains formatting that cannot be duplicated in Web pages, you'll be notified of the problem areas and will have the option of canceling or continuing with the save.

■ You should preview your presentation in a Web browser to see how it will actually look on the Web. If you're not satisfied with the Web version, refer to *Web presentations* in PowerPoint Help.

■FAQ Can I show my presentation with an overhead projector?

Typically, you'll connect your computer to a projection device, then display the presentation directly from PowerPoint. However, sometimes you won't have access to a computer and projection device, which means you might have to display your presentation the old-fashioned way—with transparency film and an overhead projector. You'll lose the transitions, animations, and sound effects, but at least you'll be able to display the content of your PowerPoint slides while you make your comments.

Figure 9-10

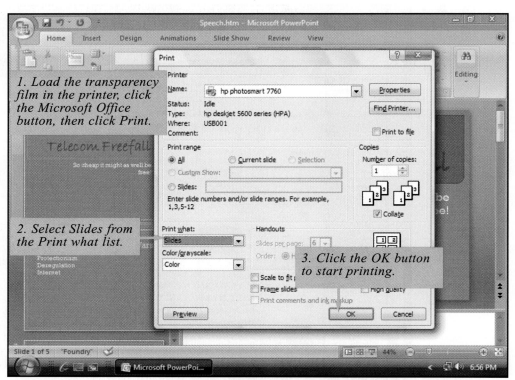

1. Load the transparency film in the printer, click the Microsoft Office button, then click Print.

2. Select Slides from the Print what list.

3. Click the OK button to start printing.

You can purchase transparency film from an office supply store. The type of film you purchase depends on whether you are printing on a laser printer or an ink jet printer. Read the packaging carefully to make sure you buy the right kind of transparency film.

■ If your printer allows it, you can put transparency film into the paper feeder and print directly onto the transparencies. However, you might have to print on regular paper and use a xerographic copier to create the transparencies. Read your printer manual for details.

■ A color printer that accepts transparency film can be used to create color transparencies. If you don't have access to a color printer, you should select the Pure Black and White option in the Print dialog box to create slides with the most readable grayscales your black and white printer can produce.

QuickCheck A

1. [_____] notes help you remember what to say when each slide is displayed during a presentation.

2. A(n) [_____] effect controls the way bullets appear in a bulleted list.

3. A(n) [_____] controls the way a slide replaces the previous slide during a presentation.

4. True or false? Transparencies can only be used to display black and white versions of the slides in a PowerPoint presentation. [_____]

5. If you're going to put your presentation on the Web, you should always include a slide with the [_____] where the presentation will be located.

Check It!

QuickCheck B

Indicate the letter of the desktop element that best matches the following:

1. The Slide Sorter view button [____]

2. The Increase List Level button [____]

3. The Increase Font Size button [____]

4. The Slide Show view button [____]

5. The Normal view button [____]

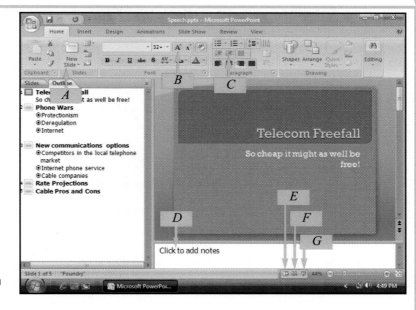

Check It!

Get It?

A Skill Set A: Sorting slides and changing fonts

B Skill Set B: Transitions and spell checking

C Skill Set C: Adding animation and sound to bullets

D Skill Set D: Adding speaker notes and saving slides as Web pages

Chapter 10
Creating a Database

What's inside and on the CD?

Microsoft Access is the component of the Microsoft Office suite best suited for working with large collections of data called databases. As database software, Microsoft Access provides a powerful set of tools for entering and updating information, deleting information, sorting data, searching for specific data, and creating reports.

The databases you create with Access are technically referred to as "relational databases." A **relational database** contains data organized into easy-to-visualize tables. A table is composed of fields and records. A **record** contains information about a single "entity" in the database—a person, place, event, or thing. A **field** contains a single unit of information, such as a name, birth date, or ZIP code.

A relational database can contain more than one table and you can define relationships between these tables so that they can be used in conjunction with each other. For example, a video store database might include a table of movies and a table of customers. Suppose a customer checks out one of the *Star Wars* movies. If the movie is never returned, the relationship between the movie and customer tables allows the clerk to contact the appropriate customer about returning the movie. The customer number, which was entered in the *Star Wars* record when the movie was checked out, acts as a link to the customer table that displays the customer's address, phone number, and credit card billing information.

■FAQ How is data organized in a database?

Because it's useful for organizing many types of data, database software, such as Microsoft Access, can be complex. A few simple concepts, however, should provide you with the background necessary to start working with this important data management tool. An Access database consists of tables. Each table is similar to a stack of index cards. Each card in the stack has the same kind of data written on it, which relates to a single entity. A database record is equivalent to one index card, as shown in the figure below.

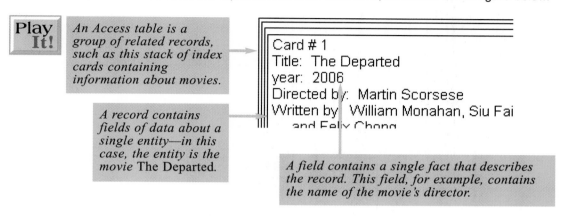

An Access table is a group of related records, such as this stack of index cards containing information about movies.

A record contains fields of data about a single entity—in this case, the entity is the movie The Departed.

Card # 1
Title: The Departed
year: 2006
Directed by: Martin Scorsese
Written by: William Monahan, Siu Fai and Felix Chong

A field contains a single fact that describes the record. This field, for example, contains the name of the movie's director.

The data in a database can be displayed in different ways. Most of the time, you'll work with the data arranged in a table, such as the one shown below. Data arranged in this way uses the same records and fields as the index cards shown above—it just looks different because of its arrangement. In the figure below, each row contains one record, equivalent to one index card. Each cell in a row contains the data for one field. The table includes all fields in all rows—equivalent to the entire stack of index cards.

Figure 10-1

An Access table consists of rows and columns.

A row contains one record—equivalent to one index card.

Each cell in a row contains one field of data.

One advantage of this arrangement is that each column contains the same field of data for each record. This column, for example, contains the director of every movie in the table.

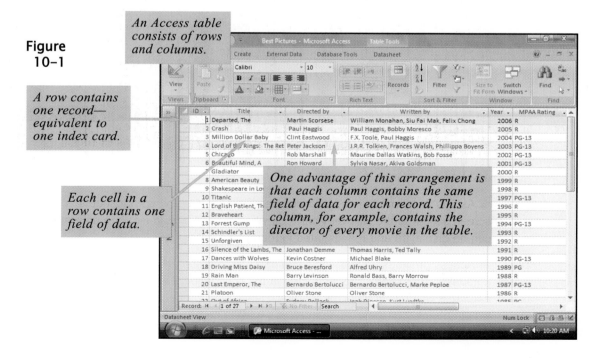

■FAQ What's in the Access window?

To start Access, click Start, point to All Programs, click Microsoft Office, then click Microsoft Office Access 2007. Unlike other Microsoft Office applications, Access doesn't automatically display an empty document window when you start the program. When you start Access, the Getting Started with Microsoft Access window appears. You can use this window to connect to Microsoft Office Online, search for an existing file, create a new database, or open an existing database.

Figure
10-2

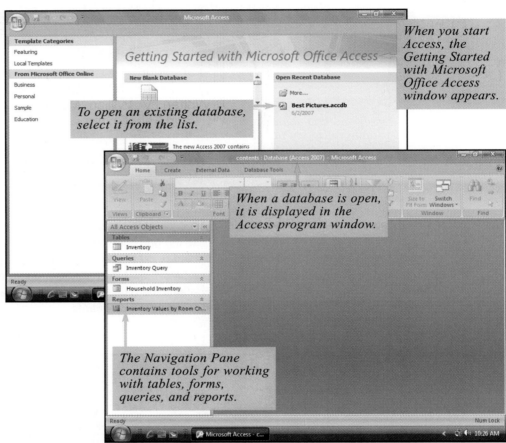

When you start Access, the Getting Started with Microsoft Office Access window appears.

To open an existing database, select it from the list.

When a database is open, it is displayed in the Access program window.

The Navigation Pane contains tools for working with tables, forms, queries, and reports.

■ When you work with Access, you typically will not create a new database each time you use the program. Instead, you'll open an existing database in order to add to, or edit, the data it contains.

■ As you've learned in previous chapters, documents and spreadsheets appear on-screen similar to the way they will look when printed. Databases are different—their data can be displayed and manipulated in many different ways.

■ Access provides several tools you can use to create, modify, and display data in the database. These tools are contained in the Navigation Pane on the left side of the database window. In this chapter, you'll learn how to use these tools to create tables and simple queries. In the next chapter, you'll learn how to use additional tools to create simple forms and reports.

■ Access also offers many different ways to use each of the tools. You should remember that Access is complex software. In order to simplify your introduction to Access, you will learn some basic ways to use the most common tools.

■FAQ How do I create a new database or open an existing database?

Creating a database is different from creating a document, worksheet, or presentation. With Word, for example, you typically enter some text into a new document before you save it. With Access, first you save an empty database, then you create the elements that make up the database. These elements include tables, reports, forms, and queries.

Do It!

Figure 10-3

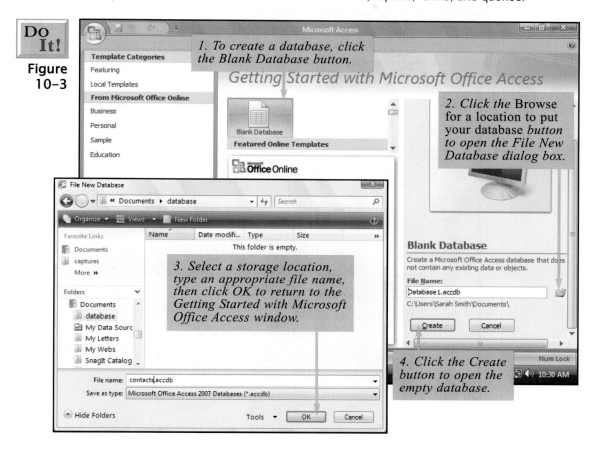

1. To create a database, click the Blank Database button.

2. Click the Browse for a location to put your database *button to open the File New Database dialog box.*

3. Select a storage location, type an appropriate file name, then click OK to return to the Getting Started with Microsoft Office Access window.

4. Click the Create button to open the empty database.

Blank Database
Create a Microsoft Office Access database that does not contain any existing data or objects.

■ You only have to save a database once, when you first create it. As you add or change data in the database, the changes are automatically saved in the database file. When you're finished using the database, you just close it—there's no need to save it because all changes are saved as you make them.

■ If you have already created a database, select the name of the database from the Getting Started with Microsoft Office Access window.

■ To open a database, you can use the Open Recent Database list or the 📂 More link on the Getting Started with Microsoft Office Access window. Select the appropriate storage device and file name, then click the Open button.

■FAQ How do I create a table using a Table Template?

Before you can enter data in a database, you must specify the structure of the tables, records, and fields in your database. A table contains records. Each record consists of one or more fields, and each field contains a particular type of data, such as a name or date. When Access creates a new database, it creates an empty table called Table1 for you to modify. If you quit Access before modifying the table, the table is not saved and the database will be empty the next time you open it. Table Templates make it easy to create tables for common business and personal databases. Table Templates also help you create fields correctly.

Figure 10-4

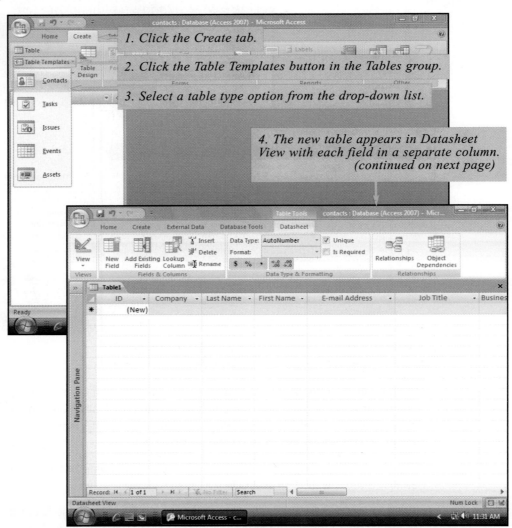

1. *Click the Create tab.*

2. *Click the Table Templates button in the Tables group.*

3. *Select a table type option from the drop-down list.*

4. *The new table appears in Datasheet View with each field in a separate column.*
(continued on next page)

■ Access includes sample tables for common business and personal databases. Select the most appropriate table type from the Table Templates list.

■ The sample tables include many fields, and some might not be necessary for your database.

■ **How do I create a table using a Table Template? (continued)**

Figure
10–5

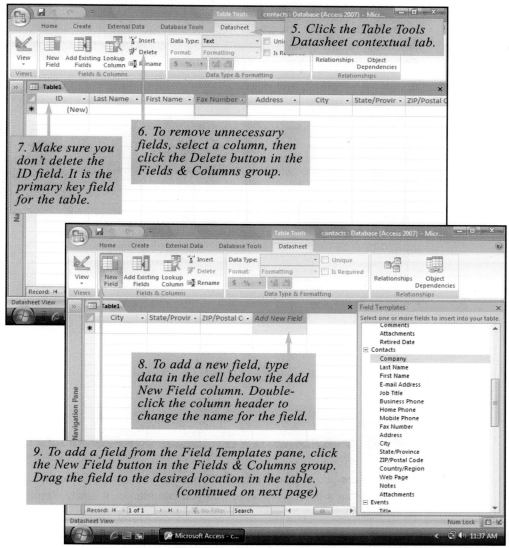

5. *Click the Table Tools Datasheet contextual tab.*

6. *To remove unnecessary fields, select a column, then click the Delete button in the Fields & Columns group.*

7. *Make sure you don't delete the ID field. It is the primary key field for the table.*

8. *To add a new field, type data in the cell below the Add New Field column. Double-click the column header to change the name for the field.*

9. *To add a field from the Field Templates pane, click the New Field button in the Fields & Columns group. Drag the field to the desired location in the table.*
(continued on next page)

■ A **primary key** is a field that uniquely identifies each record. It's very important that no two records are ever assigned the same value for this unique field. For this reason, it's usually best to have Access create the primary key. Access is then responsible for assigning a unique value to each record. As an alternative, you can select your own primary key. For example, you could use each contact's Social Security number as the primary key. To modify the primary key field, you will need to be in Design View. You'll learn more about Design View later in this chapter.

■ Each table in the database is assigned its own primary key. In a relational database, these fields are used to link the tables together, as described in the introduction to this chapter.

■ How do I create a table using a Table Template? (continued)

After you have finished modifying the table fields, the completed table is displayed and ready for data entry. The title of each field is displayed at the top of each column. The first blank record appears as the first row of fields in the table. Continue on to the next FAQ, where you'll learn how to enter data.

Figure
10-6

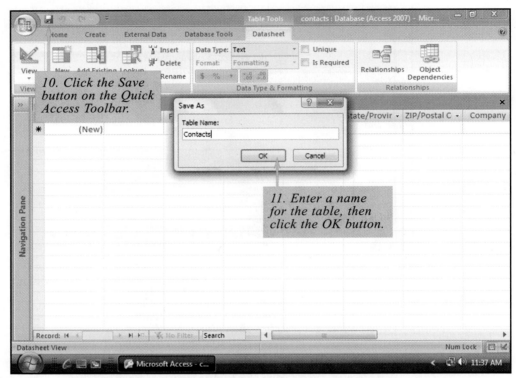

■ Make sure you click the Save button when you are done modifying the table fields. Give the table a unique name so that you can identify it easily. You don't have to save it again when you exit Access—just close the Access program window when you're through.

■ The name you enter when you save the table is the name for the table, which is not necessarily the same as the name for the database. For example, a database called "Contacts.mdb" might have tables called "Contacts," "Meetings," and so on. All tables in the database are stored in the same database file.

■ If you are saving on a floppy disk, leave the disk in the floppy disk drive until the Access window closes. If you remove the disk too soon, your database file could become corrupted and some of your data could be lost.

■ To open the database the next time you start Access, click the file name from the Getting Started with Microsoft Office Access window or click the More link to display the Open dialog box.

■ ■ ■

■FAQ How do I enter and edit data in a table?

Once you've defined the fields for a table, you can enter data. The data for each entity in your table, such as a person or an inventory item, becomes one record, or row, in the table.

If you have just created a table using a Table Template, the table is open. If the table is not open, double-click the name of the table in the Navigation Pane.

Figure 10-7

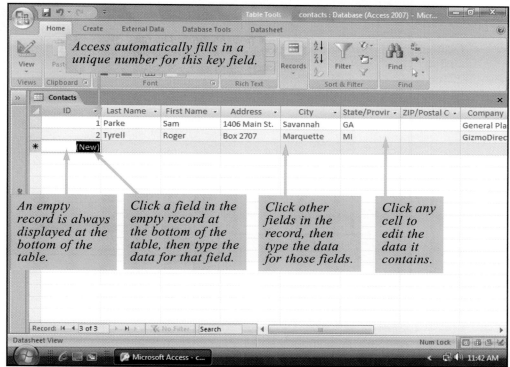

■ An empty record is always displayed at the bottom of a table. Each time you enter data into that empty record, a new empty record appears.

■ Be careful to enter data in a consistent manner. For example, don't use inconsistent entries, such as MI and Michigan, in the same database. If you're entering state names, always use either the state abbreviation or the entire state name. Later, when the database contains many records, it will be easier to locate the records that contain specific data if the data has been entered consistently. In this example, if you ask the database to list all of the contacts in the state of "MI," any records for contacts in "Michigan" might not be included in the list.

■ To edit data, click the cell containing the data. Use the left-arrow and right-arrow keys to move the insertion point within the field. Use the Backspace and Delete keys to delete text to the left or to the right of the insertion point.

■ To delete an entire record, right-click the row header containing the record. Click Delete Record on the shortcut menu, then click the Yes button.

■FAQ How do I create a table in Design View?

If the sample tables offered in the Table Templates list don't meet your needs, you can create your own table using Design View. This option requires just a bit more planning because you must specify a data type for each field. A **data type** determines what kind of data can be entered into a field.

Figure 10–8

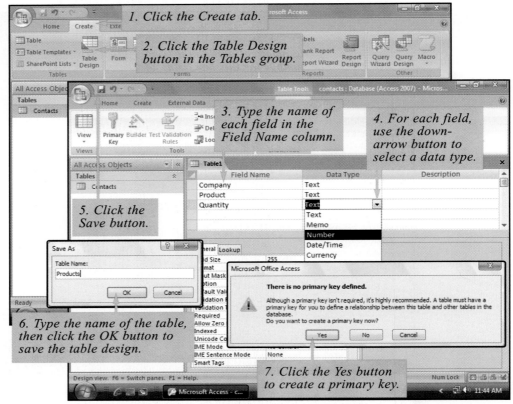

1. Click the Create tab.

2. Click the Table Design button in the Tables group.

3. Type the name of each field in the Field Name column.

4. For each field, use the down-arrow button to select a data type.

5. Click the Save button.

6. Type the name of the table, then click the OK button to save the table design.

7. Click the Yes button to create a primary key.

■ Use the **Text data type** for fields that contain words and symbols of up to 255 characters in length.

■ Use the **Memo data type** for fields that contain variable length data, such as comments, notes, and reviews.

■ Use the **Number data type** for fields that contain numeric data. Don't use the Number data type for data that looks like a number, but that will never be calculated. For example, the data type for telephone numbers should be defined as Text.

■ Use the **Date/Time data type** for dates and times. This special data type makes it much easier, for example, to determine if one date occurs before or after another date.

■ When you allow Access to define the primary key, the ID field is created using the **AutoNumber data type**. A unique number is automatically entered in this field as you enter each new record.

■ The **Yes/No data type** can be useful for fields designed to hold simple Yes/No or True/False data. For example, you might use a Yes/No data type for the field "Subtitled?"

■ When you have defined all the fields, save and then close the Table window to begin entering data into your new table.

■FAQ How do I create a query using a Wizard?

After you have organized your data into one or more tables, you can manipulate the data in many ways. For example, you can search a company database for all customers in a specific state or search an inventory database for all products that cost more than $10. You can create a **query** to search your database for records that contain particular data. A query contains criteria that specify what you would like to find. You can also use a query to display some, but not all, of the fields in a table. The Query Wizard offers a quick way to create simple queries and use them to locate data.

Figure 10-9

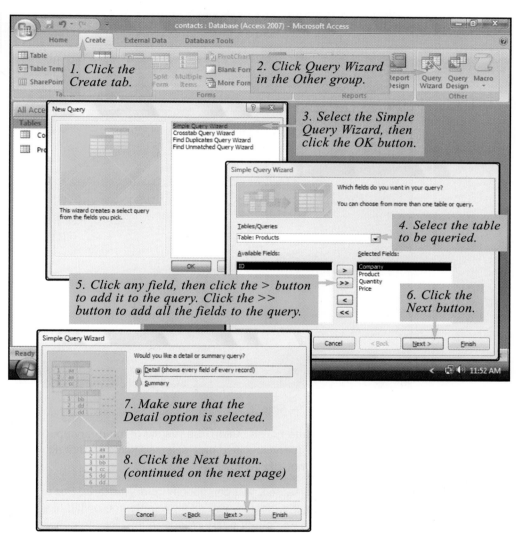

1. Click the Create tab.

2. Click Query Wizard in the Other group.

3. Select the Simple Query Wizard, then click the OK button.

4. Select the table to be queried.

5. Click any field, then click the > button to add it to the query. Click the >> button to add all the fields to the query.

6. Click the Next button.

7. Make sure that the Detail option is selected.

8. Click the Next button. (continued on the next page)

Simple Query Wizard - Step 1

■ Click a field, then click the `>` button to add an individual field to the query. Click the `>>` button to add all fields to the query. Click the `<` button to remove a field from the query. Click the `<<` button to remove all fields from the query.

Simple Query Wizard - Step 2

■ Selecting the Detail option shows all of the specified fields for the records, whereas selecting the Summary option only displays how many records match your criteria.

How do I create a query using a Wizard? (continued)

Figure
10-10

Simple Query Wizard - Step 3

■ After you click the Finish button, the results of the query appear in a new window. In this example, the query specified only selected fields so that all records are displayed, but the ID field is not displayed.

■ To further refine a search, you can specify **query criteria**. For example, instead of a query that returns all the records, you might want to see only those records for products that cost more than $10. To add query criteria, right-click the query tab at the top of the window, then click Design View on the shortcut menu. Type >10 in the criteria row under the Price field. Click the ![Run] Run button in the Results group on the Query Tools Design contextual tab to display the query results. Records that match the criteria are displayed in the query results window.

■ When you close the query window after viewing the results of a query for which you specified query criteria, you'll see a message asking *Do you want to save changes to the design of query 'Query Name'?* Click Yes if you would like to use the same query criteria every time you use this query.

■ After a query is saved, you can run it repeatedly to display all the records—including new and updated data—that match the criteria you've specified.

QuickCheck A

1. True or false? A relational database contains information that is organized into tables containing columns and rows. [_____]

2. A(n) [_____] contains a single piece of information, such as a name or ZIP code.

3. A(n) [_____] contains fields of information about a single entity in the database, such as a person, event, or thing.

4. True or false? Each time you enter new data into a database table, you must save the table. [_____]

5. A(n) [_____] contains criteria that specify the data you want to find in the database.

Check It!

QuickCheck B

Indicate the letter of the desktop element that best matches the following:

1. A text field [____]

2. A number field [____]

3. A primary key field [____]

4. A currency field [____]

5. A blank field in a new record [____]

ID	Company	Product	Quantity
1	General Plastic	6 oz mug	47
2	AwardTech	drink holder	13
3	General Plastic	12 oz mug	52
4	General Plastic	8 oz cup	38
5	AwardTech	car compass	24
6	GizmoDirect	sun visor	41
7	GizmoDirect	dash protector	17
8	AwardTech	insulated mug	61
9	General Plastic	car broom	13
10	GizmoDirect	drink holder	48
*	(New)		

All Access Objects

Tables
- Contacts
- Products

Queries
- Products Query

Forms
- Contacts

Reports
- Products
- Products Query

Check It!

Get It?

A Skill Set A: Creating a new database

B Skill Set B: Creating a table with a Table Template

C Skill Set C: Creating a table in Design View

D Skill Set D: Creating a query with a Wizard

Chapter 11

Finalizing a Database

What's inside and on the CD?

In this chapter, you'll learn how to manipulate a database to create forms, generate reports, print reports, and convert reports into Web pages.

A **form** allows you to customize the way Access displays records by selecting particular fields, specifying the field order, and adding descriptive field labels. Forms are designed to simplify the data entry process by making the screen-based record look like a printed form.

A **database report** is typically a printed document containing data selected from a database. Like a query, a report can be based on criteria that determine which data is included in the report. Reports can be formatted in various ways. Many reports are formatted in columns, with headings at the top of each column and data from each record displayed below each heading. Reports also often include totals and subtotals. In addition to printing reports, Microsoft Access makes it easy to export reports to Web pages.

■FAQ How do I create a form using a Wizard?

You can organize your data into rows and columns using a table, which is the best way to view the data contained in a large number of records. Another way to display your data is with a form. A form allows you to view your data one record at a time, with the fields of each record arranged on your computer screen as they might be arranged on a printed form. The Form Wizard helps you design an on-screen form in which you can enter and manipulate data for each record of a database.

Figure 11-1

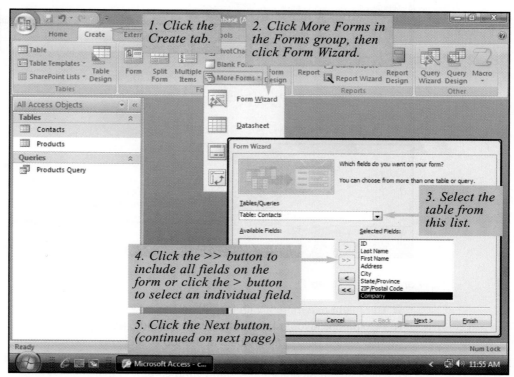

Form Wizard - Step 1

■ Most of the time, you'll want to include all fields on the form. To do so, click the `>>` button.

■ As an alternative, you can select individual fields. For example, if you are going to enter specific data, such as today's purchases, you might use a form that shows only ID, FirstName, and LastName, along with a field for the amount of purchase. You don't need to see the contact's address information while you are entering purchase data. To select a specific field, click it, then click the `>` button. Repeat these steps for each field you want to include on the form.

■ You can remove an individual field from the Selected Fields list by clicking the `<` button.

■ How do I create a form using a Wizard? (continued)

Figure 11-2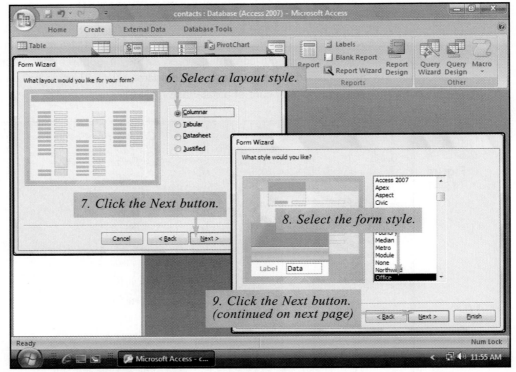

Form Wizard - Step 2

■ You might experiment with layouts to see how they work for different types of data. The Columnar layout places labels next to fields, and lists the fields in columns. The Tabular layout places field labels at the top of a column, which makes it appear like a table. The Datasheet layout resembles a spreadsheet, with cells for entering data. The Justified layout displays fields across the screen in rows, with a label above each field.

Form Wizard - Step 3

■ The form style determines the font, font color, and background for the form. Choose a style that seems appropriate for your data. The preview area to the left of the list of styles is useful for selecting a form style. The available styles are similar to the themes available in the other Office 2007 applications.

■ How do I create a form using a Wizard? (continued)

Figure 11-3

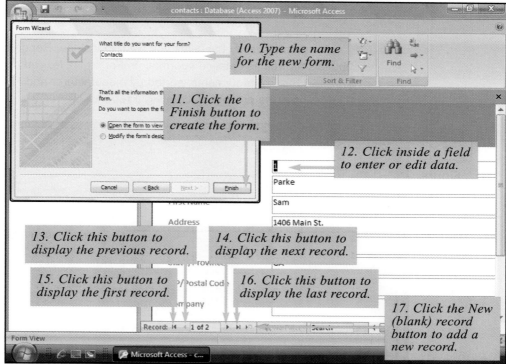

Form Wizard - Step 4

■ When the Form Wizard closes, the first record is displayed in the new form. You can now use the form to view, edit, or add records to the table. Use the navigation controls (see Steps 13 through 17 in Figure 11-3 above) to move from one record to the next and to add new records to the database.

■ The form is automatically saved in the database file, so you don't have to save the form separately. The changes you make to data while using the form automatically update the corresponding table in your database.

■ Forms created by Access are created in either a Tabular or Stacked layout. The position of the controls on the form are controlled by pre-defined parameters. You can modify the form design and layout by switching to Design View. To switch to Design View, right-click the tab at the top of the form window. Click Design View on the shortcut menu.

■ You can use the tools on the Form Design Tools contextual tabs to apply additional formatting to the form. You can change the form layout from Tabular to Stacked using the buttons in the Control Layout group on the Form Design Tools Arrange contextual tab. If you want more control over the layout of the controls on the form, you can remove the Tabular or Stacked layout from a control or the entire form with the Remove button in the Control Layout group.

■ Click any label to edit it. To move a label and the associated data field, click to select the object, move the pointer over the edge of the object until the pointer changes to a ✛ shape, then drag the label and data field to a new location. To delete a label and data field from the form, right-click the label, then click Cut on the shortcut menu.

■ As you become more familiar with Access, you might eventually want to explore creating forms using Design View. When you create a form using Design View, start with a blank form, then add the labels and controls. Design View provides maximum flexibility for designing a form, but requires more time on your part.   ■   ■   ■

■FAQ How do I create a report using a Wizard?

When you want to create a polished printout of some or all of the data in your Access database, you can create a report.

To create a report, simply specify the fields you want to include. Reports often include totals and subtotals as well as detailed information. For example, you might create a report that shows all the inventory items, sorted by manufacturer and item number. The Report Wizard simplifies the process of creating a report.

Do It!

Figure 11-4

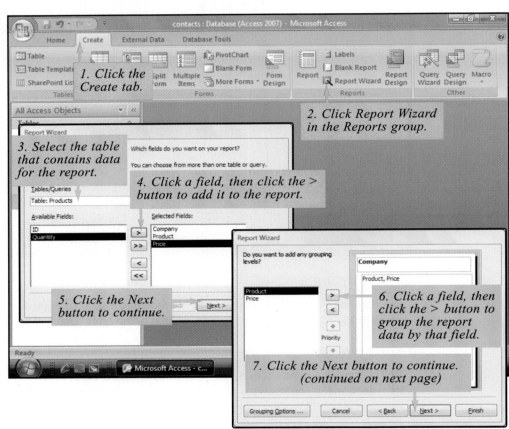

1. Click the Create tab.

2. Click Report Wizard in the Reports group.

3. Select the table that contains data for the report.

4. Click a field, then click the > button to add it to the report.

5. Click the Next button to continue.

6. Click a field, then click the > button to group the report data by that field.

7. Click the Next button to continue. (continued on next page)

Report Wizard - Step 1

■ To add individual fields to the report, click a field, then click the button. Click the button to add all available fields to the report.

Report Wizard - Step 2

■ When you add a grouping level, records are sorted according to entries in the group field. You can add several grouping levels to a report. For example, you might group a list of products by the manufacturer, then group them by item number. Grouping also helps arrange data when you want to produce a report containing subtotals.

■ ■ ■

■ How do I create a report using a Wizard? (continued)

Figure 11-5

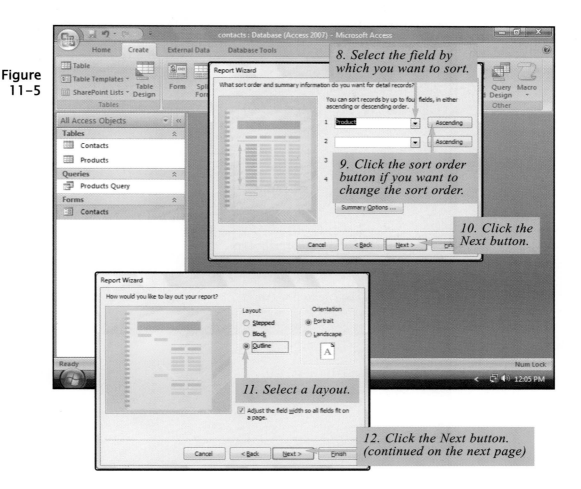

8. Select the field by which you want to sort.

9. Click the sort order button if you want to change the sort order.

10. Click the Next button.

11. Select a layout.

12. Click the Next button. (continued on the next page)

Report Wizard - Step 3

■ To sort records within a group, click the down-arrow button and select the field by which you want to sort.

■ Click the Ascending button to sort from A to Z or from low to high. Click the Descending button to sort from Z to A or high to low.

Report Wizard - Step 4

■ If you want to use a different report layout, select an option button in the Layout section. The preview area to the left allows you to select the layout that suits your individual needs.

■ How do I create a report using a Wizard? (continued)

Figure 11-6

Report Wizard - Step 5

■ Select the style that seems most suitable for your report. The preview area to the left of the list of styles is useful for selecting a report style.

Report Wizard - Step 6

■ Type a report name, which is used to identify the report so that you can open it in the future. The report layout is automatically saved in the database file along with the tables, queries, and forms that you have already created.

■ When you click the Finish button, the report is displayed in a window. Use the vertical scroll bar to view pages of the report that aren't visible. On a low-resolution screen, you can use the horizontal scroll bar to view columns on the right side of the report.

■ You can modify the report layout at any time. Right-click the report name in the Navigation Pane. Click Design View from the shortcut menu. You can use the options on the Report Design Tools contextual tabs to modify the report. Select an object on the report, then use the sizing handles to resize them. To move an object, click the object to select it, move the pointer over the edge of the object until the pointer changes to a ✛ shape, then drag the object to a new location.

■FAQ How do I print a report?

Each time you display or print a report, the contents of the report are automatically updated to reflect the current data stored in the database. For example, suppose that you print a report today. Over the next week, you add and change data in the database. If you display or print the report next week, it will include all of the updated data.

Do It!

Figure 11-7

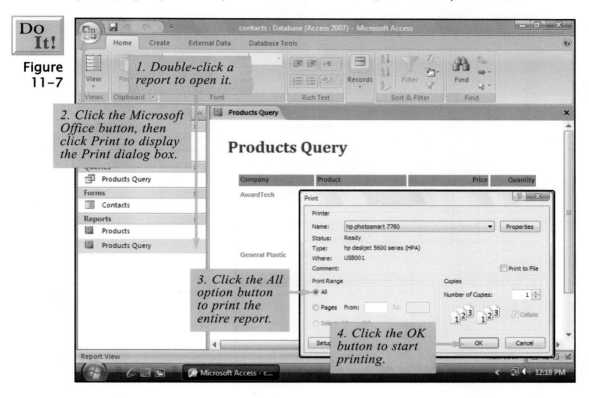

1. Double-click a report to open it.

2. Click the Microsoft Office button, then click Print to display the Print dialog box.

3. Click the All option button to print the entire report.

4. Click the OK button to start printing.

■ The data in a printed report is a "snapshot" that shows the status of your database at a particular point in time. When you edit or add data to the database, your report includes new and revised data. It is a good idea to include the date the report was printed on all pages to help readers determine if the data is current.

■ To add the date or time as a report header, right-click the report name in the Navigation Pane, then click Design View on the shortcut menu. Click the Date & Time button in the Controls group on the Report Design Tools Design contextual tab. Select the date or time formats, then click the OK button. You can move the date and time fields to any location on the report. Select both fields by holding down the Shift key while you click each field. Move the pointer over the edge of the fields until the pointer changes to a ✛ shape, then drag the fields to the desired location in the report.

■FAQ How do I save a report as a Web page?

Once you've created a report, you can print it or post it on the Web. As with other Web pages, your report must be in HTML format to be accessible to Web browsers.

Do It!

Figure 11–8

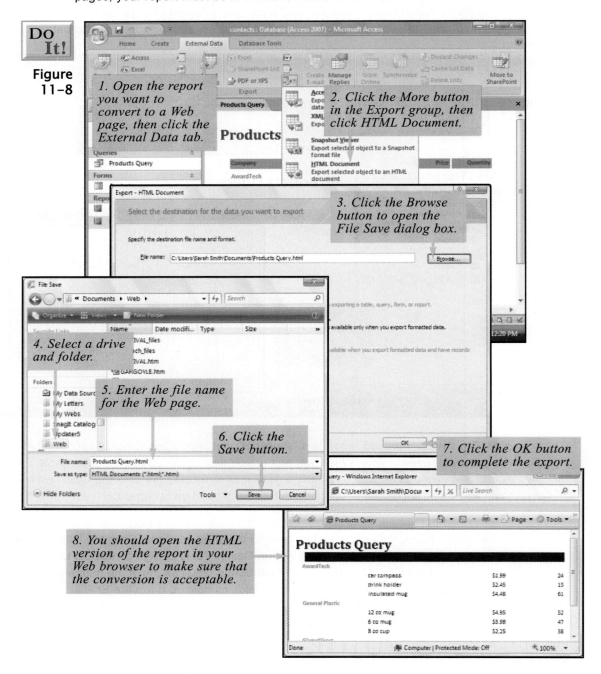

1. Open the report you want to convert to a Web page, then click the External Data tab.

2. Click the More button in the Export group, then click HTML Document.

3. Click the Browse button to open the File Save dialog box.

4. Select a drive and folder.

5. Enter the file name for the Web page.

6. Click the Save button.

7. Click the OK button to complete the export.

8. You should open the HTML version of the report in your Web browser to make sure that the conversion is acceptable.

■ Use a Web browser to preview the report as a Web page. Microsoft Access usually does a fairly good job when converting reports to Web pages, but you should check to make sure that the report layout and data appears to be correct.

■ As the data in your database changes, the Web page version of the report will become increasingly out-of-date. Periodically, you should open the report and export it again as a Web page. This action ensures that all new data is included in the Web-based version of the report.

QuickCheck A

1. A(n) [_____] displays the fields of each record arranged on your computer screen as they might be arranged on a printed form.

2. A(n) [_____] is typically a formatted printout of some or all of the data contained in a database.

3. True or false? You can use a form to view, edit, and add data to a table. [_____]

4. True or false? Reports are updated each time you display them. [_____]

5. True or false? Access automatically updates the data in Web pages every time you print a report. [_____]

Check It!

QuickCheck B

Indicate the letter of the desktop element that best matches the following:

1. A text field [____]

2. The New (blank) record button [____]

3. The First record button [____]

4. The Last record button [____]

5. The Next record button [____]

Check It!

Get It?

A — Skill Set A: Creating a form

C — Skill Set C: Printing a report

B — Skill Set B: Creating a report

D — Skill Set D: Saving a report as a Web page

Projects

∎Introduction to Projects

The projects in this section are designed to help you review and develop skills you learned by reading, watching Play It! segments, and stepping through the Do It! activities. Projects serve as a valuable intermediate step between the *Practical Office 2007* learning environment and working on your own. Even if you are not required to complete the projects for a class, you'll find that trying some of the projects can enhance your ability to use Microsoft Office 2007.

Although not required for interacting with the Play It! and Do It! segments in Chapters 1–11, Microsoft Office 2007 must be installed on the computer you use to complete the projects in this section. To discover if this software has been installed on your computer, click the Start button, click All Programs, and then look for the Microsoft Office folder on the menu. When you have located the folder, open the folder, then open Microsoft Word, Microsoft Excel, Microsoft Access, or Microsoft PowerPoint. The splash screen should display the "Microsoft Office 2007" logo.

If you don't remember how to complete a task for a project, refer to the *Practical Office 2007* book. It is designed to serve as a quick reference guide to the skills you've learned—keep it handy as you work on the projects and when working on your own.

For many of the projects, you'll start by copying project files from the CD. You can copy a project file from the CD using the Copy It! button on the first page of a project. As another option, you can use Windows Explorer or My Computer to copy the files directly from the CD supplied with this book to a floppy disk, hard disk, or USB flash drive. We suggest keeping all of the project files together in one location. We will refer to this location as your Project Folder.

At the completion of each project, you'll have created a file that demonstrates your ability to apply your Office 2007 skills. To submit a completed project to your instructor, use one of the methods indicated by the instructions at the end of the project. Most projects can be printed, turned in on a disk or removable storage device, or sent as an e-mail attachment. Your instructor might have a preference for one of these methods. You'll find additional information about printing, saving, and e-mailing projects on the next three pages.

■Submitting an Assignment as a Printout or on a Removable Storage Device

You can print or save your project files using the Microsoft Office button, as shown in the figure below.

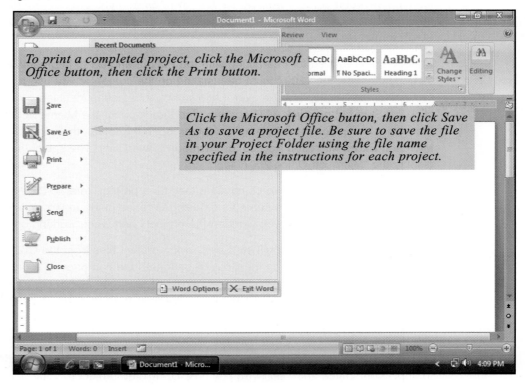

To print a completed project, click the Microsoft Office button, then click the Print button.

Click the Microsoft Office button, then click Save As to save a project file. Be sure to save the file in your Project Folder using the file name specified in the instructions for each project.

■ To print a project file:

1. Make sure that a printer is attached to your computer and that it is turned on.

2. Click the Microsoft Office button, then click Print.

3. If the printout doesn't already include your name, the project name, student ID, section number, and date, be sure to write this information on the printout.

■ To save your file on a removable storage device:

1. Click the Microsoft Office button, then click the Save As option.

2. When the Save As dialog box appears, navigate to the removable storage device.

3. In the *File name* box, enter the name specified by the project instructions.

4. Click the Save button to complete the process.

5. Before you submit your removable storage device to your instructor, make sure that you've labeled it with the project name, your name, your student ID, your section number, and date.

Note: If you saved your project file on the hard disk, you can copy it onto a disk or USB flash drive using the Copy command in Windows Explorer.

■Submitting an Assignment as an E-mail Attachment

You can typically use either Method 1 or Method 2, as explained below, to submit a Word, Excel, or PowerPoint project as an e-mail attachment. Access projects, however, require Method 1. America Online (AOL) users must use Method 1 for all projects. For information on setting up your e-mail, refer to the next page.

■ Method 1—Use your usual e-mail software to send a project

With Method 1, you'll send your project file using your usual e-mail software, such as Microsoft Outlook, Outlook Express, Eudora, Hotmail, Gmail, or AOL Mail. To use Method 1, first make sure that you have saved the project file. Next, start your e-mail software. Then, follow your software's procedures for sending an e-mail attachment. The procedure usually consists of the following steps:

1. Start a new message by using a toolbar button, such as Compose Message (Outlook Express) or Write Mail (AOL Mail).

2. Address the new message to your instructor.

3. Click the Attachment button or select the Attachment option from a menu. If you don't see an Attachment option, look for a File option on the Insert menu.

4. When prompted, specify the location that contains the attachment—usually your Project Folder—and then select the project file from the list.

5. Click the Send button to send the e-mail message and attachment.

■ Method 2—Use Microsoft Office 2007's Send feature

If Microsoft Office 2007 is set up in conjunction with your e-mail software, you can send your project file directly from Word, Excel, or PowerPoint by using the following steps:

1. After saving your project, keep your application (Paint, Word, Excel, or PowerPoint) window open.

2. Click the Microsoft Office button.

3. Select the *Send* option.

4. From the *Send* submenu, select the option *E-Mail*.

5. Enter your instructor's e-mail address in the To: box.

6. For the subject line, enter your student ID number, the project number, and your class section.

7. Click the Send button.

■   ■   ■

■E-mail attachments (continued)

■ To configure your e-mail:

You can send e-mail attachments only if your computer has an Internet connection and a functioning e-mail account. To use e-mail from a school or business computer, you should consult with your instructor or technical support person for instructions.

Using e-mail on your home computer requires an Internet connection and an e-mail account from an Internet Service Provider (ISP), such as America Online (AOL), AT&T WorldNet, or any local ISP that you might find by looking in the Yellow Pages. Many ISPs provide software that automatically creates your e-mail account. If your ISP does not supply such software, you will need to obtain the following information from your ISP and ask for help to set up your account:

The phone number that provides access to the Internet (dialup connections only)

Your e-mail address (such as hfinn5678@worldnet.att.net)

Your e-mail password (such as huck2finn)

The incoming mail server type (usually POP3)

Your incoming mail server (often the part of your e-mail address that comes after the @ symbol, e.g., aol.com)

Your outgoing SMTP mail server (such as mailhost.att.net)

The primary and secondary domain name server (DNS) numbers (such as 204.127.129.1)

As an alternative to an e-mail account through your ISP, you can sign up with a Web-based e-mail provider. For this option, you still need an ISP to provide your Internet connection. Once that connection is working, you can use it to access a Web-based e-mail provider such as www.hotmail.com, www.gmail.com, or www.yahoo.com. Follow the onscreen instructions to set up your e-mail account.

When you use a Web-based e-mail account, complete your project offline. Then connect to your Web-based e-mail account, create a new message addressed to your instructor, and then attach your project file to the message before sending it.

Microsoft Office 2007 Configuration

Microsoft Office 2007 provides many ways for you to configure and modify the way its applications look and operate. While this adaptability can be a positive feature, it can potentially cause confusion if your version of Microsoft Office 2007 is not configured to look or work the same way as the version used for the examples in the *Practical Office 2007*. Here's how to configure your software to match the settings that were used for the *Practical Office 2007* figures and animations.

■ **To configure Microsoft Word, Excel, and PowerPoint:**

1. Click the Microsoft Office button. Click either the Word Options, Excel Options, or PowerPoint Options button. On the Popular tab, make sure Show Mini Toolbar on selection and Enable Live Preview are selected.

■ **To configure Microsoft Word, Excel, PowerPoint, and Access:**

1. The entire ribbon should be visible. If it is not, double-click one of the tabs at the top of the application window.

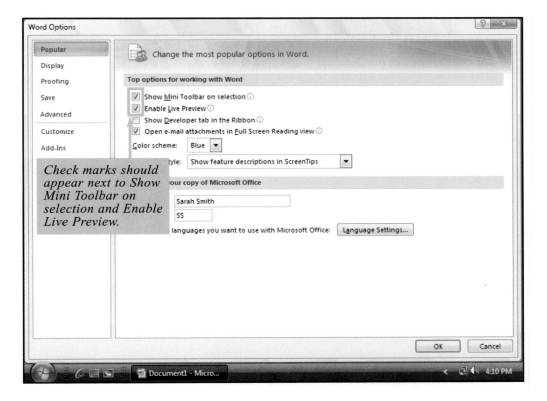

■Project AP-1: Working with Windows Applications

In this project, you'll apply what you've learned about application windows to start several programs and arrange your desktop.

Requirements: This project requires Microsoft Windows.

Project files: No project files are needed to complete this project.

1. Start the WordPad program, which is located in the Accessories group of the All Programs list on the Start menu.

2. Make sure that the WordPad window is maximized.

3. Start the Paint program, which is located in the Accessories group of the All Programs list on the Start menu.

4. Make sure that the Paint window is maximized.

5. Switch to the WordPad window.

6. Switch back to the Paint window.

7. Restore the Paint window.

8. Adjust the size and position of the Paint window so that your screen looks similar to the one on the next page.

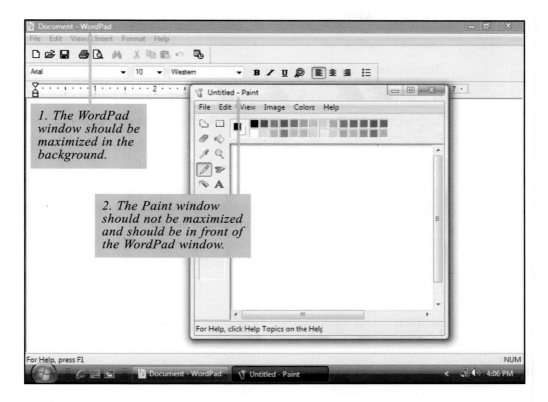

1. The WordPad window should be maximized in the background.

2. The Paint window should not be maximized and should be in front of the WordPad window.

9. Press the PrtSc or Print Screen key on your keyboard.

10. Maximize the Paint window. Click Edit on the Paint menu bar, then click Paste. If you are given the option of enlarging the bitmap, click the Yes button.

11. Save the graphic in your Project Folder as PrjAP-1-XXXXX-9999, where XXXXX is your student ID number and 9999 is your section number.

12. Use one of the following options to submit your project on disk or removable storage device, as a printout, or as an e-mail attachment, according to your instructor's directions:

■ To submit the project from your Project Folder where it is currently stored, stop the Paint program by closing its window. Copy the file to a disk or removable storage device. Include your name, student ID number, section number, date, and PrjAP-1 when you submit the file.

■ To print the project, click File on the Paint menu bar, then click Print. Click the OK button. Write your name, student ID number, section number, date, and PrjAP-1 on the printout.

■ To e-mail the file, use Method 1 as described on page 137. Type your instructor's e-mail address in the To: box. Click the Subject: box, then type PrjAP-1, your student ID number, and your class section number. Click the Send button or perform any additional steps required by your e-mail software to send an e-mail message.

■Project AP-2: Working with Files

In this project, you'll apply what you've learned about Windows applications to create, save, and open a file.

Requirements: This project requires Microsoft Windows.

Project files: No project files are needed to complete this project.

1. Start the WordPad program, which is located in the Accessories group of the All Programs list on the Start menu.

2. Make sure that the WordPad window is maximized.

3. Click anywhere in the blank section of the document window and type the following short memo. Type your own name on the FROM: line and type today's date on the DATE: line. (Hint: Press the Enter key at the end of each line.)

MEMO
TO: Professor Greer
FROM: [Your name]
DATE: [Today's date]
SUBJECT: This week's lesson
I will not be able to attend my music lesson this week.

4. Save the document in your Project Folder as PrjAP-2.txt.

5. Stop the WordPad application by closing its window.

6. Start WordPad again. Open the file PrjAP-2.txt from your Project Folder.

7. Type the word IMPORTANT so that the first line of the document reads IMPORTANT MEMO. Your document should now look like the one shown on the next page.

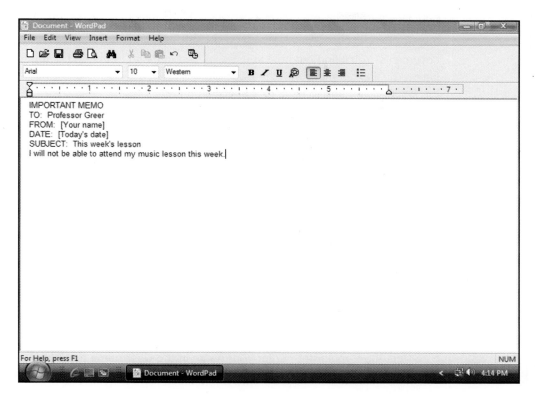

8. Save the new version of your document under a different name in your Project Folder. Use PrjAP-2-XXXXX-9999 as the new name, where XXXXX is your student number and 9999 is your section number.

9. Use one of the following options to submit your project on disk or removable storage device, as a printout, or as an e-mail attachment, according to your instructor's directions:

■ To submit the memo from your Project Folder where it is currently stored, stop the WordPad program by closing its window. Copy the file to a disk or removable storage device. Include your name, student ID number, class section number, date, and PrjAP-2 when you submit the file.

■ To print the project, click File on the WordPad menu bar, then click Print. Click the Print button. Write your name, student ID number, section number, date, and PrjAP-2 on the printout.

■ To e-mail the memo file, use Method 1 as described on page 137. Type your instructor's e-mail address in the To: box. Click the Subject: box and type PrjAP-2, your student ID number, and your class section number. Click the Send button or perform any additional steps required by your e-mail software to send an e-mail message.

■Project AP-3: Configuring Word and Navigating Documents

In this project, you'll explore how to use the Word Options dialog box to configure user information and file location settings. You'll also explore some efficient ways to move around documents. You'll find out how to use Ctrl-End to move to the end of a document in one jump. You'll experiment with the Page Up, Page Down, Home, and End keys, then use the Go To command to jump to a specified page.

Requirements: This project requires Microsoft Word.

Project files: PrjAP-3.docx

1. Copy the file PrjAP-3.docx to your Project Folder using the Copy It! button on this page in the BookOnCD.

2. Start Microsoft Word.

3. Open the file PrjAP-3.docx from your Project Folder.

4. Click the Microsoft Office button, and then click the Word Options button. When the Word Options dialog box appears, click the Save tab on the left and notice the storage device set to hold your documents. Click the Browse button to view the dialog box that allows you to change these locations. Unless you want to change these locations now, click the Cancel button to return to the Word Options dialog box.

5. Select the Popular tab. Enter your name in the User name text box if it is not already there.

6. Click the OK button to save your User Information.

7. Click the View tab, then click Print Layout.

8. Press Ctrl-End to move to the end of the document.

9. Press Ctrl-Enter to insert a page break.

10. Click anywhere in the blank section near the top of the new page and type the following:
BREAKOUT SESSION EVALUATION

Please provide comments on the effectiveness of each breakout session. Do not sign your evaluation.

11. Use the scroll bar to scroll to the beginning of the document.

12. Press the Page Down key a few times and notice how this key changes the position of the insertion point. Press the Page Up key to return to the top of the document.

13. Click in the middle of any full line of text in the document. Press the Home key and notice how this key changes the position of the insertion point. Press the End key to see what it does.

14. On the Home tab, click the down-arrow button next to Find in the Editing group, then click Go To. Type 5, click Go To, and then click Close.

15. Add the following line to the end of the memo.

Drop it off on the table at the conference room door before you leave.

The last page of your document should now look like the one shown on the next page.

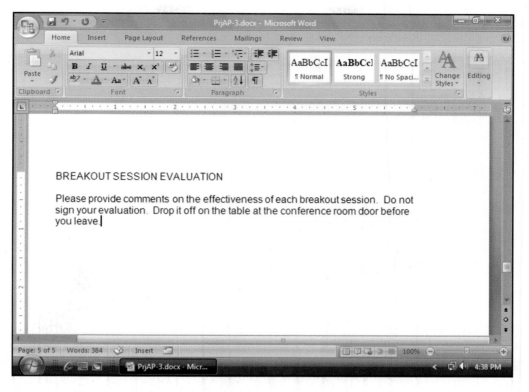

16. Save the new version of your document under a different name in your Project Folder. Use PrjAP-3-XXXXX-9999 as the new name, where XXXXX is your student number and 9999 is your section number.

17. Use one of the following options to submit your project on disk or removable storage device, as a printout, or as an e-mail attachment, according to your instructor's directions:

■ To submit the memo from your Project Folder where it is currently stored, stop the Word program by closing its window. Copy the file to a disk or removable storage device. Include your name, student ID number, class section number, date, and PrjAP-3 when you submit the file.

■ To print the project, click the Microsoft Office button, then click Print. Click the OK button. Write your name, student ID number, section number, date, and PrjAP-3 on the printout.

■ To e-mail the memo file, use Method 1 or Method 2, as described on page 137. Type your instructor's e-mail address in the To: box. Click the Subject: box and type PrjAP-3, your student ID number, and your class section number. Click the Send button or perform any additional steps required by your e-mail software to send an e-mail message.

■Project WD-1: Creating a Word Document

In this project, you'll apply what you've learned about Microsoft Word to create and modify a document.

Requirements: This project requires Microsoft Word.

Project files: No project files are needed for this project.

1. Start Microsoft Word.

2. Create a new document containing the text below, placing a blank line between each paragraph.

Dear Marjorie,

Hi! I was happy to receive your letter and learn that all is going well with you, Bob, and the kids. I really miss you all!

Your new job at the bookstore sounds great! How do you manage to keep your mind on work where there are so many fascinating books and magazines just begging to be read?

You mentioned that your first big assignment is to create a display appropriate for the month of February, but without featuring Valentine's Day or Presidents' Day. Did you know that I keep a database of offbeat events, like International Tuba Day and National Accordion Awareness Month? Let me know if you're interested and I'll create a query and send you a list of interesting events.

Sorry for the shortness of this note, but I have to run off to class. I promise to write more soon.

Good luck with the new job!

3. Compare the text that you typed with the text shown above and correct any typing mistakes that you might have made.

4. Use the Delete key to delete the phrase create a query and from the last sentence of the third paragraph. The Delete key deletes text without copying it to the clipboard.

5. Copy the phrase for the month of February from the paragraph that starts with the words You mentioned. Paste the copied phrase before the period at the end of the sentence that ends with send you a list of interesting events.

6. Select the sentence I really miss you all! in the first paragraph. Drag and drop the sentence after the sentence Good luck with the new job! at the end of the document.

7. Delete the fourth paragraph of the document, which starts with the words Sorry for the shortness.

8. Use the Undo button to restore the deleted paragraph.

9. Compare your letter with the document in the figure on the next page. Don't worry if the sentences in your document break in different places at the right margin.

Dear Marjorie,

Hi! I was happy to receive your letter and learn that all is going well with you, Bob, and the kids.

Your new job at the bookstore sounds great! How do you manage to keep your mind on work where there are so many fascinating books and magazines just begging to be read?

You mentioned that your first big assignment is to create a display appropriate for the month of February, but without featuring Valentine's Day or Presidents' Day. Did you know that I keep a database of offbeat events, like International Tuba Day and National Accordion Awareness Month? Let me know if you're interested and I'll send you a list of interesting events for the month of February.

Sorry for the shortness of this note, but I have to run off to class. I promise to write more soon.

Good luck with the new job! I really miss you all!

10. Add your name as the last line of the letter.

11. Save your document in your Project Folder using the file name PrjWD-1-XXXXX-9999, where XXXXX is your student ID number and 9999 is your class section number.

12. Use one of the following options to submit your project on disk or removable storage device, as a printout, or as an e-mail attachment, according to your instructor's directions:

■ To submit the file from your Project Folder where it is currently stored, stop the Word program by closing its window. Copy the file to a disk or removable storage device. Include your name, student ID number, class section number, date, and PrjWD-1 when you submit the file.

■ To print the project, click the Microsoft Office button, then click Print. Click the OK button. Write your name, student ID number, section number, date, and PrjWD-1 on the printout.

■ To e-mail the file, use Method 1 or Method 2, as described on page 137. Type your instructor's e-mail address in the To: box. Click the Subject: box and type PrjWD-1, your student ID number, and your class section number. Click the Send button or perform any additional steps required by your e-mail software to send an e-mail message.

■Project WD-2: Using the Mail Merge Wizard

In this project, you'll use the Mail Merge Wizard of Microsoft Word to create an address list and perform a mail merge.

Requirements: This project requires Microsoft Word.

Project file: No project files are needed for this project.

1. Start Microsoft Word.

2. Click the Mailings tab. Click Start Mail Merge in the Start Mail Merge group, then click Step by Step Mail Merge Wizard.

3. In the Mail Merge task pane, select *Letters* as the type of document, then click *Next: Starting document*.

4. In the Mail Merge task pane, select *Start from a template*, then click the *Select template* option. Select the Urban Letter template from the Letters tab, then click OK. Click *Next: Select recipients*.

5. In the Mail Merge task pane, select the *Type a new list* option, then click the *Create* option. Enter the following information in the New Address List dialog box.

First Name	Last Name	Address 1	City	State
Jim	Gallagos	1420 Elm Pass	Springfield	IL
Ed	Zimmerman	1562 River Way	Springfield	IL
Alice	Wegin	523 West Ave	Oak Grove	IL

Use the New Entry button to insert new rows. Click the OK button to close the New Address List dialog box.

6. Save the list as *address list.mdb* in your Project Folder. Click the OK button to close the Mail Merge Recipients dialog box. Click the *Next: Write your letter* option.

7. In the upper-right corner of the letter, delete the name placeholder and then replace the sender company address placeholder with the following return address:

Perfect Pizza
1320 W. Oak Grove Rd.
Springfield, IL

8. Delete the placeholders for the recipient's address and name. Click the *Address block* option from the Mail Merge task pane and then click the OK button to close the Insert Address Block dialog box.

9. Select today's date for the date placeholder.

10. Delete the placeholder for the salutation. Click the *Greeting line* option from the Mail Merge task pane, select any salutation, then click the OK button.

11. Replace the placeholder for the letter's text with:

I'm pleased to announce that Perfect Pizza has opened a new branch in your neighborhood! Stop by anytime this week for a free slice of pizza!

12. Delete the placeholder for the name at the bottom of the page. Replace the placeholder for the closing with:

Sincerely,

Paul DiCella

13. From the Mail Merge task pane, click *Next: Preview your letter*s. Use the Forward and Back buttons on the Mail Merge task pane to view the merged letters.

14. From the Mail Merge task pane, click *Next: Complete the merge*. On the task pane, click *Edit individual letters*. Click All, then click the OK button. The mail merge is complete. Scroll down the document. You should have three individually addressed letters.

15. Compare the first letter to the document shown below. Don't worry if the date is different.

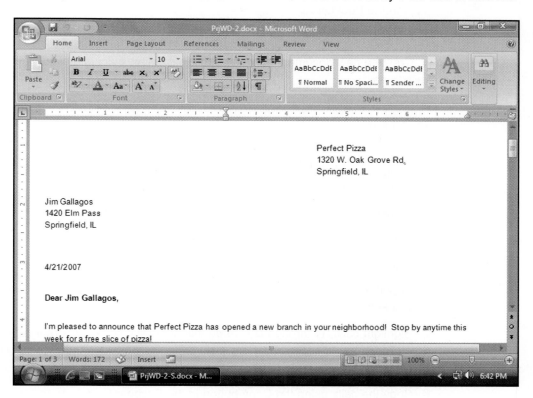

16. Save your document in your Project Folder using the file name PrjWD-2-XXXXX-9999, where XXXXX is your student ID number and 9999 is your class section number.

17. Use one of the following options to submit your project on disk or removable storage device, as a printout, or as an e-mail attachment, according to your instructor's directions:

■ To submit the file from your Project Folder where it is currently stored, stop the Word program by closing its window. Copy the file to a disk or removable storage device. Include your name, student ID number, class section number, date, and PrjWD-2 when you submit the file.

■ To print the project, click the Microsoft Office button, then click Print. Click the OK button. Write your name, student ID number, section number, date, and PrjWD-2 on the printouts.

■ To e-mail the file, use Method 1 or Method 2, as described on page 137. Type your instructor's e-mail address in the To: box. Click the Subject: box and type PrjWD-2, your student ID number, and your class section number. Click the Send button or perform any additional steps required by your e-mail software to send an e-mail message.

■Project WD-3: Cut, Copy, and Paste

In this project, you'll apply what you've learned about Microsoft Word to copy and paste text, and automatically insert special symbols such as the date and time.

Requirements: This project requires Microsoft Word and Microsoft Excel.

Project files: PrjWD-3.xlsx

1. Copy the file PrjWD-3.xlsx to your Project Folder using the Copy It! button on this page in the BookOnCD.

2. Start Microsoft Word.

3. Create a new document containing the text below, placing a blank line between each paragraph.

MEMO

To: All staff

Date:

Congratulations to Maria, winner of our quarterly sales bonus! Maria has sold over 1,000 SuperWidgets this year!

Sales totals are as follows:

4. Press the Enter key.

5. Start Microsoft Excel.

6. Click the Microsoft Office button, then click Open to open the file PrjWD-3.xlsx from your Project Folder.

7. Highlight cells A1 through D9. To do this, first click cell A1 where it says "Monthly Sales Totals by Salesperson." Next, hold down the Shift key and click cell D9, which contains $1,004.26.

8. Copy the cells using the Copy button in the Clipboard group on the Home tab. As an alternative, you can use the Ctrl-C key combination.

9. Switch back to Microsoft Word.

10. Make sure the insertion point is positioned below the last line of the document.

11. Use the Paste button in the Clipboard group on the Home tab (or press Ctrl-V) to paste the spreadsheet data into the document.

12. Switch back to Microsoft Excel. Copy the Congratulations clip art from the spreadsheet. Use the Text Wrapping options on the Picture Tools contextual tab to size and position the clip art just to the right of the memo heading lines containing MEMO, To, and Date.

13. If the Paste operation was successful, switch back to Microsoft Excel and close it.

14. In your Microsoft Word document, position the insertion point after the word "Date" on the third line of the memo. If necessary, press the Spacebar to create a space after the colon.

15. Click the Insert tab, then click Date & Time in the Text group. Choose the third option to insert the date in the format *March 16, 2007*. Click the OK button to insert the date and time.

16. Position the insertion point at the end of the word SuperWidgets.

17. On the Insert tab, click Symbols in the Symbols group, then click More Symbols. Select the trademark symbol. Click Insert, then click Close.

18. Your memo should look similar to the one below.

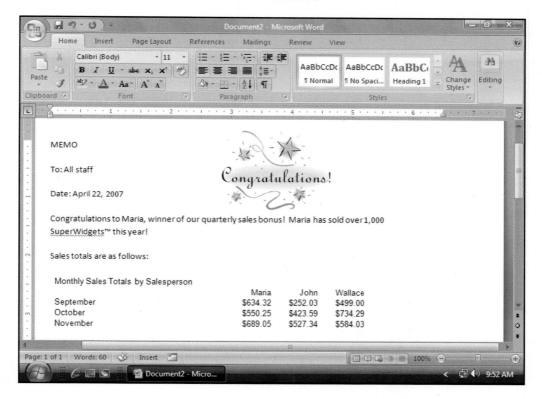

19. Save your memo in your Project Folder using the file name PrjWD-3-XXXXX-9999, where XXXXX is your student ID number and 9999 is your class section number. Use one of the following options to submit your project:

■ To submit the memo from your Project Folder where it is currently stored, stop the Word program by closing its window. Copy the file to a disk or removable storage device. Include your name, student ID number, class section number, date, and PrjWD-3 when you submit the file.

■ To print the project, click the Microsoft Office button, then click Print. Click the OK button. Write your name, student ID number, section number, date, and PrjWD-3 on the printout.

■ To e-mail the file, use Method 1 or Method 2, as described on page 137. Type your instructor's e-mail address in the To: box. Click the Subject: box and type PrjWD-3, your student ID number, and your class section number. Click the Send button or perform any additional steps required by your e-mail software to send an e-mail message.

■Project WD-4: Troubleshooting Printing Problems

Sometimes documents fail to print. In this project, you'll experiment with various techniques to troubleshoot common printing problems.

Requirements: This project requires Microsoft Word.

Project file: No files are needed for this project.

1. Start Microsoft Word.

2. Create a new document containing the title below. You can add answers to the questions posed in Steps 4–6 to the document as you go along.

Exploring Printing Problems

3. Before printing, it is important to make sure your printer is plugged in, turned on, and online. Draw a diagram of the printer currently connected to your computer and label the power switch, power light, online light, and control panel. Also, look for the brand name and model of the printer and write it down.

4. One of the most common causes of printing problems is selecting the wrong printer. Use the Microsoft Office button to select Print. When the Print dialog box appears, write the name of the printer displayed in the Name box in your Exploring Printing Problems document. Is it the same as the printer you worked with in Step 3? If not, select the correct printer using the down-arrow button on the Name box.

5. Microsoft Windows provides help for troubleshooting printing problems. Open Windows Help and Support by clicking the Start button, then clicking Help and Support. Type printer problems in the Help search box, press the Enter key, and select the *Troubleshoot printing* option to view a list of possible problems. Select three problems from this list and look at the suggested solutions. Summarize what you learn in your Exploring Printing Problems document.

6. Printers are ultimately controlled by the Windows operating system. Use the Start menu to access the Control Panel. Use the Printer option under Hardware and Sound to view a list of printers. Add the names of these printers to your Exploring Printing Problems document. Indicate which printer is the default. Check the print queue for the default printer. If it contains documents, list them and their status.

7. You can print a test page to make sure the printer is working properly. Right-click your printer, and then select Properties. From the General tab, select Print Test Page. The test page might look something like the one in the figure on the next page.

Windows
Printer Test Page

Congratulations!

If you can read this information, you have correctly installed your SnagIt 8
Printer on D7SQJZB1.

The information below describes your printer driver and port settings.

```
Submitted Time:  10:03:59 AM 4/22/2007
Computer name:   D7SQJZB1
Printer name:    SnagIt 8
Printer model:   SnagIt 8 Printer
Color support:   Yes
Port name(s):    C:\ProgramData\TechSmith\SnagIt 8\PrinterPortFile
Data format:     RAW
Share name:
Location:
Comment:
Driver name:     UNIDRV.DLL
Data file:       SNAGITP8.GPD
Config file:     UNIDRVUI.DLL
Help file:       UNIDRV.HLP
Driver version:  6.00
Environment:     Windows NT x86

Additional files used by this driver:
  C:\Windows\system32\spool\DRIVERS\W32X86\3\SNAGITD8.DLL        (8.2.1.215)
  C:\Windows\system32\spool\DRIVERS\W32X86\3\STDNAMES.GPD
  C:\Windows\system32\spool\DRIVERS\W32X86\3\UNIRES.DLL  (6.0.6000.16386
(vista_rtm.061101-2205))
  C:\Windows\system32\spool\DRIVERS\W32X86\3\SNAGITP8.INI
```

This is the end of the printer test page.

8. Save your Exploring Printing Problems document in your Project Folder using the file name PrjWD-4-XXXXX-9999, where XXXXX is your student ID number and 9999 is your class section number.

9. Print your Exploring Printing Problems document and submit it along with your printer sketch and the test printout. Write your name, student ID number, section number, date, and PrjWD-4 on all the submitted papers

■Project WD-5: Formatting a Document

In this project, you'll apply what you've learned about Microsoft Word to format an existing document.

Requirements: This project requires Microsoft Word.

Project file: PrjWD-5.docx

1. Copy the file PrjWD-5.docx to your Project Folder using the Copy It! button on this page in the BookOnCD.

2. Start Microsoft Word.

3. Open the file PrjWD-5.docx from your Project Folder.

4. Apply the bold text attribute to the line Memorandum - Novel-Tea & Coffee, Inc.

5. Apply italics to the phrase air-tight in the sentence that begins Please don't forget.

6. Apply bold and underlining to the phrase number one in the last sentence.

7. Select the Memorandum line, then change its font to Book Antiqua, size 18.

8. Center the Memorandum line.

9. Select the word Memorandum. Use the Change Case button in the Font group on the Home tab to select UPPERCASE.

10. Select the list of items starting with Bean quality, then format the list as a bulleted list.

11. Indent the first line of the main paragraphs by .4". The three paragraphs that you'll indent begin Just a reminder, Please don't forget, and Thanks for helping.

12. Change the line spacing to 1.5 lines for the paragraphs that begin Just a reminder, Please don't forget, and Thanks for helping.

13. Remove the underlining from the phrase number one in the last sentence.

14. Justify the paragraphs that begin Just a reminder, Please don't forget, and Thanks for helping so that both the left and right margins are straight.

15. For justified paragraphs, hyphenation can reduce some of the extra spacing added between words. On the Page Layout tab, click Hyphenation in the Page Setup group, then click Hyphenation Options. Place a check mark in the box *Automatically hyphenate document*. Uncheck the box *Hyphenate words in CAPS*.

16. Change the number in the Hyphenation zone box to .35" to increase the space allowed between the end of a line and the right margin. This setting produces fewer hyphens in a document, but allows the right margin to become somewhat ragged.

17. Enter the number 1 for the *Limit consecutive hyphens to* box. Professional publishers prefer not to have more than one consecutive line ending with hyphens.

18. Click the OK button to close the Hyphenation dialog box, then compare your document with the document in the figure on the next page.

MEMORANDUM - Novel-Tea & Coffee, Inc.

To: Tea n' Coffee Shop Managers
From: Food and Beverage Director, Novel-Tea & Coffee
RE: Reminder – Fundamentals of Coffee-making

Just a reminder to all Tea n' Coffee Shop managers that it takes more than our fine beans to make a quality cup of coffee. Sometimes our employees are so busy frothing cream or sprinkling cinnamon that they can forget the five key factors to creating the best possible cup of coffee. Listed below are the five fundamentals of superb coffee creation:

- Bean quality
- Water purity
- Elapsed time from roasting beans to perking
- Cleanliness of equipment
- Elapsed time from grinding beans to perking

Please don't forget to store all beans in clean, glass, *air-tight* containers to retain the freshness and aroma of the coffee beans. Beans from your weekly shipment that you don't anticipate using within the week must be kept in the refrigerator or freezer. This retains flavor by preventing chemical reactions in the beans.

Thanks for helping to make Tea n' Coffee Shops **number one** in the tri-state area.

---

19. Save your document in your Project Folder using the file name PrjWD-5-XXXXX-9999, where XXXXX is your student ID number and 9999 is your class section number.

20. Use one of the following options to submit your project on disk or removable storage device, as a printout, or as an e-mail attachment, according to your instructor's directions:

■ To submit the file from your Project Folder where it is currently stored, stop the Word program by closing its window. Copy the file to a disk or removable storage device. Include your name, student ID number, class section number, date, and PrjWD-5 when you submit the file.

■ To print the project, click the Microsoft Office button, then click Print. Click the OK button. Write your name, student ID number, section number, date, and PrjWD-5 on the printout.

■ To e-mail the file, use Method 1 or Method 2, as described on page 137. Type your instructor's e-mail address in the To: box. Click the Subject: box and type PrjWD-5, your student ID number, and your class section number. Click the Send button or perform any additional steps required by your e-mail software to send an e-mail message.

■Project WD-6: Using Tabs and Paragraph Alignment

In this project, you'll focus on font formats and tab settings.

Requirements: This project requires Microsoft Word.

Project file: PrjWD-6.docx

1. Copy the file PrjWD-6.docx to your Project Folder using the Copy It! button on this page in the BookOnCD.

2. Start Microsoft Word.

3. Open the file PrjWD-6.docx from your Project Folder.

4. Select the document title How Much Lead Is in Your Cup?, then use the Font dialog box to change the title font to size 26, dark blue, bold italic with a shadow effect.

5. Select the list of items starting with Perked coffee 90-150 mg and ending with Tea 30-70 mg. Use the Tabs dialog box to set a left tab at the 1" position. Set another left tab at the 3" position, with a dotted leader. Close the Tab dialog box.

6. Position the insertion point to the left of Perked coffee, then press the Tab key to move it to the first tab position. Place the insertion point to the left of 90-150 mg, then press the Tab key to move it to the second tab position and display the dotted leader. Use a similar process with the remaining two list items.

7. Position the insertion point at the end of the line that ends with 30-70 mg, then press the Enter key to create a new line. Add this fourth list item, with appropriate tabs: Colas 30-45 mg.

8. At the top of the document, replace Juan T. Sposito with your name.

9. Compare your completed document with the document in the figure on the next page.

Novel-Tea News
Reporter: [Student name here]

How Much Lead is in Your Cup?

Caffeine is a product found in many popular beverages. Yet most people are trying to curb their daily caffeine intake. After all, the effects of excessive caffeine have recently received a lot of press coverage.

As employees of Novel-Tea & Coffee, you will often get caffeine-related questions from customers. The following list of common drinks paired with their caffeine content may help you answer many of those questions.

Perked coffee	90-150 mg
Instant coffee	60-80 mg
Tea	30-70 mg
Colas	30-45 mg

Most customers also associate caffeine with chocolate. A typical chocolate bar contains 30 mg of caffeine. Yes, a cup of perked coffee does have three to five times the caffeine of a chocolate bar, but doesn't a chocolate bar have a few more calories than a cup of perked coffee?

So hopefully this information will help you answer commonly asked questions about caffeine and help us better serve our customers.

---

10. Save your document in your Project Folder using the file name PrjWD-6-XXXXX-9999, where XXXXX is your student ID number and 9999 is your class section number.

11. Use one of the following options to submit your project on disk or removable storage device, as a printout, or as an e-mail attachment, according to your instructor's directions:

■ To submit the file from your Project Folder where it is currently stored, stop the Word program by closing its window. Copy the file to a disk or removable storage device. Include your name, student ID number, class section number, date, and PrjWD-6 when you submit the file.

■ To print the project, click the Microsoft Office button, then click Print. Click the OK button. Write your name, student ID number, section number, date, and PrjWD-6 on the printout.

■ To e-mail the file, use Method 1 or Method 2, as described on page 137. Type your instructor's e-mail address in the To: box. Click the Subject: box and type PrjWD-6, your student ID number, and your class section number. Click the Send button or perform any additional steps required by your e-mail software to send an e-mail message.

■Project WD-7: Finalizing a Document

In this project, you'll apply what you've learned about Microsoft Word to check a document for errors, correct mistakes, set margins, use styles, display document statistics, add headers, and add footers.

Requirements: This project requires Microsoft Word.

Project file: PrjWD-7.docx

1. Copy the file PrjWD-7.docx to your Project Folder using the Copy It! button on this page in the BookOnCD.

2. Start Microsoft Word.

3. Open the file PrjWD-7.docx from your Project Folder.

4. Use the Page Setup options on the Page Layout tab to set the left margin of the document to 1.25" and the right margin to 1.5".

5. Use the right-click method to check the spelling of any words with a wavy red underline. If the spell checker catches any proper names that you'd like to add to your custom dictionary, right-click and choose Add to Dictionary.

6. Use the right-click method to correct the grammar of any phrases with wavy green underlines.

7. Use the thesaurus to select a more appropriate word or phrase to replace get in touch with in the third sentence of the paragraph that begins The deal involves.

8. Add a Blank header to the document that includes your name and your student ID number on one line; add your class section number and PrjWD-7 on a second line.

9. Add a left-justified footer that shows the word Page followed by the page number.

10. Apply the Heading 1 style to the first line in the document.

11. Press releases for the Novel-Tea & Coffee company must be fewer than 300 words. Right-click the status bar to check the word count.

12. Compare your document in Print Preview to the document shown in the figure on the next page.

[Student name], [Student ID]
[Class section number], PrjWD-7

Press Release for Immediate Publication

Novel-Tea & Coffee has selected Brooks & Barney to handle all of its public relations needs. The decision was reportedly based on the firm's excellent track record of dealing with mid-sized retail stores. Its extensive client list, as well as the satisfaction expressed by those clients, made Brooks & Barney the obvious choice, according to sources at the coffee vendor.

As specified in preliminary meetings, the retail coffee business requires a full-service approach to public relations. All press inquiries will be referred to Brooks & Barney, who will also soon update and revamp all Novel-Tea & Coffee printed materials.

The deal involves a two-year contract, and financial arrangements are yet to be finalized. Nevertheless, rumors indicate that several urgent marketing concerns dictate that the firms establish regular weekly meeting times. An effort to contact either firm to confirm these rumors was unsuccessful.

Rod McGuire, CEO for Novel-Tea & Coffee, commented, "Brooks & Barney is an excellent firm, and we are looking forward to input from its excellent staff. Let's hope this is the beginning of a long and profitable relationship for everyone involved."

Novel-Tea & Coffee and Brooks & Barney are both privately held companies.

Page| 1

13. Save your document in your Project Folder using the file name PrjWD-7-XXXXX-9999, where XXXXX is your student ID number and 9999 is your class section number.

■ To submit the file from your Project Folder where it is currently stored, stop the Word program by closing its window. Copy the file to a disk or removable storage device. Include your name, student ID number, class section number, date, and PrjWD-7 when you submit the file.

■ To print the project, click the Microsoft Office button, then click Print. Click the OK button. Write your name, student ID number, section number, date, and PrjWD-7 on the printout.

■ To e-mail the file, use Method 1 or Method 2, as described on page 137. Type your instructor's e-mail address in the To: box. Click the Subject: box and type PrjWD-7, your student ID number, and your class section number. Click the Send button or perform any additional steps required by your e-mail software to send an e-mail message.

■Project WD-8: Creating a Table

In this project, you'll apply what you've learned about Microsoft Word to create a table in a document.

Requirements: This project requires Microsoft Word.

Project file: PrjWD-8.docx

1. Copy the file PrjWD-8.docx to your Project Folder using the Copy It! button on this page in the BookOnCD.

2. Start Microsoft Word.

3. Open the file PrjWD-8.docx from your Project Folder.

4. Insert a table before the paragraph that starts Because of the special nature. The table should consist of three columns and four rows and have a fixed column width.

5. Enter the following data into the cells of the table:

COFFEE	CALORIES	FAT (grams)
Black Coffee	0	0
8 oz. Cappuccino	63	3
8 oz. Café Latte	117	3.8

6. Insert one more row into the table and enter the following data:

8 oz. Café Mocha	190	6

7. Use the Table Styles group on the Table Tools Design contextual tab to format the table using the Medium List - Accent 2 format.

8. If needed, insert a blank line so that the table is separated from the paragraphs above and below it.

9. At the top of the document, replace the reporter's name with your own name.

10. Compare your document to the document shown in the figure on the next page.

Novel-Tea News
Reporter: [Student name]

How Much Fat Is in Your Cup?

Lots of people today are trying to limit their daily calorie and fat intake. As employees of Novel-Tea & Coffee, you may be asked about the calories and the fat content of some of our standard and specialty drinks. The following list of standard drinks with their caloric and fat contents may help you answer those questions.

COFFEE	CALORIES	FAT (grams)
Black Coffee	0	0
8 oz. Cappuccino	63	3
8 oz. Café Latte	117	3.8
8 oz. Café Mocha	190	6

Because of the special nature of our monthly spotlight drinks, they are likely to be higher in both calories and fat content than any of the above drinks. We'll try to get you the data on a spotlight drink when we announce the drink.

If a customer is troubled by the calories or fat content of a particular drink, suggest a drink that's similar, but with fewer calories or less fat. For example, suggest a cappuccino instead of a café latte. Or point out that a typical one-ounce chocolate bar contains 160 calories, with 85 of those calories coming from more than 9 grams of fat. You might also point out that the specialty drinks all have considerably less caffeine than an equal amount of regular coffee.

Hopefully this information will help you answer commonly asked questions and help us better serve our customers.

---

11. Save your document in your Project Folder using the file name PrjWD-8-XXXXX-9999, where XXXXX is your student ID number and 9999 is your class section number.

12. Use one of the following options to submit your project on disk or removable storage device, as a printout, or as an e-mail attachment, according to your instructor's directions:

■ To submit the file from your Project Folder where it is currently stored, stop the Word program by closing its window. Copy the file to a disk or removable storage device. Include your name, student ID number, class section number, date, and PrjWD-8 when you submit the file.

■ To print the project, click the Microsoft Office button, then click Print. Click the OK button. Write your name, student ID number, section number, date, and PrjWD-8 on the printout.

■ To e-mail the file, use Method 1 or Method 2, as described on page 137. Type your instructor's e-mail address in the To: box. Click the Subject: box and type PrjWD-8, your student ID number, and your class section number. Click the Send button or perform any additional steps required by your e-mail software to send an e-mail message.

■Project WD-9: Using SmartArt Graphics

In this project, you'll use the SmartArt Graphics options to customize a document.

Requirements: This project requires Microsoft Word.

Project file: PrjWD-9.docx

1. Copy the file PrjWD-9.docx to your Project Folder using the Copy It! button on this page in the BookOnCD.

2. Start Microsoft Word.

3. Open the file PrjWD-9.docx from your Project Folder:

4. Position the insertion point in the text box that contains the text *SmartArt*, then delete the text.

5. With the insertion point still in the text box, click the Insert tab, then click the SmartArt button in the Illustrations group.

6. From the List tab, select the Basic Block List option, then click the OK button.

7. Insert the following items in the text boxes:

> Sledding
> Skating
> Sled Dog Racing
> Ice Sculptures

8. Delete the extra text box by selecting it, then pressing the Delete key on your keyboard.

9. From the Layouts group on the SmartArt Tools Design contextual tab, select the Vertical Box List layout.

10. From the SmartArt Styles group on the SmartArt Tools Design contextual tab, select the Subtle Effect Style.

11. Compare your document to the one on the next page.

12. Save your document in your Project Folder using the file name PrjWD-9-XXXXX-9999, where XXXXX is your student ID number and 9999 is your class section number. Use one of the following options to submit your project:

■ To submit the document from your Project Folder where it is currently stored, stop the Word program by closing its window. Copy the file to a disk or removable storage device. Include your name, student ID number, class section number, date, and PrjWD-9 when you submit the file.

■ To print the project, click the Microsoft Office button, then click Print. Click the OK button. Write your name, student ID number, section number, date, and PrjWD-9 on the printout.

■ To e-mail the file, use Method 1 or Method 2, as described on page 137. Type your instructor's e-mail address in the To: box. Click the Subject: box and type PrjWD-9, your student ID number, and your class section number. Click the Send button or perform any additional steps required by your e-mail software to send an e-mail message.

■ ■ ■

■Project EX-1: Creating a Worksheet

In this project, you'll apply what you've learned to create a worksheet using Microsoft Excel.

Requirements: This project requires Microsoft Excel.

Project file: No file is required for this project.

1. Start Microsoft Excel.

2. Use the Microsoft Office button to open the Excel Options dialog box. Use the Popular and Save tabs to make sure the user name and default file locations are correct. Click the OK button to save these settings if you have permission to modify them. Otherwise, click the Cancel button.

3. Enter the labels and values shown below:

	A	B	C	D	E	F
1	Phone Charges Per Roommate for February					
2	Basic Monthly Service Rate		20.44			
3	Long Distance Charges for Each Roommate:					
4			Jamesson	Coleman	Depindeau	Struthers
5			5.65	0.25	1.35	3.75
6			0.45	0.65	2.15	0.88
7			1.68	0.56	3.78	1.23
8				4.15	5.77	0.95
9				1.25		0.88
10				3.67		1.95
11						3.88
12	Total Long Distance					
13	Share of Basic Rate					
14	Total					

4. In cell C12, use the AutoSum button to calculate the sum of the cells in column C. Use a similar procedure to calculate the long distance call totals for Coleman, Depindeau, and Struthers in cells D12, E12, and F12.

5. In cell C13, create a formula to calculate Jamesson's share of the $20.44 basic monthly service rate by dividing the contents of cell D2 by 4. Create a similar formula for each roommate in cells D13, E13, and F13.

6. In cell C14, create a formula to calculate Jamesson's share of the total phone bill by adding the contents of cell C12 to the contents of cell C13. Create a similar formula for each roommate in cells D14, E14, and F14.

7. Change the contents of cell A1 to Feb Phone.

8. Use the Undo button to change the label in cell A1 back to the original wording.

9. Compare your worksheet to the one shown in the figure on the next page.

■   ■   ■

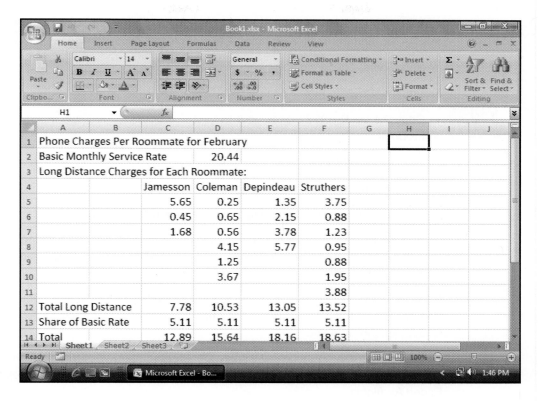

10. Save your worksheet in your Project Folder using the file name PrjEX-1-XXXXX-9999, where XXXXX is your student ID number and 9999 is your class section number.

11. Use one of the following options to submit your project on disk or removable storage device, as a printout, or as an e-mail attachment, according to your instructor's directions:

■ To submit the file from your Project Folder where it is currently stored, stop the Excel program by closing its window. Copy the file to a disk or removable storage device. Include your name, student ID number, class section number, date, and PrjEX-1 when you submit the file.

■ To print the project, click the Microsoft Office button, then click Print. Click the OK button. Write your name, student ID number, section number, date, and PrjEX-1 on the printout.

■ To e-mail the file, use Method 1 or Method 2, as described on page 137. Type your instructor's e-mail address in the To: box. Click the Subject: box and type PrjEX-1, your student ID number, and your class section number. Click the Send button or perform any additional steps required by your e-mail software to send an e-mail message.

■Project EX-2: Using Functions

In this project, you'll apply what you've learned about AutoSum plus the MAX, MIN, AVERAGE, and IF functions to complete a Microsoft Excel worksheet.

Requirements: This project requires Microsoft Excel.

Project file: PrjEX-2.xlsx

Copy It!

1. Copy the file PrjEX-2.xlsx to your Project Folder using the Copy It! button on this page in the BookOnCD.

2. Start Microsoft Excel.

3. Open the file PrjEX-2.xlsx from your Project Folder.

4. Use the AutoSum button to display the total number of flights in cells B11 and C11.

5. In cell B12, use the MIN function to display the lowest number of Mango Air flights from the list that begins in cell B4 and ends in cell B10. Enter a similar function in cell C12 for Econo Air flights.

6. In cell B13, use the MAX function to display the highest number of Mango Air flights from the list that begins in cell B4 and ends in cell B10. Enter a similar function in cell C13 for Econo Air flights.

7. In cell B14, use a function to display the average number of Mango Air flights from the list that begins in cell B4 and ends in cell B10. Enter a similar function in cell C14 for Econo Air flights.

8. In cell D3, enter the label Most Flights and adjust the column width so the label fits in a single cell.

9. In cell D4, use the Logical button in the Function Library group on the Formulas tab to create an IF function that compares the number of flights for Mango Air and Econo Air. The IF function should display Econo Air in cell D4 if that airline has the most flights for Costa Rica. It should display Mango Air in cell D4 if that airline has the most flights. *Hint*: Place quotation marks around "Econo Air" and "Mango Air" when you create the function, and remember that the Insert Function dialog box provides help and examples.

10. Use the Fill button in the Editing group on the Home tab to copy the IF function from cell D4 down to cells D5 through D10.

11. Enter your name in cell E1.

12. Compare your worksheet to the one shown in the figure on the next page, but don't save it yet. You have one change to make in Step 13.

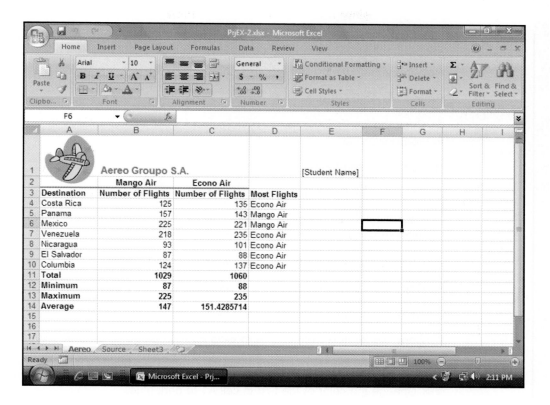

13. Change the number in cell C9 to 85.

14. Save your worksheet in your Project Folder using the file name PrjEX-2-XXXXX-9999, where XXXXX is your student ID number and 9999 is your class section number.

15. Use one of the following options to submit your project on disk or removable storage device, as a printout, or as an e-mail attachment, according to your instructor's directions:

■ To submit the file from your Project Folder where it is currently stored, stop the Excel program by closing its window. Copy the file to a disk or removable storage device. Include your name, student ID number, class section number, date, and PrjEX-2 when you submit the file.

■ To print the project, click the Microsoft Office button, then click Print. Click the OK button. Write your name, student ID number, section number, date, and PrjEX-2 on the printout.

■ To e-mail the file, use Method 1 or Method 2, as described on page 137. Type your instructor's e-mail address in the To: box. Click the Subject: box and type PrjEX-2, your student ID number, and your class section number. Click the Send button or perform any additional steps required by your e-mail software to send an e-mail message.

∎Project EX-3: Formatting a Worksheet

In this project, you'll apply what you've learned about Microsoft Excel to complete and format a worksheet.

Requirements: This project requires Microsoft Excel.

Project file: PrjEX-3.xlsx

1. Copy the file PrjEX-3.xlsx to your Project Folder using the Copy It! button on this page in the BookOnCD.

2. Start Microsoft Excel.

3. Open the file PrjEX-3.xlsx from your Project Folder.

4. Click the ▨ empty block between the "A" and "1" labels in the upper-left corner of the worksheet to select the entire worksheet.

5. Change the font size of the entire worksheet to 12 point.

6. Copy the formula from cell C6 to cells D6 and E6.

7. Copy the formula from cell C15 to cells D15 and E15.

8. Copy the formula from cell F4 to cells F5 through F6, and F9 through F15.

9. Insert a new, empty row before row 15.

10. Change the color of the text in cell A1 to dark blue.

11. Change the font in cell A1 to Times New Roman, size 14, bold.

12. Merge the contents of cells A1 through F1 so that the title is centered across those columns.

13. In cell A2, enter today's date.

14. Use the Dialog Box Launcher in the Number group to open the Format Cells dialog box. Select a date format that displays dates in the format *Wednesday, March 14, 2001*.

15. Merge the contents of cells A2 through F2 so that the date is centered.

16. Format cells A3 through F3 as bold text. Format cells A8 and A16 as bold text.

17. Format the numbers in cells C4 through E16 as currency.

18. Format the numbers in cells F4 through F16 as percentages (no decimal places).

19. Right-align the labels in cells C3 through F3.

20. Add both inside and outline borders to two cell ranges: B4 through F5 and B9 through F13.

21. Adjust the width of all columns so that all labels and values fit within the cells.

22. Now, explore what happens when you align some of the worksheet labels at a 90° angle. Select cells C3 through F3. Click the Orientation button in the Alignment group, then click Angle Counterclockwise.

23. Aligning column headings at a 90° angle is useful for worksheets that have many narrow columns. On this worksheet, however, the labels looked better at the normal angle, so use the Undo button in the Quick Access Toolbar to undo the 90° angle.

24. Compare your worksheet to the one shown below.

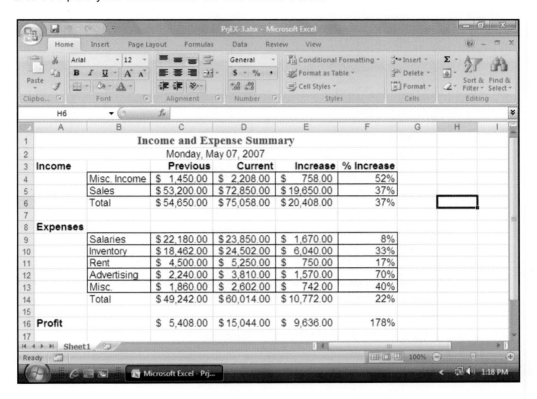

25. Save your worksheet in your Project Folder using the file name PrjEX-3-XXXXX-9999, where XXXXX is your student ID number and 9999 is your class section number.

26. Use one of the following options to submit your project on disk or removable storage device, as a printout, or as an e-mail attachment, according to your instructor's directions:

■ To submit the file from your Project Folder where it is currently stored, stop the Excel program by closing its window. Copy the file to a disk or removable storage device. Include your name, student ID number, class section number, date, and PrjEX-3 when you submit the file.

■ To print the project, click the Microsoft Office button, then click Print. Click the OK button. Write your name, student ID number, section number, date, and PrjEX-3 on the printout.

■ To e-mail the file, use Method 1 or Method 2, as described on page 137. Type your instructor's e-mail address in the To: box. Click the Subject: box and type PrjEX-3, your student ID number, and your class section number. Click the Send button or perform any additional steps required by your e-mail software to send an e-mail message.

■Project EX-4: Using Absolute and Relative References

In this project, you'll apply what you've learned about absolute and relative references to complete a sales commission worksheet.

Requirements: This project requires Microsoft Excel.

Project file: PrjEX-4.xlsx

1. Copy the file PrjEX-4.xlsx to your Project Folder using the Copy It! button on this page in the BookOnCD.

2. Start Microsoft Excel.

3. Open the file PrjEX-4.xlsx from your Project Folder.

4. Notice that cell B2 contains a sales commission rate. Each salesperson receives a commission equal to his or her total sales multiplied by the commission rate. The commission rate changes periodically. The worksheet will be set up so that if the sales manager changes the rate in cell B2, all the sales commissions will be recalculated.

5. Create a formula in cell B10 to calculate the sales commission for column B by multiplying the Total Sales in cell B9 by the Commission Rate in cell B2. (Hint: You must use an absolute reference for the Commission Rate in the formula.)

6. Copy the formula from cell B10 to cells C10 through E10.

7. Check the results of the copied formulas to make sure that they show the correct results. If cells C10 through E10 contain zeros, you did not use the correct absolute reference for the formula that you entered in Step 5. If necessary, modify the formula in B10, then recopy it to cells C10 through E10.

8. Compare your worksheet to the worksheet shown in the figure on the next page, but don't save it until you complete Steps 9 and 10.

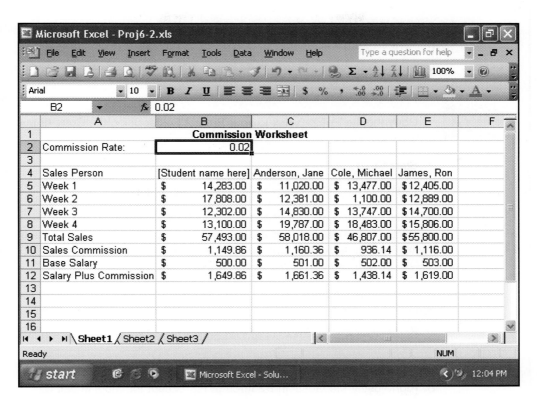

9. Change the contents of cell B2 to 0.03.

10. Enter your name in cell B4.

11. Save your worksheet in your Project Folder using the file name PrjEX-4-XXXXX-9999, where XXXXX is your student ID number and 9999 is your class section number.

12. Use one of the following options to submit your project on disk or removable storage device, as a printout, or as an e-mail attachment, according to your instructor's directions:

■ To submit the file from your Project Folder where it is currently stored, stop the Excel program by closing its window. Copy the file to a disk or removable storage device. Include your name, student ID number, class section number, date, and PrjEX-4 when you submit the file.

■ To print the project, click the Microsoft Office button, then click Print. Click the OK button. Write your name, student ID number, section number, date, and PrjEX-4 on the printout.

■ To e-mail the file, use Method 1 or Method 2, as described on page 137. Type your instructor's e-mail address in the To: box. Click the Subject: box and type PrjEX-4, your student ID number, and your class section number. Click the Send button or perform any additional steps required by your e-mail software to send an e-mail message.

■Project EX-5: Finalizing a Worksheet

In this project, you'll apply what you've learned about Microsoft Excel to complete a worksheet, freeze its titles, and finalize it for printing.

Requirements: This project requires Microsoft Excel.

Project file: PrjEX-5.xlsx

1. Copy the file PrjEX-5.xlsx to your Project Folder using the Copy It! button on this page in the BookOnCD.

2. Start Microsoft Excel.

3. Open the file PrjEX-5.xlsx from your Project Folder.

4. Scroll down the worksheet and notice that data for the miniature gargoyles is not complete. Select cell B19 and use the Fill option and then the Series option to consecutively number the products. For example, The Miniature Dragon Gargoyle should have a product number of 359 and the Miniature War Horse should be 381.

5. All of the miniatures are the same size, weight, price, and shipping cost. Use the Fill command to duplicate the information from C17 through F17 for all miniature gargoyles.

6. Select Cell B2. Use the Wrap Text button in the Alignment group to wrap the text.

7. Adjust the width of column B so that Product Number fits on two lines.

8. Right-justify the labels in B2 through F2, except the label in cell C2.

9. Notice that when you scroll the worksheet, the title and column headings are no longer visible. To freeze the titles at the top of the screen, click cell A3. You've clicked this cell because you want the titles above row 3 to remain fixed in place when you scroll.

10. Click the View tab, click Freeze Panes, then click Freeze Panes. Now scroll the worksheet and make sure that rows 1 and 2 remain in view.

11. Sort the data in cells A3 through F42 in ascending order by Description.

12. Check the spelling of the worksheet and correct misspellings as needed.

13. Add a right-justified custom header to the worksheet that includes your name, your student ID, your section, today's date, and Project EX-5.

14. Add a centered footer to the worksheet that includes the word Page followed by the page number.

15. Use the Page Setup options to print the page on a single piece of paper.

16. Preview your worksheet. It should look similar to the worksheet shown in the figure on the next page.

[Student name]
[Student ID]
[Section]
[Date]
PrjEX-5

Gothic Gargoyle Collection

Description	Product Number	Size	Weight	Price	Shipping
Ancient Burden Gargoyle	872	4"Wx2"H	16	$32.95	$5.95
Dwarf Dragon Gargoyle	561	3"Wx5"H	4	$12.95	$5.95
Dwarf Dragon Gargoyle	731	3"Wx7"H	5	$19.95	$5.95
Dwarf Florentine Gargoyle	810	2"Wx4"H	9	$14.95	$5.95
Dwarf Gnawing Gargoyle	994	3"Wx7"H	8	$10.95	$5.95
Dwarf Gothic Gruff	741	3"Wx7"H	7	$19.95	$5.95
Gargoyle Candelabra	782	3"Wx4"H	11	$22.95	$5.95
Gothic Gargoyle Snow Globe	792	3"Wx4"H	18	$12.95	$5.95
Guardian of the Flame Gargoyle	736	3"Wx4"H	14	$29.95	$5.95
Guardians of the Gate Gargoyle	824	4"Wx2"H	15	$34.95	$5.95
Keeper of the Castle Gargoyle	777	3"Wx4"H	7	$27.95	$5.95
Keeper of the Castle Gargoyle	721	4"Wx2"H	19	$32.95	$5.95
Le Petite Florentine Gargoyle	731	3"Wx4"H	7	$15.95	$5.95
Miniature Dragon Gargoyle	359	1"Wx1"H	0.5	$10.98	$3.95
Miniature Dragon Rampant Gargoyle	369	1"Wx1"H	0.5	$10.98	$3.95
Miniature Dragon-Slayer	371	1"Wx1"H	0.5	$10.98	$3.95
Miniature Dwarf Gnawing Gargoyle	357	1"Wx1"H	0.5	$10.98	$3.95
Miniature Elf with Bow	376	1"Wx1"H	0.5	$10.98	$3.95
Miniature Emmett Gargoyle	361	1"Wx1"H	0.5	$10.98	$3.95
Miniature Eregon Gargoyle	365	1"Wx1"H	0.5	$10.98	$3.95
Miniature Fang Gargoyle	367	1"Wx1"H	0.5	$10.98	$3.95
Miniature Female Warrior	378	1"Wx1"H	0.5	$10.98	$3.95
Miniature Fire-Breathing Gargoyle	368	1"Wx1"H	0.5	$10.98	$3.95
Miniature Florentine Gargoyle	360	1"Wx1"H	0.5	$10.98	$3.95
Miniature Gargoyle	356	1"Wx1"H	0.5	$10.98	$3.95
Miniature Gothic Gruff	358	1"Wx1"H	0.5	$10.98	$3.95
Miniature Guardian of the Flame Gargoyle	362	1"Wx1"H	0.5	$10.98	$3.95
Miniature Hobbit	375	1"Wx1"H	0.5	$10.98	$3.95
Miniature Keeper of the Castle Gargoyle	363	1"Wx1"H	0.5	$10.98	$3.95
Miniature Le Roi Gargoyle	364	1"Wx1"H	0.5	$10.98	$3.95
Miniature Lion Gargoyle	370	1"Wx1"H	0.5	$10.98	$3.95
Miniature Mounted Knight	372	1"Wx1"H	0.5	$10.98	$3.95
Miniature Ring-Bearer	373	1"Wx1"H	0.5	$10.98	$3.95
Miniature Smaug Gargoyle	366	1"Wx1"H	0.5	$10.98	$3.95
Miniature Troll	374	1"Wx1"H	0.5	$10.98	$3.95
Miniature War Horse	381	1"Wx1"H	0.5	$10.98	$3.95
Miniature Warrior with Axe	380	1"Wx1"H	0.5	$10.98	$3.95
Miniature Warrior with Pike	379	1"Wx1"H	0.5	$10.98	$3.95
Miniature Warrior with Sword	377	1"Wx1"H	0.5	$10.98	$3.95
The Emmett Gargoyle	735	3"Wx4"H	11	$12.95	$5.95

Page 1

17. Save your worksheet in your Project Folder using the file name PrjEX-5-XXXXX-9999, where XXXXX is your student ID number and 9999 is your class section number.

18. Use one of the following options to submit your project on disk or removable storage device, as a printout, or as an e-mail attachment, according to your instructor's directions:

■ To submit the file from your Project Folder where it is currently stored, stop the Excel program by closing its window. Copy the file to a disk or removable storage device. Include your name, student ID number, class section number, date, and PrjEX-5 when you submit the file.

■ To print the project, click the Microsoft Office button, then click Print. Click the OK button. Write your name, student ID number, section number, date, and PrjEX-5 on the printout.

■ To e-mail the file, use Method 1 or Method 2, as described on page 137. Type your instructor's e-mail address in the To: box. Click the Subject: box and type PrjEX-5, your student ID number, and your class section number. Click the Send button or perform any additional steps required by your e-mail software to send an e-mail message.

■   ■   ■

■Project EX-6: Creating Charts

In this project, you'll apply what you've learned about Microsoft Excel to create a column chart and a pie chart for an e-commerce worksheet.

Requirements: This project requires Microsoft Excel.

Project file: PrjEX-6.xlsx

1. Copy the file PrjEX-6.xlsx to your Project Folder using the Copy It! button on this page in the BookOnCD.

2. Start Microsoft Excel.

3. Open the file PrjEX-6.xlsx from your Project Folder.

4. Select the data in cells B3 through C6. Use the Insert tab to create a 3-D pie chart. Add the chart title, Which Activities Lead?, above the chart. Use the Data Labels button to show percentages on the pie slices. Place the chart on a new sheet and name the sheet Comparison Chart.

5. Change the style of the chart to *Style 12* in the Chart Styles group on the Design contextual tab.

6. Change the chart background color to *Subtle Effect, Accent 2* in the Shape Styles group on the Format contextual tab.

7. Select the data in cells H4 through H9. Use the Insert tab to create a Clustered Column chart. Click the Select Data button in the Data group on the Design contextual tab. Click the Edit button for the Horizontal (Category) Axis Labels, then select cells G4 through G8, click the OK button to close the Axis Labels dialog box, then click the OK button to close the Select Data Source dialog box. Add the chart title, U.S. Projections, above the chart. Add a vertical Y-axis title, $ Billions. Remove the legend from the chart. Place the chart on a new sheet and name the sheet Growth Chart.

8. Change the chart type to *Line with markers* in the Type group on the Design contextual tab. Click the OK button to apply the chart type.

9. Examine the charts to ensure that the spreadsheet data is accurately represented. One easy verification technique is to identify data trends and see if the trend is shown both in the data and on the chart. A trend in this data is the trend for projected growth to increase from one year to the next. Verify that the line chart corresponds to this trend by making sure the line moves up as it moves to the right.

Use care when identifying trends; make sure the conclusions you draw are accurate. Be aware of what can and can't be concluded from data. For example, although this data shows that 52% of e-commerce business activity is from business to consumer, it would be incorrect to assume that 52% of monetary transactions on a given day are from consumers to businesses.

10. Copy both charts to the E-Commerce tab.

11. Size and position the pie chart so that the top-left corner of the chart is in cell A10 and the bottom-right corner is in cell E23.

12. Size and position the line chart so that the top-left corner of the chart is in cell G11 and the bottom-right corner is in cell L23.

13. Click a blank cell in the worksheet, then open the Print Preview. Use Page Setup options to change the page orientation to Landscape and fit the worksheet on one page. The worksheet preview should look like the one shown in the figure below.

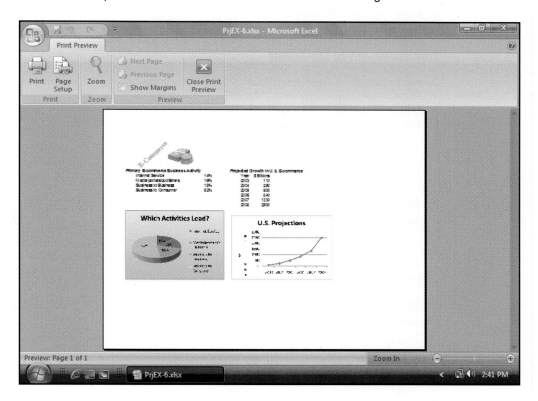

14. Save your worksheet in your Project Folder using the file name PrjEX-6-XXXXX-9999, where XXXXX is your student ID number and 9999 is your class section number.

15. Use one of the following options to submit your project on disk or removable storage device, as a printout, or as an e-mail attachment, according to your instructor's directions:

■ To submit the file from your Project Folder where it is currently stored, stop the Excel program by closing its window. Copy the file to a disk or removable storage device. Include your name, student ID number, class section number, date, and PrjEX-6 when you submit the file.

■ To print the project, click the Microsoft Office button, then click Print. Click the OK button. Include your name, student ID number, section number, date, and PrjEX-6 on the printout.

■ To e-mail the file, use Method 1 or Method 2, as described on page 137. Type your instructor's e-mail address in the To: box. Click the Subject: box and type PrjEX-6, your student ID number, and your class section number. Click the Send button or perform any additional steps required by your e-mail software to send an e-mail message.

▪Project PP-1: Creating a Presentation

In this project, you'll apply what you've learned to create a "tongue-in-cheek" PowerPoint presentation about e-commerce business trends.

Requirements: This project requires Microsoft PowerPoint.

Project file: No file is required for this project.

1. Start Microsoft PowerPoint.

2. Create a new presentation using any theme. The example on the next page shows the Trek theme.

3. Add a title slide, then enter Money Machine as the title. Enter your name as the subtitle.

4. Add a Title and Content slide. Enter The Web Economy as the slide title. Enter the following items as bullets:

> Growth is more important than profit.
> Scalability is crucial–we must be able to grow faster than the competition.
> It's OK to lose money–as long as we keep growing.

5. Add a Two Content slide. Enter We don't need profits because: as the slide title. Add the following items as bullets:

> Even if we lose money on every item, we can make it up on volume.
> What we can't make up in volume, we'll make up by selling banner ads.

Add whatever clip art you decide is appropriate.

6. Add a Title and Content slide. Enter Here's the Plan! as the slide title. Add the following items as bullets:

> Quickly expand to credit card sales!
> Expand into major international markets!

7. Compare your slides to those shown in the figure on the next page.

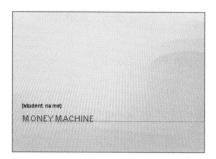

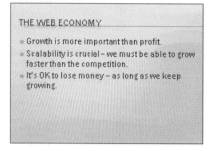

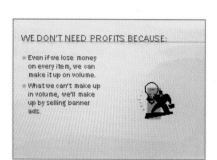

8. Save your presentation on a Project Disk using the file name PrjPP-1-XXXXX-9999, where XXXXX is your student ID number and 9999 is your class section number.

9. Use one of the following options to submit your project on disk or removable storage device, as a printout, or as an e-mail attachment, according to your instructor's directions:

■ To submit the file from your Project Folder where it is currently stored, stop the PowerPoint program by closing its window. Copy the file to a disk or removable storage device. Include your name, student ID number, class section number, date, and PrjPP-1 when you submit the file.

■ To print the project, click the Microsoft Office button, then click Print. In the Print dialog box, look for the *Print what* section and use its pull-down list to select Handouts. Make sure that the *Handouts* section specifies 6 slides per page in Horizontal order. Also, make sure that the *Scale to fit paper* check box contains a check mark. Click the OK button. Write your name, student ID number, section number, date, and PrjPP-1 on the printout.

■ To e-mail the file, use Method 1 or Method 2, as described on page 137. Type your instructor's e-mail address in the To: box. Click the Subject: box and type PrjPP-1, your student ID number, and your class section number. Click the Send button or perform any additional steps required by your e-mail software to send an e-mail message.

■Project PP-2: Creating Slides with Charts and Tables

In this project, you'll apply what you've learned about charts and tables to create PowerPoint slides for a fitness center.

Requirements: This project requires Microsoft PowerPoint.

Project file: PrjPP-2.pptx

1. Copy the file PrjPP-2.pptx to your Project Folder using the Copy It! button on this page in the BookOnCD.

2. Start Microsoft PowerPoint.

3. Open the file PrjPP-2.pptx from your Project Folder.

4. Add a Title and Content slide. Enter Target Heart Rates as the slide title. Add a table consisting of three columns and four rows, then enter the following data into the table:

Age	Minimum Rate	Maximum Rate
20	120	170
30	114	162
40	108	163

Resize and reposition the table so that it fits proportionately on the slide.

5. Select the slide you just made, and duplicate it. Change the slide title to Caloric Expenditures by Body Weight. Delete the table, and create a column chart that shows the following data:

	125 Lbs.	175 Lbs.
Jogging	7.3	10.4
Swimming	6.9	9.8

Make sure you have the weight categories as the labels for the X-axis.

6. Compare your slides to those shown in the figure on the next page.

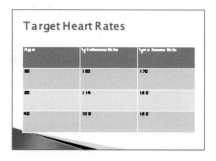

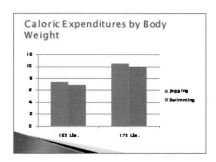

7. Save your presentation in your Project Folder using the file name PrjPP-2-XXXXX-9999, where XXXXX is your student ID number and 9999 is your class section number.

8. Use one of the following options to submit your project on disk or removable storage device, as a printout, or as an e-mail attachment, according to your instructor's directions:

■ To submit the file from your Project Folder where it is currently stored, stop the PowerPoint program by closing its window. Copy the file to a disk or removable storage device. Include your name, student ID number, class section number, date, and PrjPP-2 when you submit the file.

■ To print the project, click the Microsoft Office button, then click Print. In the Print dialog box, look for the *Print what* section and use its pull-down list to select Handouts. Make sure that the *Handouts* section specifies 6 slides per page in Horizontal order. Also, make sure that the *Scale to fit paper* check box contains a check mark. Click the OK button. Write your name, student ID number, section number, date, and PrjPP-2 on the printout.

■ To e-mail the file, use Method 1 or Method 2, as described on page 137. Type your instructor's e-mail address in the To: box. Click the Subject: box and type PrjPP-2, your student ID number, and your class section number. Click the Send button or perform any additional steps required by your e-mail software to send an e-mail message.

■Project PP-3: Using Animations, Transitions, and Sounds

In this project, you'll apply what you've learned to add animations, transitions, and sounds to a PowerPoint presentation.

Requirements: This project requires Microsoft PowerPoint.

Project file: PrjPP-3.pptx

Copy It!

1. Copy the file PrjPP-3.pptx to your Project Folder using the Copy It! button on this page in the BookOnCD.

2. Start Microsoft PowerPoint.

3. Open the file PrjPP-3.pptx from your Project Folder.

4. On the first slide, change the subtitle text The time is right! to Book Antiqua, size 44, bold, and italic.

5. Add the Uncover Down transition to the second slide.

6. Add the Fade Through Black transition to the third slide.

7. Add the Fly In animation (coming from the left) to the bulleted list on the third slide in the presentation.

8. View the presentation to see how the transition and animation effects work.

9. Switch to Slide Sorter view. You should see transition and animation icons under slides 2 and 3, as shown on the next page. Note: Don't worry about spelling errors. You will have an opportunity to fix them in the next project.

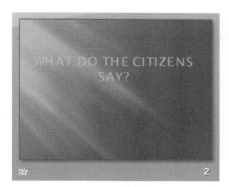

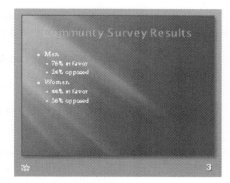

10. Save your presentation in your Project Folder using the file name PrjPP-3-XXXXX-9999, where XXXXX is your student ID number and 9999 is your class section number.

11. Use one of the following options to submit your project on disk or removable storage device, as a printout, or as an e-mail attachment, according to your instructor's directions:

■ To submit the file from your Project Folder where it is currently stored, stop the PowerPoint program by closing its window. Copy the file to a disk or removable storage device. Include your name, student ID number, class section number, date, and PrjPP-3 when you submit the file.

■ To print the project, click the Microsoft Office button, then click Print. On the Print dialog box, look for the *Print what* section and use its pull-down list to select Handouts. Make sure that the *Handouts* section specifies 6 slides per page in Horizontal order. Also, make sure that the *Scale to fit paper* check box contains a check mark. Click the OK button. Write your name, student ID number, section number, date, and PrjPP-3 on the printout.

■ To e-mail the file, use Method 1 or Method 2, as described on page 137. Type your instructor's e-mail address in the To: box. Click the Subject: box and type PrjPP-3, your student ID number, and your class section number. Click the Send button or perform any additional steps required by your e-mail software to send an e-mail message.

■Project PP-4: Finalizing a Presentation

In this project, you'll apply what you've learned as you finalize a version of the Microsoft PowerPoint presentation that you worked with in Project PP-3.

Requirements: This project requires Microsoft PowerPoint.

Project file: PrjPP-4.pptx

1. Copy the file PrjPP-4.pptx to your Project Folder using the Copy It! button on this page in the BookOnCD.

2. Start Microsoft PowerPoint.

3. Open the file PrjPP-4.pptx from your Project Folder.

4. Use Slide Sorter view to move the Questions & Answers? slide to the end of the presentation.

5. Move the Best Site slide so that it comes immediately after the Potential Sites slide.

6. In Normal view, add the following speaker note to the first slide in the presentation: Introduce team members Jill Smith, David Byrne, and Tom Woods.

7. Add the following speaker note to the Questions & Answers? slide: Let's get a general idea of your reaction to the proposed golf course... raise your hand if you would like the project to proceed.

8. Delete the We need to proceed as quickly as possible! slide.

9. Check the spelling of all slides and make any necessary corrections.

10. In Slide Sorter view, compare your presentation to the one shown in the figure on the next page.

11. Save your presentation in your Project Folder using the file name PrjPP-4-XXXXX-9999, where XXXXX is your student ID number and 9999 is your class section number.

12. Use one of the following options to submit your project on disk or removable storage device, as a printout, or as an e-mail attachment, according to your instructor's directions:

■ To submit the file from your Project Folder where it is currently stored, stop the PowerPoint program by closing its window. Copy the file to a disk or removable storage device. Include your name, student ID number, class section number, date, and PrjPP-4 when you submit the file.

■ To print the project, click the Microsoft Office button, then click Print. On the Print dialog box, look for the *Print what* section and use its pull-down list to select Handouts. Make sure that the *Handouts* section specifies 6 slides per page in Horizontal order. Also, make sure that the *Scale to fit paper* check box contains a check mark. Click the OK button. Write your name, student ID number, section number, date, and PrjPP-4 on the printout.

■ To e-mail the file, use Method 1 or Method 2, as described on page 137. Type your instructor's e-mail address in the To: box. Click the Subject: box and type PrjPP-4, your student ID number, and your class section number. Click the Send button or perform any additional steps required by your e-mail software to send an e-mail message.

■Project PP-5: Creating an Organization Chart

In this project, you'll explore the graphics capabilities of PowerPoint to create a presentation that includes an organization chart.

Requirements: This project requires Microsoft PowerPoint.

Project file: No file is required for this project.

1. Start Microsoft PowerPoint.

2. Create a new blank presentation. Select the first slide and change the layout to *Title and Content*.

3. Add the title Company Hierarchy.

4. Select the Insert SmartArt Graphic content icon. Select the Organization Chart option from the Hierarchy category.

5. Delete all boxes except the top tier by selecting the box, then clicking the Delete key. Add the title President to the top of the organization chart. Click the down-arrow button on the Add Shape button in the Create Graphic group on the SmartArt Tools Design contextual tab to create a second tier with three boxes containing the following text: VP Marketing, VP Research, and VP Operations.

6. Click any blank area of the President box. If you click the text and see an insertion bar, try again until the box itself is selected, not the text inside the box. Click the down-arrow button on the Add Shape button in the Create Graphic group to create an Assistant for the President.

7. Add the text Administrative Assistant to the new box.

8. Add 4 subordinates to the the VP Marketing box. Type Marketing Rep in each subordinate box.

9. Select the VP Marketing box, select Layout in the Create Graphic group, and then select Left Hanging.

10. Remove one Marketing Rep box by selecting it, then clicking the Delete key.

11. Compare your slide to the one shown in the figure on the next page.

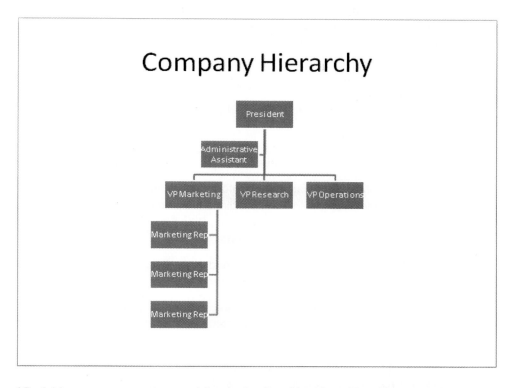

12. Add your name as a second line in the President box. To add text, click the text in the box. Use the End key to jump to the end of the line, and then press the Enter key. When the insertion point is on a new line, type the additional text.

13. Use the SmartArt Styles group to change the style for the organization chart to Subtle Effect.

14. Save your presentation in your Project Folder using the file name PrjPP-5-XXXXX-9999, where XXXXX is your student ID number and 9999 is your class section number.

15. Use one of the following options to submit your project on disk or removable storage device, as a printout, or as an e-mail attachment, according to your instructor's directions:

■ To submit the file from your Project Folder where it is currently stored, stop the PowerPoint program by closing its window. Copy the file to a disk or removable storage device. Include your name, student ID number, class section number, date, and PrjPP-5 when you submit the file.

■ To print the project, click the Microsoft Office button, then click Print. On the Print dialog box, look for the *Print what* section and use its pull-down list to select Handouts. Make sure that the *Handouts* section specifies 6 slides per page in Horizontal order. Also, make sure that the *Scale to fit paper* check box contains a check mark. Click the OK button. Write your name, student ID number, section number, date, and PrjPP-5 on the printout.

■ To e-mail the file, use Method 1 or Method 2, as described on page 137. Type your instructor's e-mail address in the To: box. Click the Subject: box and type PrjPP-5, your student ID number, and your class section number. Click the Send button or perform any additional steps required by your e-mail software to send an e-mail message.

■   ■   ■

■Project AC-1: Creating a Database Table

In this project, you'll apply what you've learned about Microsoft Access to create a database, create a table, and enter data into the table. You'll also explore data formats and validation rules.

Requirements: This project requires Microsoft Access.

Project file: No project file is required for this project.

1. Start Microsoft Access.

2. Create a new blank database in your Project Folder. Name the database PrjAC-1.accdb.

3. Use the Table Template option to create a table. Select the Contacts sample table. Include the following fields in the table: ID, Company, LastName, FirstName, Job Title, Business Phone, Fax Number, Address, City, State/Province, Zip/PostalCode, and Country/Region. Name the table Contacts.

4. In Design View, add a field at the end of the field list called ContactDate, with a data type of Date/Time.

5. Select ContactDate, and change the format of the field to General Date. To do this step, use the Format option on the General tab in the Field Properties box near the bottom of the window.

6. Create a validation rule to restrict the dates entered in the ContactDate field to later than 1/1/2007. Select ContactDate, and type >=#1/1/2007# in the Validation Rule box found on the General tab under Field Properties. In the Validation Text box, enter Please enter a date later than 1/1/2007.

7. Select Zip/PostalCode, and change the Field Size to 5 using the Field Size option on the General tab under Field Properties. Note that changing format options, such as field size, might result in changes to data in your database. For example, for records that include Zip/PostalCodes greater than 5 characters long, changing the field size to 5 characters would result in some fields being truncated. Save the changes to the table, then switch to Datasheet View.

8. Move the ContactDate column heading and drag it so that it is positioned just to the right of the FirstName column.

9. Delete the Company column.

10. Add the following record to the database. Leave fields, such as Fax Number, blank if you don't have the data. If you can't see the full text for a field, drag the dividing line between field headers to resize the column.

Last Name	First Name	Contact Date	Business Phone	Address	City	State/ Province	ZIP/ Postal Code	Country/ Region
Brown	Luke	5/9/2007	(812) 928-3828	4702 Lakewood Lane	Stone's Throw	GA	83928	USA

11. What happens to the Zip/PostalCode when you enter the following record?

Last Name	First Name	Contact Date	Business Phone	Address	City	State/ Province	ZIP/ Postal Code	Country/ Region
Cho	Alison	9/30/2008	(702) 737-2781	337 Center Street	Stockton	KY	83748-7707	USA

12. What happens when you try to add the data for the following record?

Last Name	First Name	Contact Date	Business Phone	Address	City	State/ Province	ZIP/ Postal Code	Country/ Region
McGuire	Joe	10/10/2002	(303) 383-7478	1147 Old Mill Road	Hanover	OH	57373	USA

Enter today's date instead of 10/10/2002, and then complete the record.

13. Check the data you entered and correct any typing mistakes. Your table should look similar to the one in the figure below.

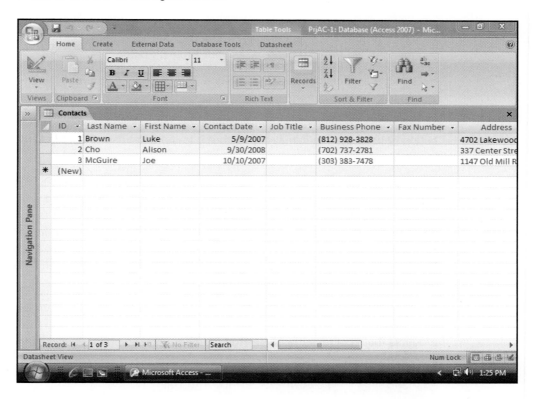

14. Use one of the following options to submit your project on disk or removable storage device, as a printout, or as an e-mail attachment, according to your instructor's directions:

■ To submit the file from your Project Folder where it is currently stored, stop the Access program by closing its window. Copy the file to a disk or removable storage device. Include your name, student ID, section number, date, and PrjAC-1 when you submit the file.

■ To print the file, make sure that the Contacts table is open. Click the Microsoft Office button, click Print, then click OK. Write your name, student ID, section number, date, and PrjAC-1 on the first page of the printout.

■ To e-mail the file, exit Access and start your usual e-mail program. Type your instructor's e-mail address in the To: box. Type PrjAC-1, your student ID number, and your class section number in the Subject: box. Attach the file PrjAC-1.accdb from your Project Folder to the e-mail. Click the Send button or perform any additional steps required by your e-mail software to send an e-mail message.

■Project AC-2: Creating Queries

In this project, you'll apply what you've learned about Microsoft Access to find specific records and create queries for finding specific information in a database.

Requirements: This project requires Microsoft Access.

Project file: PrjAC-2.accdb

1. Copy the file PrjAC-2.accdb to your Project Folder using the Copy It! button on this page in the BookOnCD.

2. Start Microsoft Access.

3. Open the file PrjAC-2.accdb from your Project Folder.

4. Select the Contacts table and delete it. When asked if you really want to delete this table, click the Yes button.

5. Suppose you hadn't intended to delete this table. If you remember to click the Undo button right away, you can easily restore it to the database. Click the Undo button on the Quick Access Toolbar.

6. Open the Products table and find the first Description that matches "Signal Kit." To complete this step, click the Home tab and then click Find in the Find group to open the Find and Replace dialog box. This dialog box allows you to type the text you want to find and select options such as which table to search and how to match the criteria. Enter Signal Kit in the *Find What* box. Set the *Look In* box to Products. Set *Match* to Whole Field. Set *Search* to All. Click the Find Next button to initiate the search. When the record has been located, click the Cancel button.

7. Use the Query Wizard to create a query that includes all fields from the Products table. Name the query Products Under $10. Add query criteria to limit the query results to products that cost less than $10. Run the query and compare your results to those shown in the figure below:

Products Under $10			✕
ID ▾	Product Number ▾	Description ▾	Price ▾
1	72838	8 oz Coffee Mug	$3.45
2	82892	12 oz Coffee Mug	$4.15
3	18372	Cup Holder	$2.85
5	83827	Auto Trash Bag	$7.95
7	23702	Lock De-icer	$2.89
8	37027	Windshield Scraper	$3.25
* (New)	0		$0.00

Save and close the updated query.

8. Use the Query Wizard to create a query that includes only the State/Province and EmailName fields from the Contacts table. Name the query Ohio E-mail Addresses. Add query criteria to limit the query results to records of people located in the state of Ohio (OH). Uncheck the Show check box to Show the State/Province field from the query. Run the query and compare your results to those shown in the figure below.

Save and close the updated query.

9. Use one of the following options to submit your project on disk or removable storage device, as a printout, or as an e-mail attachment, according to your instructor's directions:

■ To submit the file from your Project Folder where it is currently stored, stop the Access program by closing its window. Copy the file to a disk or removable storage device. Include your name, student ID, section number, date, and PrjAC-2 when you submit the file.

■ To print the project, make sure that the Products Under $10 query is open, then click the Microsoft Office button, click Print, then click OK. Close the Products Under $10 query, then open the Ohio E-mail Addresses query. Click the Microsoft Office button, click Print, then click OK. Staple the pages together, then write your name, student ID number, class section number, date, and PrjAC-2 on the first page.

■ To e-mail the file, exit Access and start your usual e-mail program. Type your instructor's e-mail address in the To: box. Type PrjAC-2, your student ID number, and your class section number in the Subject: box. Attach the file PrjAC-2.accdb from your Project Folder to the e-mail. Click the Send button or perform any additional steps required by your e-mail software to send an e-mail message.

■Project AC-3: Creating Forms

In this project, you'll apply what you've learned about Microsoft Access to create forms that would allow a data entry person to easily update the Products and Contacts tables.

Requirements: This project requires Microsoft Access.

Project file: PrjAC-3.accdb

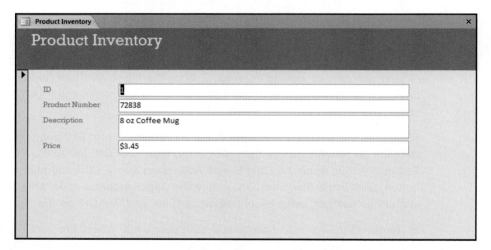

1. Copy the file PrjAC-3.accdb to your Project Folder using the Copy It! button on this page in the BookOnCD.

2. Start Microsoft Access.

3. Open the file PrjAC-3.accdb from your Project Folder.

4. Use the Form Wizard to create a form containing all the fields from the Products table. Specify the Columnar layout and the Foundry style. Enter Product Inventory as the form title.

5. Compare your form to the one shown below:

Product Inventory	✕
Product Inventory	

ID	1
Product Number	72838
Description	8 oz Coffee Mug
Price	$3.45

6. Use the Product Inventory form to add a new record for product number 54431, which is Fix-a-Flat, priced at $1.89.

7. Close the Product Inventory form.

8. Use the Form Wizard to create a form containing the following fields from the Contacts table: LastName, FirstName, and EmailName. Use the Justified layout and the Foundry style. Enter E-Mail List as the form title.

9. Compare your form to the one shown on the next page.

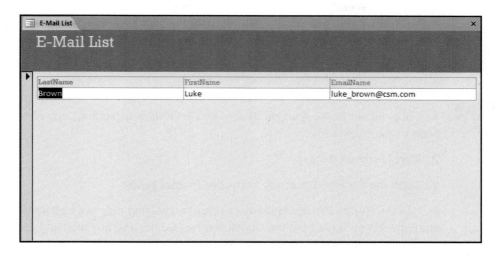

10. Add your own name and e-mail address to the list. If you don't have an e-mail address, just make one up.

11. Close the E-Mail List form.

12. Use one of the following options to submit your project on disk or removable storage device, as a printout, or as an e-mail attachment, according to your instructor's directions:

■ To submit the file from your Project Folder where it is currently stored, stop the Access program by closing its window. Copy the file to a disk or removable storage device. Include your name, student ID, section number, date, and PrjAC-3 when you submit the file.

■ To print the data as it appears in the form, make sure that the Product Inventory form is open. Click the Microsoft Office button, click Print, then click OK. Close the Product Inventory form and open the E-Mail List form. Click the Microsoft Office button, click Print, then click OK. Staple the pages together, then write your name, student ID number, class section number, date, and PrjAC-3 on the first page.

■ To e-mail the file, exit Access and start your usual e-mail program. Type your instructor's e-mail address in the To: box. Type PrjAC-3, your student ID number, and your class section number in the Subject: box. Attach the file PrjAC-3.accdb from your Project Folder to the e-mail. Click the Send button or perform any additional steps required by your e-mail software to send an e-mail message.

■Project AC-4: Creating Reports

In this project, you'll apply what you've learned about Microsoft Access to generate printed reports.

Requirements: This project requires Microsoft Access.

Project file: PrjAC-4.accdb

Copy It!

1. Copy the file PrjAC-4.accdb to your Project Folder using the Copy It! button on this page in the BookOnCD.

2. Start Microsoft Access.

3. Open the file PrjAC-4.accdb from your Project Folder.

4. Use the Report Wizard to create a report containing only the LastName, FirstName, and EmailName fields from the Contacts table. Do not add any grouping levels. Sort the records by LastName in ascending order. Use the Tabular layout and the Foundry style for the report. Enter Contact E-Mail Addresses for the report title.

5. Compare your report to the one shown in the figure below, then close the report.

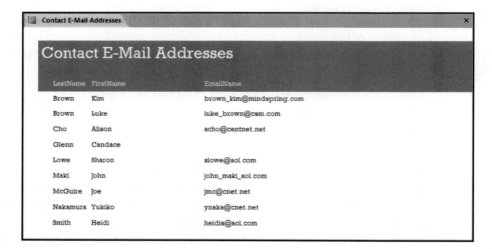

6. Use the Report Wizard to create a report containing all fields *except the ID field* in the *Query: Products Under $10* table. Group by Department. Sort the records by Description in ascending order. Use the Stepped layout and Foundry style for the report. Enter Products Under $10 by Department for the report title.

7. Compare your report to the one shown in the figure below, then close the report.

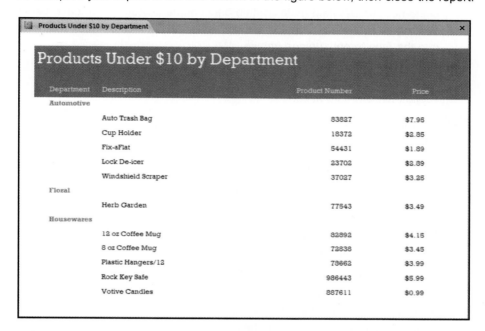

8. Use one of the following options to submit your project on disk or removable storage device, as a printout, or as an e-mail attachment, according to your instructor's directions:

■ To submit the file from your Project Folder where it is currently stored, stop the Access program by closing its window. Copy the file to a disk or removable storage device. Include your name, student ID, section number, date, and PrjAC-4 when you submit the file.

■ To print the project, open the Contact E-Mail Addresses report, click the Microsoft Office button, click Print, then click OK. Open the Products Under $10 by Department report, click the Microsoft Office button, click Print, then click OK. Staple the pages together, then write your name, student ID, section number, date, and PrjAC-4 on the first page.

■ To e-mail the file, exit Access and start your usual e-mail program. Type your instructor's e-mail address in the To: box. Type PrjAC-4, your student ID number, and your class section number in the Subject: box. Attach the file PrjAC-4.accdb from your Project Folder to the e-mail. Click the Send button or perform any additional steps required by your e-mail software to send an e-mail message.

■Project AC-5: Indexing and Filtering

In this project, you'll explore how indexes can be used to make databases more efficient. You'll also find out how to use filters to create a quick "query by example."

Indexes are used to find and sort records quickly. A primary key is an example of an index. It is a good idea to create an index on any fields commonly used as a sort or search field. Indexes also can be used to restrict fields to unique values. For example, a customer number field must contain only unique customer numbers, because no two customers can share a customer number. A "No Duplicate" index restricts values entered into the field to only unique values.

Requirements: This project requires Microsoft Access.

Project file: PrjAC-5.accdb

Copy It!

1. Copy the file PrjAC-5.accdb to your Project Folder using the Copy It! button on this page in the BookOnCD.

2. Start Microsoft Access.

3. Open the file PrjAC-5.accdb from your Project Folder.

4. Create an index by opening the Contacts table in Design View. Select the State/Province field and select *Yes (Duplicates OK)* from the Indexed option on the General tab under Field Properties.

5. Select the ID field and use the General tab to verify that the index for this field does not allow duplicates. Close Design View and save the changes you just made. Now that you have indexes for the State/Province field and ID field, sorts and searches on these fields will require less time—especially in databases that contain thousands of records. You can't tell the difference with a short database that fits on a removable storage device, but keep this important database design technique in mind for your own large databases.

6. Now explore the way filters help you quickly sift through a table to find records. Open the Contacts table. Click the down-arrow button on the column header in the State/Province field. Remove the check marks from all of the selections except OH, then click the OK button.

7. Compare your screen to the one shown on the next page, then cancel the filter by clicking the Toggle Filter button in the Sort & Filter group on the Home tab.

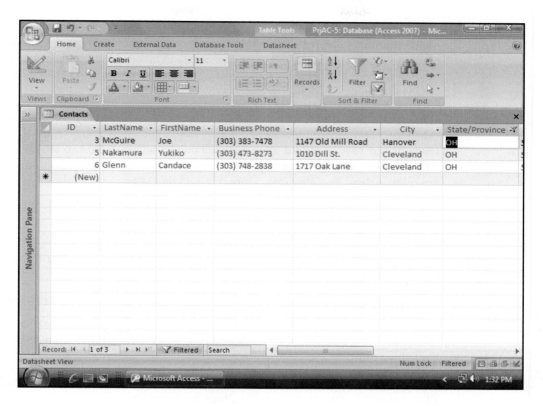

8. Use one of the following options to submit your project on disk or removable storage device, as a printout, or as an e-mail attachment, according to your instructor's directions:

■ To submit the file from your Project Folder where it is currently stored, stop the Access program by closing its window. Copy the file to a disk or removable storage device. Include your name, student ID, section number, date, and PrjAC-5 when you submit the file.

■ To print the project, open the Contacts table, set the filter, click the Microsoft Office button, click Print, then click OK. Write your name, student ID, section number, date, and PrjAC-5 on the printout.

■ To e-mail the file, exit Access and start your usual e-mail program. Type your instructor's e-mail address in the To: box. Type PrjAC-5, your student ID number, and your class section number in the Subject: box. Attach the file PrjAC-5.accdb from your Project Folder to the e-mail. Click the Send button or perform any additional steps required by your e-mail software to send an e-mail message.

■Project AC-6: Creating Relationships

In this project, you'll learn how to create and use one-to-many relationships. A one-to-many relationship links one record in a table to one or more records in another table. Examples of one-to-many relationships include customers to orders (one customer can place many orders), authors to titles (one author can write multiple books), and classes to students (several students can take one class).

To complete this project, you'll create a one-to-many relationship between students and classes so that you can use the data from both tables in a single report. One-to-many relationships require a third table containing links between the two tables in the relationship. The project database provides you with three tables, so that you will create the relationships and generate a report based on the linked data.

Requirements: This project requires Microsoft Access.

Project file: PrjAC-6.accdb

1. Copy the file PrjAC-6.accdb to your Project Folder using the Copy It! button on this page in the BookOnCD.

2. Start Microsoft Access. Open the file PrjAC-6.accdb from your Project Folder.

3. Click the Database Tools tab, then click Relationships in the Show/Hide group. Click the Show Table button in the Relationships group on the Relationship Tools Design contextual tab.

4. Hold down the Ctrl key while you click Classes, click Students, then click Rosters. Click the Add button, then click the Close button to close the Show Table dialog box. The Relationships window now contains three field lists—one for each of the tables. Drag the borders of the field lists so that you can see their entire contents.

5. Drag the field list title bars so that Rosters is between Classes and Students.

6. Note that the Classes table and the Rosters table both include a ClassID field. To create a relationship between these tables, drag ClassID from the Classes table and drop it on ClassID in the Rosters table.

7. When the Edit Relationships window appears, make sure it says *One-to-Many* at the bottom, and then click the Create button. If the window says *One-to-One*, click the Cancel button, then repeat Step 6, making sure to drop on the word ClassID.

8. Next, create a one-to-many relationship between the Rosters table and the Students table using the StudentID field.

9. Close the Relationships window and save the changes.

10. With the relationships created, you can generate a class roster report. Click the Create tab, then click Report Wizard in the Reports group.

11. Choose all the fields from the Classes table by first choosing *Table: Classes* from the Tables/Queries list, then clicking the >> button to move all the fields to the Selected Fields list.

12. Choose *Table: Students* from the Tables/Queries list, select LastName, and click > . Also, add the FirstName field. Click the Next button to continue.

13. Verify that the next dialog box indicates that you'll view your data by Classes, and click the Next button.

14. Do not choose any grouping levels, and click the Next button.

15. Sort records by student last names in ascending order by choosing LastName. Click Next.

16. Choose to lay out your report using the *Outline* layout. Click Next.

17. Choose the Foundry style, and click Next.

18. Type Class Roster as the report title. Verify that *Preview the report* is selected, and click the Finish button.

19. Compare your results to those shown below.

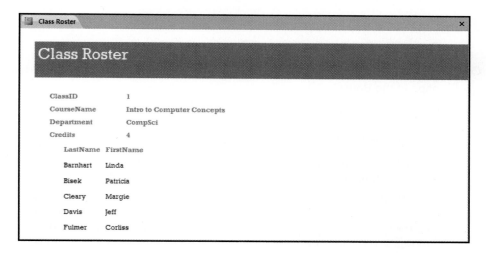

20. Use one of the following options to submit your project on disk or removable storage device, as a printout, or as an e-mail attachment, according to your instructor's directions:

　■ To submit the file from your Project Folder where it is currently stored, stop the Access program by closing its window. Copy the file to a disk or removable storage device. Include your name, student ID, section number, date, and PrjAC-6 when you submit the file.

　■ To print the relationships, open the relationships window. Click the Relationship Report button in the Tools group on the Relationship Tools Design contextual tab. Click the Print button in the Print group on the Print Preview tab, then click OK. Close the Print Preview. Save and close the relationships report using the default report name. Write your name, student ID, section number, date, and PrjAC-6 on the printouts.

　■ To e-mail the file, exit Access and start your usual e-mail program. Type your instructor's e-mail address in the To: box. Type PrjAC-6, your student ID number, and your class section number in the Subject: box. Attach the file PrjAC-6.accdb from your Project Folder to the e-mail. Click the Send button or perform any additional steps required by your e-mail software to send an e-mail message.

■Project AC-7: Setting Up Referential Integrity

In this project, you'll explore how to use relationships to maintain referential integrity between tables, and how to create queries that use relationships.

Referential integrity can be used to ensure that data entered in tables is correct in the context of the database. Let's suppose you are working with two tables from a school database. One table contains a list of classes. The other table contains prerequisites. The school uses two tables for this data because the database designer did not want to waste disk space to store empty fields for classes that have no prerequisites.

Assume that a class can have no more than one prerequisite. You can activate referential integrity to make sure that prerequisites cannot be added for a course that does not exist. You can also use it to avoid entering more than one prerequisite for a class.

Requirements: This project requires Microsoft Access.

Project file: PrjAC-7.accdb

1. Copy the file PrjAC-7.accdb to your Project Folder using the Copy It! button on this page in the BookOnCD.

2. Start Microsoft Access.

3. Open the file PrjAC-7.accdb from your Project Folder.

4. Click the Database Tools tab, then click Relationships in the Show/Hide group. Click the Show Table button in the Relationships group on the Relationship Tools Design contextual tab. Hold down the Shift key while you click Classes, and then click Prerequisites. Click the Add button, then click the Close button. The Relationships window now contains two field lists—one for the Classes table and one for the Prerequisites table. Drag the borders of the field lists so that you can see their entire contents.

5. Note that both tables include a ClassID field. To create a relationship between these tables, drag ClassID from the Classes table to the Prerequisites table.

6. When the Edit Relationships window appears, make sure the box for *Enforce Referential Integrity* contains a check mark.

7. Click the Create button to create a one-to-one relationship between Classes and Prerequisites.

8. The line that connects the two tables indicates the one-to-one relationship you just created. Close the Relationships window and save the changes.

9. Take a look at the Prerequisites table by double-clicking the table name. The ClassID field lists classes by number. If you want to find the name of a class, you can simply click the + sign next to it. What is the name of class 4? If you click the + sign, you'll see that it is Applied Math. Click the minus sign to hide the class name. The PrerequisiteName field lists the title of the prerequisite course. For example, the prerequisite for course 4 is Math Basics.

10. Now, what happens when you try to enter a prerequisite of English 101 for a class (numbered 11) that does not exist? Add a new record with the following values: *Class ID:* 11, *Prerequisite Name:* English 101. Press the Tab key to move to the next record. A warning message appears because no classes exist with a Class ID of 11. Therefore, no prerequisites for that class can be added. Click the OK button to close the warning message.

11. Now, try to change the Class ID to 6. Press the Tab key twice to move to the next record. Another warning message appears because you can see from the record above that class 6 already has a prerequisite of English 101.

12. Click the OK button and enter the following data:

ClassID: 1 PrerequisiteName: Math Basics

13. Create a query using the query wizard that includes all the fields from the Classes table and the Prerequisite Name field from the Prerequisites table. Save the query with the name Classes and Prerequisites.

14. Run the query and compare your results to those shown below.

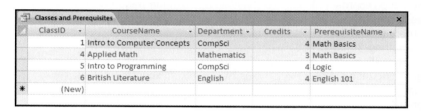

	ClassID	CourseName	Department	Credits	PrerequisiteName
	1	Intro to Computer Concepts	CompSci	4	Math Basics
	4	Applied Math	Mathematics	3	Math Basics
	5	Intro to Programming	CompSci	4	Logic
	6	British Literature	English	4	English 101
*	(New)				

15. Use one of the following options to submit your project on disk or removable storage device, as a printout, or as an e-mail attachment, according to your instructor's directions:

■ To submit the file from your Project Folder where it is currently stored, stop the Access program by closing its window. Copy the file to a disk or removable storage device. Include your name, student ID, section number, date, and PrjAC-7 when you submit the file.

■ To print the project, make sure that the Classes and Prerequisites query is open, click the Microsoft Office button, click Print, then click OK. Write your name, student ID number, class section number, date, and PrjAC-7 on the first page.

■ To e-mail the file, exit Access and start your usual e-mail program. Type your instructor's e-mail address in the To: box. Type PrjAC-7, your student ID number, and your class section number in the Subject: box. Attach the file PrjAC-7.accdb from your Project Folder to the e-mail. Click the Send button or perform any additional steps required by your e-mail software to send an e-mail message.

The Skeleton in the Closet

To my very scary pair, Spence and Dylan
—A.S.

For Mum, thanks for leaving the light on. All my love.
—C.J.

Library of Congress Cataloging-in-Publication Data
Schertle, Alice.
    The skeleton in the closet / By Alice Schertle ; illustrated by Curtis
Jobling. — 1st ed.
        p.   cm.
    Summary: A scary skeleton terrorizes a boy in his bedroom while it
searches his closet for clothes to wear.
    ISBN 0-688-17738-7 — ISBN 0-688-17739-5 (lib. bdg.)
    [1. Skeleton—Fiction. 2. Clothing and dress—Fiction. 3. Stories in
rhyme.] I. Jobling, Curtis, ill. II. Title.
PZ8.3.S29717 Sk 2003   2002005643
[E]—dc21   CIP
                                                                 AC

Typography by Al Cetta and Drew Willis
1 2 3 4 5 6 7 8 9 10

First Edition

The Skeleton in the Closet

by Alice Schertle
illustrated by Curtis Jobling

HarperCollinsPublishers

Late one night I was sound asleep,
snoring like a motorcycle, cuddled down deep
in my crocodile comforter, snug as a clam,
when I thought I heard a knocking—

BAM! BAM! BAM!

Someone at the door! I sat up straight.
Who would come a-knocking on my door so late?
In my spaceman jams I crept downstairs
and tiptoed to the window in my bedroom slipper bears.

I moved the curtain and peeked through the crack—
Two empty eyeholes stared right back!

White bones,
bright bones,
night bones glowing,
bare bones, scare bones, teeth all showing
in a big, wide, petrified, skeleton grin.

A deep-down voice said,
"*Let me in!*"

I ran like a rabbit.
I took the stairs
three at a time in
my bedroom slipper bears.
Into the bedroom!
Slam the door!

I stood there shaking in the middle of the floor.
Suddenly a noise made my knees grow weak—
Someone on the staircase!

creak . . . creak . . . creak . . .

Bones on the first step—
What do they want?

Second step ... third step ...
bones on a haunt,

fourth, fifth, sixth step . . .
white bones walking,

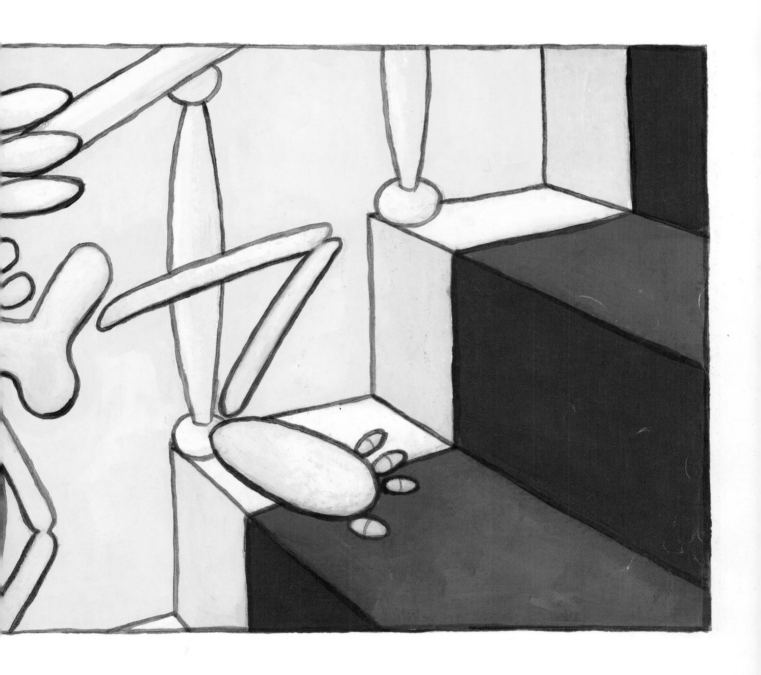

seventh step . . . eighth step . . .
night bones *talking*.

Ninth step, tenth—bones coming upstairs!
I jumped right out of my bedroom slipper bears
and dived inside of my nice safe bed
with my nice safe pillow on top of my head—
but I heard
every word
that the bone man said:

"I got a big hollow head bone,
ribs in a row,
got hip bones, thigh bones,
knee bones below,
got two shiny shin bones and little bone toes,
but I'm wearin' no skin, so EVERYTHING shows—
Comin' up to find some skeleton clothes!"

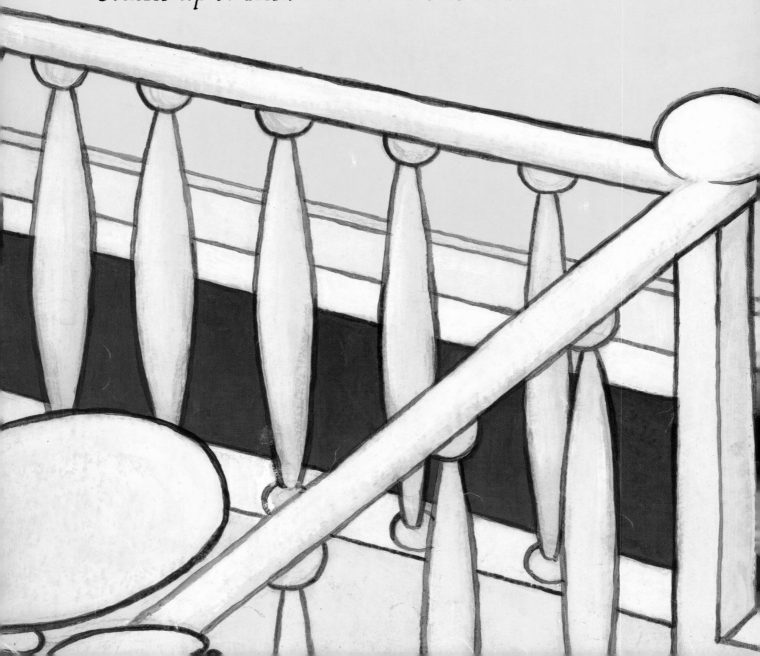

Fourteen . . . fifteen . . . very last stair. . . .

He was looking for something his bones could wear!

What did he mean by skeleton clothes?
Waterproof skin and a nose that blows?

Bones out shopping—
Good-bye skin!

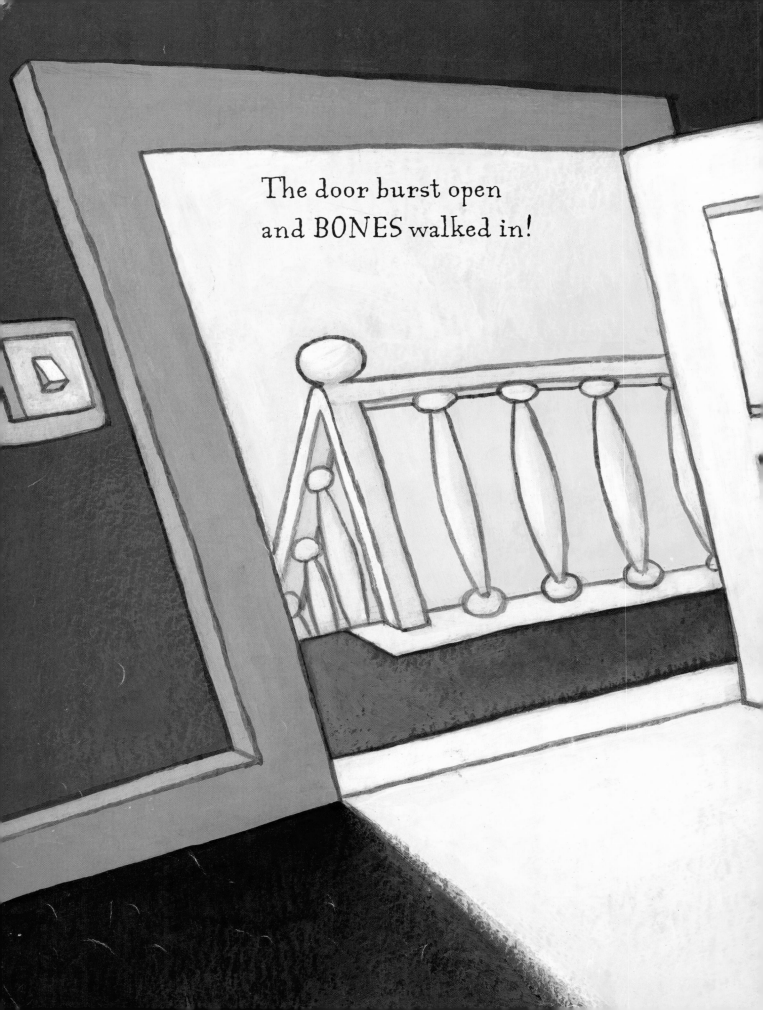

He walked straight to the closet and helped himself to whatever he found on the underwear shelf:

spaceman underpants,
polka dots, plaid,
tanks and T-shirts—whatever I had,

trying on jackets, tying on ties,
buttoning buttons, zipping up flies,

rattling hangers, banging around,
trying and tossing whatever he found,

but when he came out I'd have to say
he was looking good, in a skeleton way.

He boogied across the bedroom floor,
gave me thumb-bones-up and was out the door.

He was gone at last, I don't know where,
but wherever he is, his bones aren't bare.

So . . .

if a skeleton calls on *you* tonight,

and he's wearing clothes, they're mine, all right,

but
you might not
hear him
when he climbs your stairs.

He'll be

quiet,

quiet,

quiet,

in my bedroom slipper bears.